Comparative Histories of Crime

Comparative Histories of Crime

Edited by

Barry S. Godfrey
Clive Emsley
Graeme Dunstall

WILLAN
PUBLISHING

Published by

Willan Publishing
Culmcott House
Mill Street, Uffculme
Cullompton, Devon
EX15 3AT, UK
Tel: +44(0)1884 840337
Fax: +44(0)1884 840251
e-mail: info@willanpublishing.co.uk
website: www.willanpublishing.co.uk

Published simultaneously in the USA and Canada by

Willan Publishing
c/o ISBS, 5824 N.E. Hassalo St,
Portland, Oregon 97213-3644, USA
Tel: +001(0)503 287 3093
Fax: +001(0)503 280 8832
e-mail: info@isbs.com
website: www.isbs.com

First published 2003

ISBN 1-84392-036-0 (paperback)
ISBN 1-84392-037-9 (hardback)

British Library Cataloguing-in-Publication Data
A catalogue record for this book is available from the British Library

Cover photo copyright Barry Godfrey. The photograph shows part of an exhibition of
Australian history at 'Nostalgia Town', Pacific Paradise, Queensland, Australia.
Project management by Deer Park Productions
Typeset by GCS, Leighton Buzzard, Beds
Printed and bound by T.J. International, Padstow, Cornwall

Contents

Foreword by Martin Wiener   *vii*

Acknowledgements   *ix*

Notes on the editors and contributors   *xi*

1   Introduction: do you have plane-spotters in New Zealand?
    Issues in comparative crime history at the turn of modernity   1
    Barry S. Godfrey, Clive Emsley and Graeme Dunstall

2   It's a small world after all? Reflections on violence in
    comparative perspectives   36
    John Carter Wood

3   Moral panics and violent street crime 1750–2000:
    a comparative perspective   53
    Peter King

4   'The great murder mystery' or explaining declining
    homicide rates   72
    Maria Kaspersson

5 Strangers, mobilisation and the production of weak ties:
   railway traffic and violence in nineteenth-century South-
   West Germany   89
   Susanne Karstedt

6 'Inventing' the juvenile delinquent in nineteenth-century
   Europe   110
   Heather Shore

7 'Scoundrels and scallywags, and some honest men ...'
   Memoirs and the self-image of French and English
   policemen c.1870–1939   125
   Paul Lawrence

8 Policing the seaside holiday: Blackpool and San Sebastián
   from the 1870s to the 1930s   145
   John K. Walton

9 'The greatest efficiency': British and American military
   law, 1866–1918   159
   Gerry Oram

10 The decline and renaissance of shame in modern penal
    systems   178
    John Pratt

11 Practical and philosophical dilemmas in cross-cultural
    research: the future of comparative crime history?   195
    Bronwyn Morrison

Index   *213*

Foreword

Martin Wiener

Comparative history is an approach to the past long urged by many but actually practised by few. This is not surprising: it is difficult and time-consuming, for it demands a mastery of more than one body of sources and, if it is nationally comparative (as is usually the case), of more than one body of scholarship. Of course, as Barry Godfrey, Clive Emsley and Graeme Dunstall note in their enlightening introduction, all history is fundamentally comparative: historians cannot help at least implicitly comparing the present in which they live to the past they study. Yet as the historical profession continues to specialise, the need for specifically comparative historical work becomes ever clearer. Comparison alone makes it possible to understand just what is particular about particular histories to give them their proper place in the larger picture.

The history of crime and criminal justice is still a young branch of study, and its scholars have been preoccupied with establishing basic understandings of national patterns of crime over time and of the workings of national systems of criminal administration. By now, however, sufficient knowledge about crime and criminal justice in particular locales and eras has begun to accumulate to permit serious comparative work to begin. Eric Monkkonen has pointed to 'a growing international standard of definition and communication' which is now making cross-national comparisons feasible. Some guidelines may be appropriate for this sort of scholarship. Comparison seems to work best when its subjects are different but not too different: when they have enough in common to make their differences revealing, for example comparison between England (or Britain, bearing in mind the unique Scottish system of law) and her settlement colonies, or between two or more of those colonies. Here a legal and to a significant degree a social and cultural heritage is shared, and differences can highlight other differences – in environment, politics and society – as well as the omnipresent influence of contingency. Another potentially rewarding approach is comparison between England and the United States; here again, a shared early history and legal framework can bring into sharp relief differences emerging over several centuries of divergent development. A third angle of attack is to compare European states, as wholes or in part. In each of these approaches what is shared can provide a meaningful context for highlighting and examining differences, and can suggest fruitful generalisations for further exploration. The essays in this collection all adopt one or other of these approaches, and each in its own way advances our understanding of the complex contours of 'crime' and its 'administration' in the western world in the past two centuries.

Martin J. Wiener
Mary Gibbs Jones Professor of History
Rice University, Texas

Acknowledgements

The editors would like to thank all those who took part in the international conference 'Comparative Histories of Crime' held at Keele University in 2002. The papers presented there and the subsequent discussions they provoked have contributed to a greater understanding of crime histories in a national and international perspective.

We would also like to thank John Locker and Bronwyn Morrison who helped to organise that conference and the British Academy who sponsored the event. Not least we thank the authors who contributed to this edited collection promptly and with grace despite demanding deadlines.

Notes on the editors and contributors

Editors

Graeme Dunstall is Senior Lecturer in History at University of Canterbury, New Zealand. He researches and teaches New Zealand social history and criminal justice history. His publications include *A Policeman's Paradise? Policing a Stable Society 1918–1945* (*The History of Policing in New Zealand*, Vol. 4) (1999), having jointly edited *Southern Capital. Christchurch: Towards a City Biography, 1850–2000* (2000) and made a contribution to the *Oxford History of New Zealand*.

Clive Emsley is Professor of History at the Open University where he also directs a research group on the history of policing. Since 1995 he has been President of the International Association for the History of Crime and Criminal Justice. Publications include *Policing and its Context 1750–1870* (1983), *Crime and Society in England 1750–1900* (2nd edn, 1996), *The English Police: A Political and Social History* (2nd edn, 1996) and *Gendarmes and the State in Nineteenth-Century Europe* (1999).

Barry S. Godfrey is Senior Lecturer in Criminology at Keele University where he teaches the course on the history of crime. He has approximately twenty publications in this area, and has recently completed research projects on the decline of prosecuted violence in England, Australia and

New Zealand. He is now engaged on further comparative work in those countries.

Contributors

Susanne Karstedt is Professor of Criminology at Keele University. Current research projects focus on cross-national criminology, particularly a comparative study of the moral economy of consumer societies (with Stephen Farrall), cross-cultural research on corruption and violence, and crime in transition countries in Central and East Europe. Her historical research includes work on social movements in the nineteenth century, on early Nazis and right-wing extremists in Germany, and on public opinion on the Nuremberg trials and de-nazification in postwar Germany. She has authored many articles in leading journals and is currently editing a volume on *Legal Institutions and Collective Memories*.

Maria Kaspersson graduated in Stockholm with a thesis on homicide and infanticide in a historical perspective and is currently Lecturer in Criminology at the Institute of Criminal Justice Studies, Portsmouth University. Her research interests include homicide, infanticide and concepts of honour and masculinity in relation to violence. Forthcoming publications include 'Homicide and Infanticide in Interwar Stockholm' in the *Journal of Scandinavian Studies of Crime and Crime Prevention* and 'Homicide in a Domestic Context' in N. Loucks, (ed.) *Killing in Perspective*.

Peter King is Professor of Social History at University College Northampton. He is also a trained social worker who has worked for Social Services. Books include *Chronicling Poverty. The Voices and Strategies of the Labouring Poor 1640–1840* (joint ed., 1997) and *Crime Justice and Discretion in England 1740–1820* (2000).

Paul Lawrence is Lecturer in European History at the Open University. Since 1998, he has been working on a comparative analysis of the relationships between the police and the poor in France and England 1850–1939 as part of a European-wide project considering notions of 'social control'. He also specialises on the perception and treatment of immigrants in France during the interwar period, and has published articles in *Crime, History and Society, French History, Immigrants and Minorities* and *Contemporary European History*.

Bronwyn Morrison has worked as a researcher at the Institute of Criminology at Victoria University of Wellington, and the Policing Development Group of the New Zealand Police. She has researched the history of punishment and civilisation, arson, residential burglary and crime prevention. In 2000 she was the recipient of a New Zealand Government 'Bright Future Scholarship', and is currently completing her doctoral thesis on women, alcohol and mechanisms of social control in Victorian and Edwardian England at Keele University.

Gerald Oram is a Lecturer in Modern History at the Open University. He has published numerous articles and books on the development of military law and punishments in European armies during the nineteenth and twentieth centuries. His forthcoming book *Military Executions during World War I* reflects his interest in the social and cultural dimension of this little understood topic. He is now developing a new line of research into the formation of military codes, martial law, rules for the conduct of war, and war crimes in Europe and North America since 1500.

John Pratt is a Reader in Criminology at Victoria University of Wellington, New Zealand. He has published extensively in the area of the sociology and history of punishment, including *Punishment in a Perfect Society* (1993), *Governing the Dangerous* (1998) and *Punishment and Civilization* (2002). He is also editor of the *Australian and New Zealand Journal of Criminology*.

Heather Shore is a Lecturer in Social and Cultural History at the University of Portsmouth. She is the author of *Artful Dodgers: Youth and Crime in Nineteenth Century London* (1999), co-author with Pamela Cox of *Becoming Delinquent: British and European Youth, 1650–1950* (2002), and with Tim Hitchcock of *The Streets of London: From the Great Fire to the Great Stink* (2003). She has also authored a number of chapters and journal articles. She is currently working on a social and cultural history of the idea of the criminal 'underworld' since 1700.

John K. Walton is Professor of Social History at the University of Central Lancashire, Preston. He has published extensively on regional history and identity, popular culture and the history of tourism, especially in England and Spain. His most recent books are *Blackpool* (1998), *The British Seaside: Holidays and Resorts in the Twentieth Century* (2000) and (ed. with F. J. Caspistegui) *Guerras danzadas: fútbol e identidades regionales y locales en Europa* (2001).

Martin Wiener, Mary Gibbs Jones Professor of History at Rice University, was President of the North American Conference on British Studies from 2001 to 2003. He is the author of *Between Two Worlds: The Political Thought of Graham Wallas* (1971), *English Culture and the Decline of the Industrial Spirit, 1850–1980* (1981) (awarded the Schuyler Prize of the American Historical Association and translated into Italian and Japanese), *Reconstructing the Criminal: Culture, Law and Policy in England 1830–1914* (1990) and, to appear in 2004, *'Men of Blood': Contesting Violence in Victorian England*. He is now writing a book examining the treatment of inter-racial violent crime in the empire, tentatively entitled 'An Empire of Law? Violence, Race and Imperial Authority in the British Empire'.

John Carter Wood teaches at the University of Bayreuth. Along with continuing research interests on the topic of violence, he is in the early stages of a collaborative project on images of Germany in postwar Britain. He is the author of 'Self-Policing and the Policing of the Self: Violence, Protection and the Civilising Bargain in Britain', *Crime, Histoire et Sociétés/ Crime, History and Societies*, 7, 1 (2003) and *Violence and Crime in Nineteenth-Century England: The Shadow of Our Refinement* (forthcoming).

Chapter 1

Introduction: do you have plane-spotters in New Zealand? Issues in comparative crime history at the turn of modernity

Barry S. Godfrey, Clive Emsley and Graeme Dunstall

> A cultural gulf seems to lie at the heart of the detention of 12 British plane-spotters in Greece. The Greeks, progenitors of philosophies and the idea of the well-rounded life, just don't get the notion of grown men (and the occasional woman) standing for hours on end looking at planes and jotting down their numbers. There are, it seems, some things that EU harmonisation can never reconcile. (*The Guardian*, 23 November 2001)

At the time when this edited collection was first proposed, the English newspapers reported that a Greek court's inability to recognise the eccentric 'English' hobby of collecting numbers from various forms of transport – railway trains or aeroplanes normally – had had serious repercussions for a group of twelve tourists 'caught' taking photographs of Greek jet aircraft. The sentences of between one and three years imprisonment for the crime of espionage (*The Guardian*, 27 April 2002) were a salutary reminder that laws and criminal justice systems are embedded within cultural norms, and that legal codes emerge from specific cultural contexts that have evolved over time. In this case, the specificities of Greek culture and history had produced an outcome that would be unlikely in an English court. Cultural differences and their displacements, of course, are very much the theme of this edited collection, this introduction to which will sketch out some of the issues and concerns that have arisen in comparative research over recent years; and also (in the second part) offer a commentary both on the historiography of comparative crime history in general and the specific contributions made by the essays in this volume.

The past and future of comparative criminology

As Durkheim noted, all sociological inquiry is fundamentally comparative in both content and method (Durkheim, 1895: ch. 6). However, comparative criminology exists as a separate sub-discipline today, though the borders between it and mainstream criminology have become much more blurred over the last few years. From a position of under-representation in the sociological canon, there is now a growing body of criminological work that seeks to investigate the similarities in approaches to crime and disorder across national boundaries (see Nelkin, 1996, and his modified view in the 2002 edition), or to invigorate developing models of justice – the reliance of theories of restorative justice on indigenous and traditional shaming and punishment practices for example (Braithwaite, 1997; Karstedt, 2001: 295), and also to undermine and critique the harmful generalisations that have pervaded imperial and 'first-world' approaches to non-westernised countries. The organising dynamics for comparative research are therefore both evaluative and critical, and its ecumenical inclusivity has allowed various methodological and theoretical traditions to flourish within its realm. Where some researchers have examined one or two countries in considerable depth, some have expanded their scope to take in huge parts of the globe; some researchers have juxtaposed countries that are fundamentally different in ways which immediately present themselves, while others have focused on groups of countries that can be moulded together to outline, say, a European perspective (Cox and Shore, 2002: ch. 1).

Understanding 'the other' – the possibilities of comparison?

Underpinning all categories of comparative approach is the belief that researchers can disaggregate, interrogate and theorise a culture that is not their own. No social scientific research would be possible if we could not understand 'the other' to some extent (Leavitt, 1990), but this issue is a more explicit one for comparative researchers. It reduces to a set of interlinking beliefs in effect:

- That the cultural world in which the researcher was socialised is not a straitjacket which forever inhibits comprehension of other cultures

Culture is inalienable and insoluble, being, as Susanne Karstedt terms it, 'a specific social force' (Karstedt, 2001: 288) which forms an integral part of the human condition. The transmission of social and behavioural norms begins at birth and ends with death: no one escapes culture. That is not to say, however, that this social force is fixed and monolithic. Researchers can understand differing cultural codes through the study of ritual, symbol and the exchange of various forms of information. Although, even over time, the understanding may not be complete, it is possible to gain what we might term a 'functional understanding', which allows all (perhaps) but the subtlest of understandings to be 'read'. It is also the case that some put down one set of cultural 'clothes' and pick up another – to adopt a set of cultural attributes, consciously or unconsciously, that grants them admission to a different cultural milieu. Historically this can be seen in the sailors who jumped ship in New Zealand and became 'Pakeha (European) Maori' in the early nineteenth century, adopting the moko (tattoos) and Maori modes of dress and behaviour (see Bentley, 1999; see also Colley, 2002 for stories of coercive identity shifts during the Imperial period); or, to take another example from modern anthropology, Liza Dalby adopting the life of a Maiko (trainee Geisha) in 1970s Japan (Dalby, 2000).[1] Although we are discussing the ability to understand rather than 'be', many people successfully exchange one culture for another and come to belong to the new group, although this process is usually dependent on initial acceptance by the 'insiders'. To the extent that they can adapt to new situations and acquire the necessary linguistic competency, empathetic researchers should have the ability to approach the study of different cultures with some confidence of success.

- That universal phenomena exist but are conditioned by specific contextual and local factors

Gottfredson and Hirshi, as is well known, attempted to suppress local differences in order to prioritise a general theory of crime.[2] It has not been disputed that universals exist: that men feature more prominently in modern criminal justice systems; that youths offend more than adults; that the poor are successively disadvantaged at every stage of the criminal justice system, and so on. Yet grand unifying theories do not, and cannot, account for the infinite variety that general truths present in different cultural settings.

For example, all modern societies prohibit the arbitrary murder of one person by another – this is a universal given. Yet some countries permit judicial homicide in exceptional circumstances, while others do not. While countries with different policies could justifiably claim that they are acting in accordance with other universal values – harm limitation, the exercise of powerful authority in order to safeguard the weak, and so on – markedly different legal, policing and political situations have arisen. The ecologies of justice that have evolved around the globe all balance the interplay of competing universals, and with different results, which will be discussed in this book.

- That cultural shifts can create new realities

This last tenet of belief stresses that culture is not ahistorical or immune to historical change. When cultures change, they bring along a new set of realities. This is, of course, well known to cultural historians, and also to historical criminologists. Researchers of, say, declining rates of violence in the late nineteenth century (see summary of this work in Godfrey, 2003) are well aware of the impact on prosecution rates of the apparent growth of civilisation (see debates on violence and Elisian/Foucauldian notions of civilisation and 'governmentality' in Pratt, 2002 and also Wood, forthcoming 2003). The shifts and manoeuvrings of cultural change, the motors that drive it and the implications it has for various forms of social phenomena are important areas for study. Changes over time, changes in physical, psychic and social geographies, all necessitate and demand comparative frameworks of understanding.

With these three beliefs in mind, it seems clear that comparability is possible, indeed desirable, and that by adopting appropriate methodologies, we can begin to understand 'the other' – but, as the following section shows, 'otherness' as a social construct is grounded in a concept of modernity which is being increasingly challenged by postmodern theorists.

Eurocentricity and modernity – moving towards global postmodern fracture

Dussel, among many others, has described how exclusive notions of Eurocentric modernity came to dominate the landscape from the Middle Ages through to the twentieth century (Dussel, 1998: 3–4; see also Albrow, 1996). A distinctive prism of civilisation with its shared semiotics, language and set of moral understandings characterises those countries said by some to be the heirs to the 'Enlightenment' project (Hegel, 1975 translation; von Ranke, 1973 translation; Toynbee, 1935: 54; see summary and critique of this view in Callinicos, 1995; Dirlik, 2000). By marginalising non-European (and later non-western) modes of thinking, western ontological frameworks have become dominant. Indeed, paradoxically, western values have become universal while still defined against oriental 'others' – the 'civilised' West, the 'irrational' East. After September 11 (will we ever need to add the year to *that* date?) this has again become a fashionable rhetoric for the media – Afghanis referred to as 'Stone Age people' never having experienced western 'Enlightenment' (*Time Magazine*, December 2001). It might be that the end of the twentieth century witnessed the high point of this process, however, with scholars from differing theoretical viewpoints resisting traditional overarching modernist narratives. To take a specific example, Maori researcher Moana Jackson asserted the need to adopt a 'Maori methodology' and 'conceptual framework' with 'Maori concepts of causation, analysis and inter-pretation' in his study of Maori crime rates. He argued that previous research on the issue had 'produced little understanding' because of its 'monocultural' (or Eurocentric) nature. In his findings Jackson focused upon the deleterious effects of colonisation resulting in a 'sense of cultural and socio-economic deprivation' among Maori and the institutional racism of the New Zealand justice system (Jackson, 1988).

At a more general level, postmodern theorists have also critiqued Enlightenment/modernist historical explanations. These scholars reprise non-western knowledge and tradition, are more inclusive of popular cultures and tend to question orthodox hierarchical belief systems. The critique of modernism, as it found expression in the West, has encouraged relativism and, in its own way, democracy. Over recent years, postmodernists have entered the mainstream. Beck in *Risk Society* (1986/ 92: 9) asserted that the prefix 'post' had become the *key* word of our times, and 'globalisation' has now joined it as a ubiquitous shorthand for the conjunction of interlinked relationships that encompass modern society. The discontinuities of political power and security that the prefix 'post' has signalled have characterised descriptions of the globalised world: post-colonial, post-industrial, postwar, post-communist, and post-modern. Yet description appears to be the limit of postmodern aspiration. Postmodernity seems to lack the explanatory power that modernity, and modernists, value (see Henry, 2002). The tendency for postmodernity is to fracture and shatter, not to aggregate or account for collective experience.

This should be welcome news for comparative social scientists – the relativising process should bring forth more for researchers to compare, as does the breaking down of comparative 'units' like sovereign countries into sub-national groupings of communities. But, postmodernity also challenges the terms on which comparisons are made, and the significance of difference. Comparative researchers will no doubt wrestle with those demons for many years to come.

Whither comparative history?

Where does all of this leave the comparative historian? Historical enquiry has also been blown about by the winds of postmodernity (Pecora, 1989: 243), but it is not the time or place to discuss the new historicism or the linguistic turn, except to note that historians have been less concerned with the bed-fellow of postmodernity – globalisation. Snyder and Hay once described the two fault lines in academic theory as 'between past and present, on the one hand, and between the First World and Third World, on the other' (Snyder and Hay, 1989; see also Burke, 1992: 22–8). Despite this, historians have been relatively unambitious and have remained largely rooted in the analysis of crime in one nation state, with brief reference to one or two other nation-states. Monkonnen's study of homicide in nineteenth-century New York (with reference to Liverpool) would be a good example of this (Monkonnen, 2001). As the variety of chapters in this book indicates, this situation is likely to change, assisted no doubt by geopolitical realignments:

> In the fifties … Just William kids standing at the track-side to salute the trains and their drivers. This was England at its monochrome best: smoky and proud, sadly oblivious to the political skulduggery that was going to change it for ever. But those kids have long gone … What on earth happened? No-one used to take the piss. Train-spotting was our national hobby, as English as morris dancing and looked on with indulgence. We had the best trains in the world, it was only natural that kids took an interest … Train-spotting has always been a peculiarly British hobby, though no-one has ever known exactly why. My own theory is that it was all tied up with patriotism and loyalty and Empire … (Whittaker, 1995: 10–11, 243[3])

As Whittaker's allusions to 'perfidious' Europe make clear, the extension of European integration is not only going to impinge on English distinctiveness in the future, but will also recast the historical view of traditional English cultural activities. Morris dancing, Whittaker laments, is no longer viewed as an unbroken pastime, yea since the Middle Ages, but as an example of how ill-fitting and 'strange' England was before it conformed to more European sensibilities. History will no doubt be recruited to serve various political agendas in the coming debates over England's place in the world, and when it does so, comparative histories will be at the forefront.

The 'right' to study the other

For the moment, however, there are two other significant debates in comparative history that we should mention. The first concerns entitlement or 'academic property rights'. Who has the right to study histories of 'the other'? These debates have been keenest felt in European settled/occupied nations – notably New Zealand, Australia and the United States (see the essays in Sharp and McHugh, 2001; Binney, 2001; Bull, 2001; and see also Davison, 2000). In the case of Aotearoa/New Zealand, for example, Maori have challenged the production by Pakeha historians of monocultural history which simply integrates Maori experience into the mainstream, appropriating and misinterpreting it, and often making it invisible. There, as in other areas of recent European settlement, the rewriting of a nation's history from the perspective of indigenous groups has not merely supplemented and enriched historical knowledge, but also acted as an agent for political change and raised ongoing questions as to who should write about the past, and how it should be written. It is not simply that a proper understanding of Maori beliefs, core values and custom is expected of those writing about Maori, but also accountability – the obligations of researchers to those who shared their knowledge with them (see King, 1985; Parsonson, 2001: 281-8; Walker, 1990). The view that only Maori can study Maori history, working class the working class, or more broadly that only members of a particular social group can properly study members of that group, can be (and is) contested, but the issue will not go away. Indeed, it is linked to a second issue for comparative historians, that of cultural identification, or the extent to which an 'insider's view' can or should be adopted.

Strategies for comparative crime histories

'The past is a foreign country', as Hartley famously wrote[4] – moreover, one we can never visit. Historians are therefore *obviously* involved in comparative research (though that is not often explicitly expressed) and cross-national historians to a *profound* extent. This approach does not necessarily impose an additional layer that prohibits the possibility of meaningful research, but historians need to ensure that the methodology and theoretical approach they take do not create insurmountable difficulties. In order to generate reliable data, historians who seek to make cross-national comparisons need to have an accurate knowledge of the local or insiders' meanings of categories in the sources used. However, comparative history cannot be limited to explanations framed simply in terms of the concepts of the insiders since this limits the possibilities of explanation. Furthermore, the degree to which actions and their meanings are culturally specific may be debated. A measure of common ground, as well as differences and misunderstandings, for example, was evident from the outset of cultural contact between indigenous peoples and European colonisers, and modernising European societies can also be seen to have an increasing degree of conceptual common ground. In order for historians and social scientists to make some sense of insider/outsider conceptualisations of reality within historical contexts, they may take recourse to specific strategies which make comparisons more method-ologically robust, and more meaningful – notably by 'structuring in familiarity'.

Structuring in familiarity – the basis of comparison

We can first do this by forming coherent 'units' of comparison. Each nation state has institutions, policies and practices that can be analysed and this provides a good platform for comparative research. In fact, there are still relatively few historical studies of crime that provide systematic com-parative analyses based on *national* data. Ted Robert Gurr's pioneering comparative study of crime and conflict over two centuries was based on the experience of four cities (Gurr, Grabosky and Hula, 1977). The focus of most historians of crime still remains on single societies, or on institutions, practices, groups and localities within individual states. Studies of crime in single states can be implicitly if not explicitly comparative where they are informed by common concerns, methods and bases for comparing national data. However, the potential for systematic comparison can be limited by a focus simply on what is distinctive about, or specific to, the experience of one country. Although the issue of what is distinctive is an implicitly comparative question, the degree of difference has not generally been tested by a sustained comparison of the causes ascribed to common outcomes in different countries. This may be observed, for example, with studies of New Zealand and English national data on nineteenth- and early twentieth-century violence.

After the advent of a colonial British state in New Zealand in 1840, the apparatus for criminal justice – courts, policing and gaols – developed rapidly, broadly mimicking the English system in organisation, ideology and practice (Spiller, Finn and Boast, 1995; Hill, 1986, 1989; Pratt, 1992). Publication of data on offences and offenders (distinguishing between Maori and Europeans) soon paralleled the process in England and Wales (Gatrell and Hadden, 1972) – with colonial court data from 1853, and then police and prison statistics from 1877. Though, initially, some concessions were made to Maori viewpoints and customs by resident (stipendiary) magistrates in Maori-dominated areas, this practice weakened from the 1860s as Maori were 'swamped' by Pakeha (overwhelmingly British) migrants, and it disappeared from the 1880s as the dominance of the colonial state was asserted. In fact, until the early twentieth century Maori remained mainly subject to their own mechanisms of social control, and those dealt with by the criminal justice system were proportionately very small in number (Ward, 1995; Belich, 1996, chs 9 and 11; Dunstall, 1999: 204–14). Accordingly, in terms of its institutional outcomes at least, the colonial experience of crime can be broadly compared with that of England.

In examining recorded violence by Europeans in New Zealand between 1853 and 1940, Miles Fairburn and Stephen Haslett adapted V. A. C. Gatrell's method of classifying published court statistics of violence in England and Wales (Fairburn and Haslett, 1986; Gatrell, 1980). In both the colony and the parent society, there was a long-term decline in recorded violence per capita between the 1870s and the First World War (similar to trends in other anglophone societies as well as parts of Western Europe). Following Gatrell's approach to the English data, Fairburn and Haslett see in this decline an actual and significant reduction in 'assaultive behaviour'. Like Gatrell, they see the magnitude and speed of the decline in recorded violence as too great to be explained by possible changes in recording practices, modes of policing or attitudes to prosecution. Despite the close parallelism of the colonial trend with that of English recorded violence, however, there is not a common explanation for what is ostensibly a common process – a real and coincident decline in violent behaviour. Gatrell emphasises the 'potency' of policing and accounts for the decline in English violence in terms of a broadly defined 'process of moralisation' within the working class (Gatrell, 1980: 252–61; 1990: 244–5), By contrast, Fairburn sees the high level of colonial violence in the 1850s and 1860s as a product of a migrant society initially shorn of social bonds, and the subsequent decline in recorded violence as resulting from a *reversal* in the processes of social atomisation by an ongoing decline in the proportions of young, unattached and transient adult males, and a growth in informal social controls provided by developing networks of kinship and 'associational machinery' (Fairburn, 1989: Part 3). Both Gatrell and Fairburn frame their explanations in terms of the overall social experience of one society and in reaction to interpretations prevailing in its historiography. (Accordingly, both ignore marked gender differences in trends and patterns of recorded crime common to both societies: cf. Macdonald, 1989.) Fairburn looks to identify what was 'fundamental and distinctive to the colonial social pattern', while Gatrell emphasises the role that the coercive power of the law played in the broader processes of social stabilisation in Victorian England.

Yet, to what extent might coincident trends reflect common processes? While the potentially 'criminogenic' effects of migration to and within

British cities, and as fostered by the railway, have been noted (Walton *et al.*, 1999; Ireland, 1997), the trends of recorded violence in nineteenth-century Britain have not yet been systematically examined in the terms (of social atomism and its decline) defined by Fairburn.[5] A similar view to that of Gatrell on the 'potency' of English policing has been taken by Richard Hill on the effects of policing in nineteenth-century New Zealand: frontier society was 'self-tamed' by the processes of socio-economic and cultural change, but overtly coercive modes of policing 'accelerated the process to a marked degree' (Hill, 1995: 411–12). In such global explanations of the potency of policing, however, the kinds of criminal behaviour that local police actually deterred, and how they did so, remains an issue.

Even so, further examination of policing might provide evidence of a common institutional or managerial influence (but not necessarily the dominant influence) on downward trends of *recorded* crime in the late nineteenth century. Though there continued to be locally distinctive features in the organisation of policing (New Zealand developed a centralised force by contrast to the multiplicity of forces in Britain, and there were different 'rural/small town' and 'city' styles of policing in both countries), there was apparently a broad convergence during the late nineteenth century towards shared norms and common bureaucratic processes (Hill, 1989, 1995; Dunstall, 1999). In particular, the impact on trends of recorded crime of a late nineteenth-century transition from prosecution by complainants to prosecution by police in courts of summary jurisdiction needs further investigation in New Zealand, England and Wales, and elsewhere. Hypotheses that police and prosecutors filtered out cases of petty assault and theft, or 'rationed' crime, remain to be properly tested in different jurisdictions (Davis, 1989; Weaver, 1995; Taylor, 1998; Morris, 2001). This requires comparative local studies of police and court records.

Indeed, comparative studies of crime based simply on national statistical aggregates have important limitations. National patterns and trends of recorded crime may reflect the experience of the largest subnational units (generally the main cities) and conceal significant local variations over time and space. London's nineteenth-century conviction rates paralleled the trends of English data, and patterns of crime in New South Wales were taken to be 'those of Sydney writ large', according to Gurr and his co-researchers (Gurr, Grabosky and Hula, 1977: 26, 646). Though there are now a sizeable number of local studies of English crime, the extent of their variation from a national statistical pattern remains to be systematically analysed. Using statistical measures, Haslett and Fairburn found that all provinces in colonial New Zealand followed similar and broadly simultaneous trends from high to low measures of social atomism

(Haslett and Fairburn, 1990). However, employing qualitative evidence, their critics remain unconvinced, citing localities which were apparently exceptions. Global or macro-explanatory theories, whether of (say) social atomism or the 'potency' of policing, need to be tested by local case studies: how far can the process be demonstrated on the ground (as it were)?

Micro-studies could be used comparatively, for example, to test the explanatory power of Fairburn's atomisation thesis for localities in Britain, as in the colony, where there were common outcomes in terms of the trends and patterns of violence, and to establish whether each locality had the same set of postulated causes: a predominance of young males, an imbalance of the sexes, a turnover of migrants of diverse backgrounds, weak kinship ties, and little or weak associational machinery. (For a discussion on the comparative method and 'establishing important causes' see Fairburn, 1999: 4.) Sub-national case studies, employed comparatively and using *qualitative* sources, might also examine the degree of distinctiveness of (say) a colonial legal culture and the context and uses of colonial violence. To what extent, for example, did colonial litigiousness concerning violence reflect a different economic, social and institutional environment or simply the transposition of English attitudes and practices regarding the use of violence and the courts, along with concomitant processes of 'moralisation' during the late nineteenth century? Indeed, how far in both nineteenth-century England and colonial New Zealand were the boundaries between civil and criminal law blurred in dealing with assaults which, when they came to court, could be treated more as private disputes than as public wrongs? To what extent did the 'gender gap' in recorded crime change over time in the colony and the parent society?

In establishing generalisable findings on these and other issues in comparative crime histories, micro-studies present a number of well-known problems. The first is the comparability of sources – especially of policing, courts and statistical conventions. Despite such problems, a recent study has been able to establish some broad differences between sample towns of north-west England and the Basque country with regard to crime and migration in the late nineteenth and early twentieth centuries (Walton *et al.*, 1999). Thus far, however, the focus of local English studies of crime has been largely on the participants, processes and outcomes of indictable offences in trial courts, thereby limiting (for example) comparability with similar studies in colonial New Zealand which have used the records of summary courts. A further problem for comparative sub-national studies of crime lies in establishing a valid population base within consistent boundaries over time. An inability to match statistical data of judicial and policing jurisdictions with that of the population subject to their surveillance is a fundamental limitation to comparative analysis. Above all, micro-studies always present the problem of representativeness. This can be lessened by 'putting up a strong defence for the selection of cases, demonstrating that they belong to a distinct set' (Fairburn, 1999: 95). But, overall, the nation state (preferably buttressed by local case studies) may remain the strongest unit for comparative histories of crime. Research based upon national units also offers the advantage of further integrating qualitative data into comparative studies, for example the reputation/ character/identity of nations and their inhabitants.

National characteristics and identity politics

In one of the many books dealing with national characteristics and the effect they might have on the development of international society, Platt stated, 'It is sad to see that, in spite of all that the French might have learned from the English or the Americans, *the French are still as French as ever*' (original emphasis in Platt, 1961: 71; see also Lynn, 1971). His view that national characteristics were evident in the behaviour and attitudes of their inhabitants which could be recognised by 'outsiders' is an old one. Moreover, while research on national characteristics declined in volume after the 1960s and 1970s, modern research is again beginning to focus on what and how national characteristics manifest themselves and can be accounted for – although they are now regarded as imaginary self-conceptions shaped in the main by dominant social and/or ethnic groups – rather than the tangible realities Platt believed them to be (see Peabody, 1985; Hobsbawm, 1990; Anderson, 1991; Greenfield, 1992; Hutchinson, 1994; Smith, 1995; Bedani and Haddock, 2000). Crime historians might also usefully interrogate putative national characteristics or 'identities' (a term preferred by modern researchers) for a number of reasons.

First, by studying the stories that nations like to tell about themselves, it might be possible to reveal social data which otherwise would remain hidden. Nineteenth-century public attitudes towards violence (rather than statistical indices of offences) are difficult to uncover (see Godfrey, 2003). However, published works describing putative national characteristics often referred explicitly or obliquely to attitudes regarding the safety, pacificity or aggression of their nation/nationals (though these stories are in no way unproblematic). Well-known literary figures as diverse as Arthur Bryant (1934), George Orwell (1944) and J. B. Priestley (1973) have eulogised about the 'essential Englishness of the English' (Priestley, 1973: 11). For them, Englishness meant fairness, decency, love of liberty and a respect for order (but not officiousness). Academics have gone on to explain the growth of the idea of the English character, a concept which was usually favourably juxtaposed implicitly or explicitly against, oriental despotism, 'native' emotionalism and deceit, or 'European incivilities' (Said, 1978; Colley, 1992; Sinha, 1995; Langford, 2000; Rushby, 2003) and used to justify the building of a colonial Empire (see Tidrick, 1992 among others). Englishness has also been said to find expression in its legal structures – the jury trial, the lay (non-professional) magistracy and the various doctrines of mercy.[6] These self-conceptions and self-conceits can say much about nineteenth-century images of justice as well as of concepts of orderliness and fairness (which are of interest to crime historians). Equally as useful are the contemporary views of people from other nations on Englishness (see for example Hassam, 2000 and Davie, 2001).

In recent times, Englishness has been so closely identified with Britishness (or more accurately vice versa), that the stripping away of 'Scottishness' and 'Welshness' after political devolution has caused both popular and academic commentators to strive to re-examine and redefine Englishness (Colls and Dodd, 1986; Colls, 2002; Collini, 1999; White, 1985, 1992). As this process plays out it will be interesting to see which cultural representations will 'recover' traditional qualities that are said to belong to the English.

The 'Australian story',[7] too has been examined and re-examined many times (Nicholl, 2001; Day, 1998; Hudson and Bolton, 1998; Stokes, 1997) but most agree that a predominant theme was that of 'masculine virtue in a hostile land', personified in the 'Digger', the 'Aussie Battler' and the ANZAC soldier (Murrie, 2000; Nelson, 2000; Dixson, 1976/99, 1999; Goodall, 1997). Nile, explaining why a mainly urbanised country dreamed a rural identity for itself,[8] exemplified an prominent aspect of masculine identity when he talked of Australians being born tough and 'built tough' (Nile, 2000). That is not to say that the hard-drinking, hard-bitten colonial character was a reality, or indeed that it constituted a hegemonic representation of colonial manhood, for many versions of masculinity contended (Crotty, 2001). However, it may have offered a viable role model for Australian men to fall into whenever they found themselves threatened by social or environmental situations, and may offer a partial explanation for the comparatively high rate of public violence in Australasia – particularly the predominantly 'masculine' offences, domestic violence and fighting for example. In other words, the national picture coloured everyday experiences, and can offer evidence for the high Australian crime rates to the imaginative researcher. The idea of New Zealand being a masculine heartland with all that that entailed has also held purchase in both academic research (Phillips, 1996) and popular representations (Lee, 1977; Crump, 1960). Fairburn (1989), as previously stated, has examined the differences between the colonial realities and (what we might see as) the Pakeha 'foundational myth' of New Zealand – that it was a society largely free of many of the faults and problems of the British 'motherland' – to explore New Zealand rates of violence. Therefore, the contemporary stories that illustrated or propagandised about national character become not only a 'social fact' ripe for analysis in comparative research, but an integral research factor. It is one that should be treated with caution, however. For example, to continue our example of violence, aggression can be taken as something of a *universal* masculine quality (Spierenburg, 1998) and attempts to conform to putative national characteristics could only shade the way that aggression was expressed. Moreover, *local* rather than national reputation could be a more dominant factor. For example, hyper-masculinities and over-aggressive forms of dispute-resolution were reputed to be the preserve of those men working in the heavy structural industries in Britain – mining, shipbuilding and various other forms of extraction and construction work – in the nineteenth century. These local factors may have overridden any attempt to live up to national stereotypes.

It is just becoming apparent how far contemporary conceptions of national characteristics played a part in the development and processes of criminal justice. For example, Williams has described how the post-Second World War English police service was expressed (and even designed) in opposition to the German Gestapo (Williams, 2002). The enduring image of the peaceable kingdom watched over by kindly police father-figures rather than 'jack-booted bullies' is further described by Reiner (2000). This was a useful fiction to encourage acceptance of police services among all classes in England, but also partly determined later developments in policing. For example, this image made it difficult for those wanting an armed para-military style of policing introduced in the 1970s and later. Even today, policing provision and style in England is conditioned by enduring myths of the unarmed citizen constable (see Loader, 2003).

In the nineteenth-century courts too, Martin Wiener found that the level of passion capable of being generated by Englishmen and by European 'foreigners' was evaluated by judges and jurists, and had an impact on sentencing practices (Wiener, 1999; Wiener, 2002a; Wiener, 2002b). In the streets and in the courts, the stories that promoted certain characteristics on behalf of a country and its population may have affected the levels of crime and the disposals of some individual offenders. Without more research in this area, it will be difficult to assess just how significant that impact was.

Aside from national identities, local cultural landscapes have also been excavated by modern criminologists to explain attitudes towards criminal victimisation, and more dispersed structures of feelings about risk and security. Girling, Sparks and Loader, for example, in their recent study of 'Middle England' found it impossible to separate out feelings, anxieties and fears about crime from similar worries about the condition of the locale – high levels of unemployment, declining infrastructure and so on (Girling *et al.*, 2000). Ian Taylor *et al.*'s *A Tale of Two Cities* (1996) had already found a similar story in Manchester and Sheffield in the last quarter of the twentieth-century. Indeed, the north of England is a fruitful area of research, with Jewell, and later Kirk, finding that the North of England can be understood as a coherent regional 'other' (Jewell, 1994; Kirk, 2000). It would also be possible to make supra-national comparisons. Jeremy Black found that the eighteenth- and nineteenth-century English upper classes had more in common with their European counterparts than with the labouring classes of their own country (Black, 1996, 2001) and crime historians can construct larger units of comparison. Supporters of the federal European project and its discontents would both acknowledge that the countries of Western Europe share cultural/political – certainly economic – frameworks that bind them together and make them/us different from, say, the inhabitants of the Near or Far East (see Dunkerley *et al.*, 2002).

However, the effect of putative national or local/regional characteristics must be considered alongside local cultural, economic and social conditions (and not least the legal structures), factors which may have much more of a bearing on explaining the levels and nature of criminality in any one district or country.

The colonial legacy and its uses

Stories and myths about nations and their peoples shift and evolve over time, as do the social/political circumstances that help to shape those 'national tales'. Changes in legislation and the way it was enacted and operationalised change over time too, naturally, and historians have devoted considerable time to understanding the processes of change and the forces that forced them. It is a great advantage to those studying former colonies that they can rely on the use of court records written in English, a culture based largely on Anglo-European values and legislation rooted in English common law with similar laws passed across the Commonwealth (see Riles, 1999[9]). Moreover, the transmission overseas of Anglo-attitudes towards law and order was not mystical but mechanical, with the transmission of judicial norms and practices being reliant on legislation passed in England and the physical movement of judicial personnel to the colonies. Those routes can be traced (Howard, 1965; Kercher, 1995; Karstedt, 2002*)*. So, just as it is possible to explain why cricket is played in most Commonwealth countries (having been a popular game in the eighteenth century it travelled with English colonists to Australia, New Zealand, Africa and the Indian subcontinent), and why they have few trainspotters in New Zealand or Australia (that pastime becoming popular in the 1930s – after the Victorian settlement of Australasia, but relatively unpopular by the time the 1960s '£10 poms' emigration wave was under way), so can the transmission of Anglo-attitudes abroad. The similarities and differences between Britain and, say, colonial Australia or New Zealand, are therefore both more discernible and more readily comprehended. However, it is not only a matter of fortune that colonial criminal records and English court records are so similar, but also crucial to the understanding of how power was manifested through colonial governance, how crime policies 'travel' (a matter of considerable importance to modern criminologists) and how local socio-economic forces produced variation in the policing and punishment of offenders over time in different contexts. How and in which ways historians and criminologists have applied a comparative framework to these and other questions forms the basis of the following section.

A brief historiography of comparative crime history literature

The last thirty years or so have witnessed an explosion of academic research into the history of crime. Most of the work has been rooted in the experience of a single country, sometimes a region, sometimes just a town or city. Some of it draws on, or at least feels some need to engage with the broad, wide-ranging historical theses of Émile Durkheim, Norbert Elias and Michel Foucault. The history of punishment provides a particularly good example. The Dutch historian Pieter Spierenburg has used Elias's hypothesis regarding changing sensibilities and state formation in the early modern period to explore the changes in punishment, and particularly the decline in public executions and the development of carceral institutions (Spierenburg, 1984, 1991). In *The Spectacle of Suffering*, for example, he focuses on the specific case of Amsterdam, but situates this in the much broader context of a civilising process. It was not, he subsequently insisted, that the civilising process ameliorated punishment on a simple cause and effect model, but rather 'that the penal transformations of the late eighteenth and nineteenth centuries reflected the interdependence of increasing sensitivity to violence and suffering on the one hand and the emergence of stronger and less personally governed states on the other' (Spierenburg, 1995: 26). The powerful and sophisticated assessments of capital punishment in England and Germany by, respectively, V. A. C. Gatrell (1994) and Richard J. Evans (1996) follow the more typical path of British empiricism by getting the theory out of the way early on. In Evans's case, however, he provides an extensive introductory chapter assessing the theoretical perspectives employed with reference to the history of both capital punishment and death. Moreover, throughout the book he draws some important parallels with execution and punishment practice elsewhere, particularly in England and France.

Potentially, penal institutions and penal policies make some of the easiest topics for comparison. Moreover, given the popularity of Michel Foucault's *Discipline and Punish* (1975), it is surprising that rather more monograph comparisons have not been attempted. Comparative work has been mainly confined to collected essays. *The Oxford History of the Prison* (Morris and Rothman, 1995) is slanted towards England and the United States, while *The Emergence of Carceral Institutions*, edited by Spierenburg in 1984, looks specifically at continental Europe, is very much shorter and ten years older. Foucault's theories have most commonly informed or fostered work on single national experiences. Not surprisingly, perhaps, it gave rise to significant debates on the development of the prison in France (Perrot, 1980; O'Brien, 1982). It also informed Michael Ignatieff's challenging reappraisal of the development of the prison in England, though Ignatieff is critical of Foucault's 'fatalism' (Ignatieff, 1978). The sharpest and most perceptive comparative work in this area has been that of David Garland which, rather than 'history', the author calls 'work in the sociology of punishment, or, more precisely, in the sociology of criminal law, criminal justice, and penal sanctioning' (Garland, 1990: 10). Garland's work provides a penetrating critique of the historical theories framed to assess the changing patterns of punishment, or at least deployed to that end, and it is consciously addressed towards contemporary problems, something that at one time many academic historians often studiously appeared to avoid.

A significant change in this avoidance of contemporary debate became apparent at the turn of the millennium with debates in the United States on the topics of gun control and murder rates. In these debates historians and criminologists have deployed a variety of both conventional historical evidence and cliometrics. Some of this work has involved international comparison. For example, Joyce Lee Malcolm (2002) has sought to demonstrate that, in comparison with the modern United States, crime rates have begun to soar in the United Kingdom because, since the early twentieth century, successive governments have systematically removed the Englishman's right to bear arms. Some have looked comparatively within the United States, contrasting gun homicides across different states, across different cities and across time. In the autumn of 2001 a round table debate at the Social Science History Association Conference sought to pull some threads together and map out an agenda for future work (Roth, 2002).

The police, like prisons and other penal institutions, constitute entities that can be compared relatively easily. Again there have been a series of collections with essays ranging across national contexts. Some of these have had a fairly soft focus such as the collections edited by Jean-Noël Luc (2002) on gendarmeries during the nineteenth century with particular concentration on France, and by Jean-Marc Berlière and Denis Peschanski (1997), which ranges widely across the twentieth century and, in so doing, demonstrates the need for the development of some organisational framework for analysis. Alf Lütdke (1992) suggests interesting and potentially useful organising themes for the history of policing during the nineteenth and twentieth centuries with the concepts of 'security' and 'welfare'. The essays in Lütdke's edited volume chart the swings between regulatory social service policing and a militarised crime-busting model but, unfortunately, the comparisons are limited almost entirely to the German lands, and it would be useful to see these concepts deployed analytically in assessing policing elsewhere. Mark Mazower's edited survey (1997) of political policing in the twentieth century ranges much more widely geographically, and his authors are virtually unanimous in gloomily charting the erosion of that nineteenth-century situation in which a liberal public opinion could successfully circumscribe a range of police and state powers. Two volumes edited by David Anderson and David Killingray (1991 and 1992) respectively explore first the varieties of policing in the British Empire and the role of the police in maintaining the empire, and second the changing responsibilities and experiences of the police in the period of decolonisation. Whether or not police institutions lend themselves more easily to comparison than prisons and penal policies, individual historians have also produced monographs of comparative police history.

Professional bureaucratic police, like prisons, emerged in significant numbers across the western world during the nineteenth century. David Bayley situated the development of modern policing in the transformation of the organisation of political power and the extent of violent popular resistance that accompanied the emergence of the modern nation state (Bayley, 1975). In broad terms there can be little controversy about this, though the extent of cultural exchange and of the reshaping of models of policing are issues that Bayley tends to ignore and might merit further comparative analyses. Clive Emsley has provided two examples of how this could be done with a typology of nineteenth-century police that concentrates on command, control and administration (Emsley, 1999a), and with a comparison of the development of gendarmerie-style policing across nineteenth-century Europe (Emsley, 1999b). The former delineates three forms of police, commonly functioning side by side across the western world: state civilian, responsible directly to the national government and often largely confined to capital cities; municipal civilian, recruited by and answerable to local government; and the gendarmeries, state military police most often to be found in the countryside symbolising the nation state for the peasantry. The gendarmeries, Emsley suggests in his book, were based on a model exported under the Napoleonic imperium that suited well both emergent nation states and multinational empires seeking to tax, domesticate and win the loyalty of their peasantries. Rather more ambitious are the monographs of Hsi-Hui Liang (1992) and Mathieu Deflem (2002). Liang sets out to demonstrate how the development of modern police in Europe and its role in establishing and maintaining internal stability were central to the deployment of diplomacy and the organisation of national defence from the fall of Napoleon to the Second World War. His principal focus is on high or political police rather than on what he labels 'order police', but the nebulous nature of some of his conceptualisation leaves the argument interesting but ultimately frustrating. Deflem's interest is the development of international police cooperation from the mid-nineteenth century. Deflem never loses sight of his conceptual framework that interweaves Max Weber's theories of bureaucratisation with theories of globalisation to chart what he sees as increasing claims for, and the increasing achievement of autonomy by police agencies, particularly with reference to cross-border cooperation.

The centrality of the nation state to developments in criminal justice has informed several collections from the French-speaking world, not least, perhaps, because of the impact of the Napoleonic legal code imposed along with an effective, centralised system of government across much of Europe in the wake of the Napoleonic armies. The essays in the collection edited by Xavier Rousseaux, Marie-Sylvie Dupont Bouchat and Claude Vael (1999) focus specifically on the revolutionary and Napoleonic period teasing out how the relationships between the state, its justice and its citizens were reworked and modified through a mixture of Enlightenment and revolutionary ideology, and the presence of, or opposition to, the French imperium. Rousseaux, this time with René Lévy (1997), has also edited a second volume, with a much wider chronology, that takes the growth of the state as a key conceptual tool for analysing developments in the history of crime and criminal justice from the Middle Ages.

Various English-language collections have ranged more widely.

Margaret Arnot and Cornelie Usborne edited an important volume focusing on the concept of gender, and how gender norms were reflected and reinforced by both legal practices and forms of deviant behaviour (Arnot and Usborne, 1999). Eric Johnson and Eric Monkkonnen (1996) have employed Elias's concept of the civilising process to bind together a collection exploring the shifting patterns of violent behaviour in Europe since the Middle Ages. The collection edited by V. A. C. Gatrell, Bruce Lenman and Geoffrey Parker (1980) cannot be said have a clear organising theme. Nevertheless, this volume contains several essays that have become central to the understanding and subsequent development of the history of crime, notably the wide-ranging, comparative introductory essay by Lenman and Parker, and the important analysis of the Victorian and Edwardian crime statistics for England and Wales by Gatrell.

Crime statistics provide a means for measuring the scale and the pattern of crime, but they are also fraught with danger. Moreover, as Hermann Mannheim demonstrated more than half a century ago, since different states employ different categories for various offences, international comparisons are especially risky (Mannheim, 1940: 48–9). Nevertheless, drawing on Durkheim's work for his conceptual tools, Howard Zehr has produced a convincing comparative analysis of the patterns of property crime and violence in France and Germany during the nineteenth century (Zehr, 1976). More recently several historians have drawn cautiously on homicide statistics to assess the reality of a decline in violence across the western world since the Middle Ages (Eisner, 2001).

The history and the value of judicial statistics in Belgium, France, Germany and the Netherlands have been usefully addressed in a special edition of the French criminology journal *Déviance et société* in 1998 ('*La statistique ...*'). The early nineteenth-century determination to know about crime through the new science of statistics was followed hard by new theories of criminality and degeneration. Daniel Pick has explored these issues across England, France and Germany from the mid-nineteenth century until the end of the First World War (Pick, 1989). He charts an interrelationship between Darwinian evolutionary thought, criminal anthropology and psychiatry; he stresses how these ideas went far beyond the new science of criminology and were absorbed into a cross section of cultural, medical, political and social thinking. The international meetings and debates between criminologists at the close of the nineteenth-century form a crucial part of Robert Nye's discussion of the concern about national decline in France on the eve of the First World War. And he concludes this book with an important comparison of the similar fears to be found in Britain and Imperial Germany (Nye, 1984).

Broad, comparative, single-authored studies of either crime in general or of particular varieties of crime have been relatively infrequent. Michael Weisser attempted a broad survey of crime and criminal justice in Europe when the subject was just gaining academic interest and respectability. His survey (1979), while important at the time, now has its weaknesses highlighted by the detailed research undertaken since it was published. Trevor Dean's recent study of crime in the late medieval period is more successful since there is now a significant research literature on which such a synthesis can be based (Dean, 2001). The same is true for Julius Ruff's important discussion of violence in early modern Europe that usefully rehearses the theoretical perspectives and surveys the range of violent behaviour from that of private individuals to the emerging states (Ruff, 2001). Sadly, as yet, no one has had the courage to address the significant two hundred years from roughly 1750. This was, after all, the period when 'crime' and 'criminals' came to be defined as such as a result of a new perspective on the individual's responsibility for his or her actions. It was the period when new legal codes and new police structure were developed within the new nation states, and when the courts of these states took responsibility for a much greater proportion of criminal offences. Wim Mellaerts's comparison of criminal justice in three provincial towns in England, France and the Netherlands at the close of the nineteenth century is both unique and an exemplar of what might be done in comparing legal cultures and the relationship between criminal justice and different states (Mellaerts, 1997, 2000).

The one criminal offender who has been assessed comparatively in detail is the bandit. Eric Hobsbawm's *Bandits* was first published in 1969; the book was a mere hundred pages of text including illustrations. Hobsbawm's focus was the 'social bandit', the Robin Hood character who was a popular hero with the poor and a literary hero with just about everyone. Hobsbawm's work became the starting point, or at least the theoretical perspective that every subsequent historian of bandit activity had to address even though, early on, his 'social bandit' was the target of a fierce critical analysis by Anton Blok (1972/2001). Blok, a Dutch anthropologist, has worked extensively on both the nineteenth-century Sicilian *mafia* and the eighteenth-century Dutch bandit gangs known as the *Bokkeryders*, and for him few bandits ever showed much sympathy or consideration for poor peasants. Subsequent editions of Hobsbawm's book have sought to take note of Blok's critique. The social bandit, and a variety of other bandits across Europe during the old regime, are also addressed in the multi-lingual collection edited by Gherardo Ortalli (1985) and with an introduction by Hobsbawm.

From a history of 'civilised' punishment to bandits, together these published works have provided a substantial foundation for comparative historical research, and the essays in this volume take up many of the themes and strategies adopted by the authors discussed above. But comparison is no easy option. There are a variety of ways in which it can be done, but there are also problems and pitfalls. In the last of the essays that follow Bronwyn Morrison highlights some of these difficulties. From painful personal experience she stresses that it is not possible to draw a hypothesis from one country and to assume that it can be explored similarly in a contrasting national context. At the same time she draws attention both to the pressures that have developed in recent years that urge comparison as a 'good thing', and the alternative pressures that emphasise cultural distinctions. Comparisons can focus on both similarities and differences, and the historian embarking on comparative crime research must recognise this and be prepared constantly to reshape and reform the questions and hypotheses being deployed.

Around forty years ago, when academic historians first began to take crime seriously as a subject for study, property crime was a central focus. French historians were particularly interested in the notion of a shift from interpersonal violence to property crime going hand in hand with the shift from medieval to modern. Anglo-Saxon historians working on the eighteenth and nineteenth centuries suspected that new notions of property and changing work patterns over the period of the Industrial Revolution fostered an increase in appropriation by the burgeoning working classes. These hypotheses have worked themselves out, and with little to substantiate the earlier enthusiasm with which they were pursued. The apparent decline in violence, however, implicit in the *violence-vol* hypothesis, can be seen to have some links with Norbert Elias's conceptualisation, and it continues to act as a spur for research. Several of the essays that follow touch on these issues, particularly with reference to Elias's theory of the process of civilisation.

Maria Kaspersson's essay is typical of much of the contemporary research on homicide. Using particularly extensive statistics from Stockholm she is able to chart a significant decline in homicide over 400 years, with a particularly sharp downward trend during the seventeenth century. This ties in with the specific conclusions drawn by historians such as Roth (2001) and the general overview established by Eisner (2001). The problem, of course, is to account for the decline. Kaspersson interrogates the usual suspects, but concludes that while they may be able to explain some of the changing patterns of homicide, they do not readily account for them all. Implicitly this raises a recurring problem of theory and historical data which some out-and-out empiricists seek to resolve by claiming that theory is best rejected in preference for an emphasis on nothing but 'the facts'. Yet theory in some form remains essential for setting up questions, exploring data and, ultimately, for writing a cogent narrative.

Susanne Karstedt takes theory as her starting point. She rehearses Elias's civilising process and Foucault's emphases on the emergence of disciplinary and confining practices. These theories, as already noted above, have been instrumental in informing and shaping research over the last quarter of a century. But, as Karstedt stresses, there are other sociological and historical theories that are relevant to long-term change and yet these seem scarcely to have been considered in the analyses of criminal and especially violent behaviour. Focusing on the south-west German state of Würtemberg and drawing her inspiration from theories of modernisation and mobilisation, Karstedt looks at the interrelationship between the railway and the decline of violence. The railway was the first mass-impact technology, and one that created new forms of both isolation and integration. In Württemberg, moreover, with its small cities and towns and its slow but steady introduction to industrialisation, the railway was also, she argues, something that can be seen to have contributed in a measurable way to changes in mentalities and habits of violent behaviour.

One of the key continuities in the greater proportion of incidents of interpersonal violence across time, implicit in Karstedt's and explicit in Kaspersson's essays, is the fact that most of such violence is committed by men. This issue is taken up in the essay by John Carter Wood in which he rehearses some of the different methodologies deployed to explain violent behaviour. Since the Enlightenment students of criminal behaviour have assumed cross-cultural similarities in interpersonal violence with various evolutionary biological and psychological explanations being proposed. Wood touches on the broad explanations for the overall decline in violence, but his real interest is on how historians can use comparison to explore violence and the meaning of violence across different boundaries – the boundaries of time, of states and of regions being the most obvious – and to assess how narratives of violence and violent actions might interact in different cultural settings. Wood's essay echoes some of the cautions expressed by Morrison.

The comparison of narratives of violence from different cultural settings is the organising concept behind the essay by Peter King. King draws attention to the striking parallels between a press-generated panic in mid-eighteenth-century England and a similar phenomenon from the United States in the late twentieth century. His re-examination of theories of moral panics builds a bridge between history and criminology, both of which could profit from a closer relationship. Moreover, his paper challenges the assumptions that are sometimes made about the discontinuities that characterise the 'modern world' from earlier periods.

Violent behaviour, for example, is often seen as something more common in 'primitive' or early modern societies. A superficial reading of Elias's civilising process and the old *violence-vol* hypothesis would support such a perspective. Yet, invariably, research suggests that the reality is more complex. John Pratt's discussion of the decline and renaissance of restorative justice is illuminating here. Shaming punishments, which commonly involved an element of physical violence, virtually disappeared in Victorian Britain. Yet they continued, with appalling violence and viciousness, in the southern states of the USA. The reason, Pratt suggests, is not to be found in notions of the primitive, but in the development and particularly the strength and authority of the state. Shifts in this strength and authority have contributed to the resurgence of the shaming punishment. The problem for contemporary societies is what form of the shaming punishment will become the dominant: that which is stigmatic and humiliating, or that which is favoured by a modern group of penologists under the label of 'restorative justice'.

An Anglo-American comparison is also the basis of Gerard Oram's essay. Here the focus of the investigation is the persistence of legitimate violence within a central state institution – the military. Historians of crime have tended to shy away from the military, which is odd given, first, that the armed forces of a country generally consist of young men – the group within society that is responsible for most offending – and, second, that it was common for English courts, if not others, to comment during wartime that criminal trials at home had fallen. Oram demonstrates that in both countries the army was able to maintain considerable autonomy with respect to its law, not least because, unlike the nineteenth-century conscript armies of continental Europe, the rank and file were largely kept separate from society as a whole. Military law in Britain and America thus remained much harsher until a redefinition of the relationship between the soldier and the state in the wake of the First World War. Implicitly Oram demonstrates the need for more awareness of military law and for some assessment of the volume of criminal behaviour carried out by soldiers.

It has already been stressed that while in some instances comparison works, in others it does not. John Walton begins his essay noting a difficulty similar to that described by Morrison but involving an entire research team – the foundering of a comparative quantitative project on the history of crime in the north-west of England and the Basque country of northern Spain. On the other hand, as Walton goes on to show, it is possible to make useful comparisons and contrasts between Blackpool and San Sebastián in the late nineteenth and early twentieth centuries. Both towns developed as pleasure resorts, presenting similar problems of crowds of transient holidaymakers, new levels of social mixing and new forms of social space, notably the beach. These added up to new experiences and new tasks for policing authorities. And it is in the nature of comparative analysis that work such as Walton's should highlight, in addition to the similarities, the significant contrasts between, for example, legal, policing and other cultural structures and ideologies.

How different legal systems understand and address similar problems and how the same profession can encompass different cultural perspectives in different national contexts are explored further in the chapters by Heather Shore and Paul Lawrence. Shore argues that the nineteenth century was a key moment in the formation of new attitudes to juvenile offenders and hence of new forms of juvenile justice. Moreover, many of the discourses of delinquency that became dominant in Europe then remain significant today. Lawrence, in turn, picks up on a concept popular with contemporary academic analysts of policing – cop culture – and seeks to explore elements of its past through an evaluation of police memoirs and autobiographies. The important comparative element here is how English and French police memoirs have similar emphases on, for example, the nature of and their loyalty to the job, but how there are also significant differences in the way in which they portray themselves and structure their narratives.

The kinds of comparative work offered here by Shore and Lawrence, as well as several other contributors, is not linked to wide-ranging theoretical overviews of the decline of violence or the spread of discipline and surveillance. But the comparisons work, and might well be extended to similar explorations in other national contexts. The comparative history of crime is not the easiest option, and there are issues where comparison can cloud and confuse. But comparison and contrast remain essential for testing the broad theories that are, by their very nature, explanations of broad, international changes and processes. And they are also important for drawing attention to and understanding precisely why things are different in various regional or national contexts, and over time.

Notes

1. At a lower level, people move between sub-cultures throughout their lives, exchanging one for another, or simultaneously participating in many sub-cultural worlds (see Cohen, 1972, or the many sociological texts dealing with 'frame' analysis).
2. They were not the first to suggest universal behavioural codes and their relationship to law and order. Post, for example, stated that 'human societies

tend to evolve with similar codes of behaviour, and, in time, develop legal codes that reflect this' (Post, 1889).

3. Although Whittaker accepts that there are train-spotters in other countries, he insists that only the British have a 'true' fascination for the hobby (Whittaker, 1995: 243).

4. Hartley should really have said that the past was a loose federation of lands – for the seventeenth century is as different culturally as is the nineteenth- from the twenty-first century (Hartley, 1953: 1).

5 Fairburn's theories have recently been employed in a comparative analysis of crime in dynamic New Zealand and English communities (see Dunstall and Godfrey, 2003).

6. This glorification has not been without its critics. See Renier's biting satire, *The English: Are They Human?* published in 1934, particularly pp. 105–19.

7. A recent text on Pacific history stated that 'During the late nineteenth century the colonists groped towards a distinctive sense of themselves as separate (though not apart) from the Mother Culture' (no doubt assisted by the proportion of people born in Australia reaching 80 per cent by 1900) – see Denoon *et al.* (2000: 12).

8. Early twentieth-century Australia was among the most urbanised nations in the world, yet could draw upon a vast continent-sized area of undeveloped bush should they wish to use it. It was the bush and its conquering which had held nascent Australian national identity spellbound, and which allowed a country of urbanites to develop a national identity based on heroic rural virtues.

9. Riles talks of the international plane, a geometric analogy – but it also arouses a fascinating image of criminologists peering down on the countries they study from the windows of a Boeing 747.

References

Adam, B., Beck, U. and Loon, van J. *The Risk Society and Beyond: Critical Issues for Social Theory*. Sage: London, 2000.

Albrow, M. *The Global Age. State and Society Beyond Modernity*. Cambridge: Polity, 1996.

Anderson, B. *Imagined Communities: Reflections on the Origin and Spread of Nationalism*. London: Verso, 1991.

Anderson, D. and Killingray, D. (eds) *Policing the Empire: Government, Authority and Control, 1830–1914*. Manchester: Manchester University Press, 1991.

Anderson, D. and Killingray, D. (eds) *Policing and Decolonisation: Nationalism, Politics and the Police, 1917–1965*. Manchester: Manchester University Press, 1992.

Arnot, M. L. and Usborne, C. (eds) *Gender and Crime in Modern Europe*. London: UCL Press, 1999.

Barry, J. and Melling, J. 'The problem of culture: an introduction', in Barry, J. and Melling, J. (eds), *Culture in History. Production, Consumption and Values in Historical Perspective*. Exeter: University of Exeter Press, 1992.

Bayley, D. H. 'The police and political development in Europe', in Tilly, C. (ed.), *The Formation of the National States in Western Europe*. Princeton, NJ: Princeton University Press, 1975.

Beck, U. *Risk Society: Towards a New Modernity*, trans. M. Ritter. London: Sage, 1992.

Bedani, G. and Haddock, B. (eds) *The Politics of Italian National Identity. A Multidisciplinary Perspective*. Cardiff: University of Wales Press, 2000.

Beirne, P. and Nelkin, D. *Issues in Comparative Criminology*. Aldershot: Dartmouth, 1983.

Belich, J. *Making Peoples: A History of New Zealanders from Polynesian Settlement to the End of the Nineteenth Century*. Auckland: Allen Lane. The Penguin Press, 1996.

Bentley, T. *Pakeha Maori. The Extraordinary Story of the Europeans Who Lived as Maori in Early New Zealand*. Auckland: Penguin, 1999.

Berlière, J.-M. and Peschanski, D. (eds) *Pouvoirs et polices au XXe siècle*. Brussels: Editions Complexe, 1997.

Binney, J. (ed) *The Shaping of History*. Wellington: Bridget Williams Books, 2001.

Black, J. *A History of the British Isles*. London: Macmillan, 1996.

Black, J. *Europe and the World, 1650–1830*. London: Routledge, 2001.

Blok, A. 'Social banditry reconsidered', *Comparative Studies in Society and History*, 14, 1972, pp. 495–505 (including a response by E. J. Hobsbawm); reprinted in A. Blok, *Honour and Violence*. Cambridge: Polity Press, 2001.

Braithwaite, J. *Restorative Justice: Assessing an Immodest Theory and a Pessimistic Theory*. Canberra: ANU Press, 1997.

Bryant, A. *The National Character*. London: Longmans, 1934.

Bull, S. ' "The land of murder, cannibalism, and all kinds of atrocious crimes?" An overview of "Maori" crime from pre-colonial times to the present day'. Unpublished PhD thesis, Victoria University of Wellington, 2001.

Burke, P. *History and Social Theory*. London: Polity, 1992.

Callinicos, A. *Theories and narratives. Reflections on the Philosophy of History*, London: Polity, 1995.

Cohen, S. *Folk Devils and Moral Panics the Creation of the Mods and Rockers*. London: MacGibbon & K, 1972.

Colley, L. *Britains: Forging the nation, 1707–1837*. New Haven: Yale University Press, 1992.

Colley, L. *Captives. Britain, Empire and the World, 1600–1850*. London: Jonathon Cape, 2002.

Collini, S. *English Pasts. Essays in Culture and History*. Oxford: Oxford University Press, 1999.

Colls, R. *The Identity of England*. Oxford: Oxford University Press, 2002.

Colls, R. and Dodd, P. (eds) *Englishness. Politics and Culture, 1800–1920*. London: Croom Helm, 1986.

Cox, P. and Shore, H. (eds) *Becoming Delinquent: British and European Youth, 1650–1950*. Aldershot: Ashgate Publishing, 2002.

Crotty, M. *Making the Australian Male, 1870–1920*. Melbourne: Melbourne University Press, 2001.

Crump, B. *A Good Keen Man*. Auckland: Firstlight Productions, 1960.

Dalby, L. *Geisha*. London: Vintage, 2000 edition.

Davie, M. *Anglo-Australian Attitudes*. London: Pimlico, 2001.

Davis, J. 'Prosecutions and their context. The use of the criminal law in later nineteenth century London', in Hay, D. and Synder, F. (eds), *Policing and Prosecution in Britain 1750–1850*. Oxford: Oxford University Press, 1989.

Davison, G. *The Use and Abuse of Australian History*. Sydney: Allen & Unwin, 2000.

Day, D. *Australian Identities*. Melbourne: Australian Scholarly Publishing, 1998.

Dean, T. *Crime in Medieval Europe 1200–1550*. London: Longman, 2001.

Deflem, M. *Policing World Society: Historical Foundations of International Police Co-operation*. Oxford: Oxford University Press, 2002.

Denoon, D., Mein-Smith, P. and Wyndham, M. *A History of Australia, New Zealand and the Pacific*. Oxford: Blackwells, 2000.

Dirlik, A. *Postmodernity's Histories. The Past as Legacy and Project*. Lanham, MD: Rowman & Littlefield, 2000.

Dixson, M. *The Real Matilda. Women and Identity in Australia – 1788 to the Present*. Sydney: University of New South Wales Press, 1976, fourth edn 1999.

Dixson, M. *The Imaginary Australian. Anglo-Celts and Identity – 1788 to the Present*. Sydney: University of New South Wales Press, 1999.

Dunkerley, D., Hodgson, L., Konopacki, S., Spybey, T. and Thompson, A. *Changing Europe. Identities, Nations and Citizens*. London: Routledge, 2002.

Dunstall, G. *A Policeman's Paradise? Policing a Stable Society 1918–1945*. Palmerston North: Dunmore Press, 1999.

Dunstall, G. and Godfrey, B. 'Crime in Developing Communities: Timaru (NZ) and Crewe (UK)'. Paper to the Australian and New Zealand Criminology Society, Sydney, 1–4 October, 2003.

Durkheim, E. *The Rules of Sociological Method*, 1895: ch. 6; see also S. Lukes (ed.) *The Rules of Sociological Method, and Selected Texts on Sociology and Its Method*, trans. W. D. Halls. London: Macmillan, 1982.

Dussel, E. 'Beyond Eurocentrism: the world-system and the limits of modernity', in Jameson, F. and Miyoshi, M. (eds), *The Cultures of Globalization*. London: Duke, 1998.

Eisner, M. 'Modernization, self-control and lethal violence: the long-term dynamics of European homicide rates in theoretical perspective', *British Journal of Criminology*, 41, 2001, pp. 618–38.

Emsley, C. 'The nation state and the peasant in 19th century Europe', in Rousseaux, X. and Lévy, R. (eds), *Pénal dans tous les Etats: Justice, Etats, Sociétés en Europe (XII, XX, CX Siècles)*. Brussels: Publications des Facultés Universitaires Saint Louis, 1997.

Emsley, C. 'A typology of nineteenth-century police', *Crime, histoire et sociétés/Crime, history and societies*, 3, 1, 1999a, pp. 29–44.

Emsley, C. *Gendarmes and the State in Nineteenth-Century Europe.* Oxford: Oxford University Press, 1999b.

Evans, R. J. *Rituals of Retribution: Capital Punishment in Germany 1600–1987.* Oxford: Oxford University Press, 1996.

Fairburn, M. *The Ideal Society and Its Enemies. The Foundations of Modern New Zealand Society 1850–1900.* Auckland: Auckland University Press, 1989.

Fairburn, M. *Social History: Problems, Strategies and Methods.* London: Macmillan, 1999.

Fairburn, M. and Haslett, S. 'Violent crime in old and new societies – a case *Study Based* on New Zealand 1853–1940', *Journal of Social History*, 20, 1986, pp. 89–126.

Fitzpatrick, P. 'Laws of the postcolonial: an insistent introduction', in Darian-Smith, E. (ed.), *Laws of the Postcolonial.* Ann Arbor, MI: University of Michigan Press, 1999.

Foster, R., Hosking, R. and Nettelbeck, A. (eds) *Fatal Collisions. The South Australian Frontier and the Violence of Memory.* Kent Town, Adelaide: Wakefield Press, 2001.

Foucault, M. *Discipline and Punish: The Birth of the Prison*, trans. A. Sheridan. London: Allen Lane, 1997.

Garland, D. *Punishment and Modern Society: A Study in Social Theory.* Oxford: Clarendon Press, 1990.

Gatrell, V. A. C. and Hadden, T. B. 'Criminal statistics and their interpretation', in Wrigley, E. A. (ed.), *Nineteenth Century Society.* Cambridge: Cambridge University Press, 1972.

Gatrell, V. A. C, 'The decline of theft and violence in Victorian and Edwardian England', in Gatrell, V. A. C., Lenman, B. and Parker, G. (eds), *Crime and the Law: The Social History of Crime in Western Europe since 1500.* London: Europa, 1980.

Gatrell, V. A. C. 'Crime, authority and the policeman-state', in Thompson, F. M. L. (ed.), *The Cambridge Social History of Britain 1750–1950*, Volume 3, Social Agencies and Institutions. Cambridge: Cambridge University Press, 1990.

Gattrell, V. A. C. *The Hanging Tree: Execution and the English People 1770–1868.* Oxford: Oxford University Press, 1994.

Girling, E., Loader, I. and Sparks, R. *Crime and Social Change in Middle England: Questions of Order in an English Town.* London: Routledge, 2000.

Godfrey, B. 'Counting and accounting for the decline in non-lethal violence in violence in England, Australia and New Zealand, 1880–1920', *British Journal of Criminology*, 43, 2, 2003, pp. 230–55.

Goodall, H. 'Aboriginal history and the politics of information control' in White, R. and Russell, P. (eds), *Memories and Dreams. Reflections on 20th Century Australia.* Sydney: Allen & Unwin, 1997.

Greenfeld, L. *Nationalism: Five Roads to Modernity.* Cambridge, MA: Harvard University Press, 1992.

Gurr, T. R., Grabosky, P. N. and Hula, R. C. *The Politics of Crime and Conflict: A Comparative History of Four Cities.* Beverly Hills, CA: Sage, 1977.

Harring, S. *Crow Dog's Case: American Indian Sovereignty, Tribal Law, and United States Law in the Nineteenth Century.* New York: Cambridge University Press, 1994.

Hartley, L. P. *The Go-Between*. London: Hamilton Press, 1953.

Haslett, S. J. and Fairburn, M. 'Interprovincial differences in the rates of minor crimes of violence and related disorders in New Zealand 1853–1930', *Historical Social Research/Historische Soczialforschung*, 15, 4, 1990, pp. 140–83.

Hassam, A. *Through Australian Eyes. Colonial Perceptions of Imperial Britain*. Melbourne: Melbourne University Press, 2000.

Hay, D. and Snyder, F. (eds) *Policing and Prosecution in Britain, 1750–1850*. Oxford: Clarendon, 1989.

Hegel, G. *Lectures on the Philosophy of World History. Introduction: Reason in History*, translated from the German edition of Johannes Hoffmeister by H. B. Nisbet, with an introduction by D. Forbes. Cambridge: Cambridge University Press, 1975.

Heiland, H., Shelley, L. and Katoh, H. (eds) *Crime and Control in Comparative Perspectives*. Berlin: de Gruyter, 1992.

Henry, B. 'Identities of the West. Reason, myths, limits of tolerance', in Friese, H. (ed.), *Identities. Time, Difference and Boundaries*. London: Berghann Books, 2002.

Hill, R. S. *Policing the Colonial Frontier: The Theory and Practice of Coercive Social and Racial Control in New Zealand, 1767–1867*. Wellington: Government Printer, 1986.

Hill, R. S. *The Colonial Frontier Tamed: New Zealand Policing in Transition, 1867–1886*. Wellington: Government Printer, 1989.

Hill, R. S. *The Iron Hand in the Velvet Glove: The Modernisation of Policing in New Zealand, 1886–1917*. Palmerston North: Dunmore Press, 1995.

Himmelfarb, G. *The De-moralization of Society from Victorian Virtues to Modern Values*. London, IEA Health and Welfare Unit, 1995.

Hobsbawm, E.J. *Bandits*. London: Weidenfeld & Nicolson, 1969.

Hobsbawm, E. J. *Nations and Nationality since 1780: Programme, Myth, Reality*. Cambridge: Cambridge University Press, 1990.

Howard, C. *Australian Criminal Law*. Melbourne: Law Book Company, 1965.

Hudson, W. and Bolton, B. *Creating Australia, Changing Australian History*. St Leonards, NSW: Allen & Unwin, 1998.

Hutchinson, J. *Modern Nationalism*. London: Fontana, 1994.

Ignatieff, M. *A Just Measure of Pain: The Penitentiary in the Industrial Revolution 1750–1850*. London: Macmillan, 1978.

Ireland, R. W. ' "An increasing mass of heathens in the bosom of a Christian land": the railway and crime in the nineteenth century', *Continuity and Change*, 12, 1, 1997, pp. 55–78.

Jackson, M. *The Maori and the Criminal Justice System – A New Perspective: He Whaipaanga Hou*. Wellington: New Zealand Department of Justice, 1988.

Jewell, H. *The North-South Divide: The Origins of Northern Consciousness in England*. Manchester: Manchester University Press, 1994.

Johnson, E. A. and Monkkonen, E. H. (eds) *The Civilization of Crime: Violence in Town and Country since the Middle Ages*. Urbana, IL and Chicago: University of Illinois Press, 1996.

Karstedt, S. 'Comparing cultures, comparing crime: challenges, prospects and problems for a global criminology', *Crime, Law and Social Change*, 36, 2001, pp. 285–308.

Karstedt, S. 'Durkheim, Tarde and beyond: the global travel of crime policies', *Criminal Justice*, 2, 2, 2002, pp. 111–23.

Kercher, B. *An Unruly Child: A History of Law in Australia*. St. Leonards, NSW: Allen & Unwin, 1995.

King, M. *Being Pakeha*. Auckland: Hodder & Stoughton, 1985.

Kirk, N. (ed.) *Northern Identities. Historical Interpretations of 'The North' and 'Northerness'*. Aldershot: Ashgate, 2000.

'La statistique judiciaire: son histoire et ses usages scientifiques', special edition of *Déviance et Société*, 22, 1998.

Langford, P. *Englishness Identified. Manners and Character, 1650–1850*. Oxford: Oxford University Press, 2000.

Leavitt, G. 'Relativism and cross-cultural criminology', *Journal of Crime and Delinquency*, 27, 1, pp. 5–29.

Lee, J. *Roughnecks, Rolling Stones and Rouseabouts*. Christchurch: Whitcoulls, 1977.

Liang, H.-H. *The Rise of Modern Police and the European State System from Metternich to the Second World War*. Cambridge: Cambridge University Press, 1992.

Loader, I. *Policing and the Condition of England. Memory, Politics and Culture*. Oxford: Oxford University Press, 2003.

Luc, J.-N. (ed.) *Gendarmerie, état et société au XIXe siècle*. Paris: Publications de la Sorbonne, 2002.

Lüdtke, A. 'Sicherheit' und 'Wohlfahrt', *Polizei, Gesellschaft und Herrschaft im 19. und 20. Jahrhundert*. Frankfurt am Main: Suhrkamp, 1992.

Lynn, R. *Personality and National Character*. Oxford: Pergamon Press, 1971.

MacDonald, C. 'Crime and punishment in New Zealand 1840–1913: a gendered history', *New Zealand Journal of History*, 23, 1, 1989, pp. 5–21.

Malcolm, J. L. *Guns and Violence: The English Experience*. Cambridge, MA: Harvard University Press, 2002.

Mannheim, H. *Social Aspects of Crime in England between the Wars*. London: Allen & Unwin, 1940.

Mazower, M. (ed.) *The Policing of Politics in the Twentieth Century: Historical Perspectives*. Providence, RI and Oxford: Berghahn Books, 1997.

Mellaerts, W. 'Dispute settlement and the law in three provincial towns in France, England and Holland, 1880–1914'. Unpublished PhD thesis, University of East Anglia, 1997.

Mellaerts, W. 'Criminal justice in provincial England, France and Netherlands, c. 1880–1905: some comparative perspectives', *Crime, histoire et sociétés/Crime, History and Societies*, 4, 2, 2000, pp. 19–52.

Monkonnen, E. *Murder in New York City*. Los Angeles: University of Californian Press, 2001.

Morris, N. and Rothman, D. (eds) *The Oxford History of the Prison: The Practice of Punishment in Western Society*. Oxford: Oxford University Press, 1995.

Morris, R. M. ' "Lies, damned lies and criminal statistics": reinterpreting the criminal statistics in England and Wales', *Crime, histoire et societes/Crime, History and Societies*, 5, 1, 2001, pp. 111–127.

Murrie, L. 'Australian legend and Australian men', in Nile, R. (ed.), *The Australian Legend and its Discontents*. St Lucia: University of Queensland Press, 2000.

Nelkin, D. 'Understanding criminal justice comparatively', *The Oxford Handbook of Criminology*. Oxford: Oxford University Press, 1996.

Nelson, H. 'Gallipoli, Kokoda and the making of national identity', in Nile, R. (ed.), *The Australian Legend and its Discontents*. St Lucia: University of Queensland Press, 2000.

Nicoll, F. *From Diggers to Drag Queens*. Annandale: Pluto Press, 2001.

Nile, R. 'Introduction', *The Australian Legend and Its Discontents*. St Lucia: Queensland Press, 2000.

Nye, R. *Crime, Madness and Politics in Modern France: The Medical Concept of National Decline*. Princeton, NJ: Princeton University Press, 1984.

O'Brien, P. *The Promise of Punishment: Prisons in Nineteenth-Century France*. Princeton, NJ: Princeton University Press, 1982.

Ortalli, G. (ed.) *Bande armate, banditi, banditismo e repressione di guistizia negli stati europei di antico regime*. Rome: Jouvence, 1985.

Orwell. G. *The English People*. London: Collins, 1944.

Parsonson, A. 'Aotearoa/New Zealand' section in 'Race, gender and nation in history and law' in Kirkby, D. and Coleborne, C. (eds), *Law, History and Colonialism: The Reach of Empire*. Manchester: Manchester University Press, 2001.

Peabody, D. *National Characteristics*. Cambridge: Cambridge University Press, 1985.

Pecora, V. 'The limits of local knowledge', in Veesna, H. (ed.), *The New Historicism*. New York: Routledge, 1989, pp. 243–76.

Perrot, M. (ed.) *L'impossible prison. Recherche sur le système pénitentiaire au XIXe siècle*. Paris: Seuil, 1980.

Phillips, J. *A Man's Country? The Image of the Pakeha Male – a History*. London: Penguin, 1996.

Pick, D. *Faces of Degeneration: A European Disorder, c.1848–1919*. Cambridge: Cambridge University Press, 1989.

Platt, W. *National Character in Action – Intelligence Factors in Foreign Relations*. New Brunswick, NJ: Rutgers University Press, 1961.

Post. *Studien zur Entwicklungsgeschicte des Familienrechts*. 1889.

Pratt, J. *Punishment in a Perfect Society: The New Zealand Penal System 1840–1939*. Wellington: Victoria University Press, 1992.

Pratt, J. *Punishment and Civilization*. London: Sage, 2002.

Priestley, J. B. *The English*. London: Heinemann, 1973.

Purdy, J. 'Postcolonialism: the emperor's new clothes?', in Darian-Smith, E. (ed.), *Laws of the postcolonial*. Ann Arbor, MI: University of Michigan Press, 1999.

Ranke, L. von, *The Theory and Practice of History*, ed. and intro. G. G. Iggers and K. von Moltke; trans. W. A. Iggers and K. von Moltke. Indianapolis, IN: Bobbs-Merrill, 1973.

Reiner, R. *The Politics of the Police*. Hemel Hempstead: Harvester Wheatsheaf, 2000.

Renier, G. *The English: Are They Human?* Leipzig: Berhard Tauchnitz, 1932.

Reynolds, H. *Fate of a Free People. A Radical Re-examination of the Tasmanian Wars*. London: Penguin, 1995.

Richards, J. and MacKenzie, J. *The Railway Station: A Social History*. Oxford: Oxford University Press, 1988.

Riles, A. 'The view from the international plane: perspective and scale in the architecture of colonial international law', in Darian-Smith, E. (ed.), *Laws of the postcolonial*. Ann Arbor, MI, University of Michigan Press, 1999.

Roth, R. 'Homicide in Early Modern England, 1549–1800: the need for a quantitative synthesis', *Crime, Histoire et Societies/Crime, History and Societies*, 5, 2001, pp. 33–67.

Roth, R. 'Counting guns: what social scientists and historians could learn about gun ownership, gun culture, and gun violence in the United States', *Social Science and History*, 26, 2002, p. 699–708.

Rousseaux, X. and Lévy, R. (eds) *Le pénal dans tous ses États: Justice, États et sociétés en Europe (XIIe–XXe siècles)*, Brussels: Publications des Facultés universitaires Saint-Louis, 1997.

Rousseaux, X., Dupont-Bouchat, M.-S., and Vael, C. (eds) *Révolutions et justice pénale en Europe. Modèles français et traditions nationales 1780–1830*. Paris: L'Harmattan, 1999.

Ruff, J. R. *Violence in Early Modern Europe 1500–1800*. Cambridge: Cambridge University Press, 2001.

Rushby, K. *Children of Kali: Through India in Search of Bandits, the Thug Cult, and the British Raj*. London: Constable Robinson, 2003.

Said, E. *Orientalism*. London: Routledge, 1978.

Sharp, A. and McHugh, P. (eds) *Histories, Power and Loss*. Wellington: Bridget Williams Books, 2001.

Singha, R. *A Despotism of Law: Crime and Justice in Early Colonial India*. Oxford: Oxford University Press, 1998.

Sinha, M. *Colonial Masculinity. The 'Manly Englishman' and the 'Effeminate Bengali' in the Late Nineteenth Century*. Manchester: Manchester University Press, 1995.

Smith, A. *Nations and Nationalism in a Global Era*. Cambridge: Polity, 1995.

Smith, P. *Milenial Dreams. Contemporary Culture and Capital in the North*. London: Verso, 1997.

Spierenburg, P. *The Spectacle of Suffering: Executions and the Evolution of Repression from a Preindustrial Metropolis to the European Experience*. Cambridge: Cambridge University Press, 1984a.

Spierenburg, P. (ed.) *The Emergence of Carcereal Institutions: Prisons, Galleys and Lunatic Asylums*. Rotterdam: Erasmus University Press, 1984b.

Spierenburg, P. 'Elias and the history of crime and criminal justice: a brief evaluation', *Bulletin of the International Association for the History of Crime and Criminal Justice*, 20, 1995, pp. 17–30.

Spierenburg, P. *The Prison Experience: Disciplinary Institutions and Their Inmates in Early Modern Europe*. New Brunswick, NJ: Rutgers University Press, 1991.

Spierenburg, P. 'Masculinity, violence, and honour: an introduction', in Spierenburg, P. (ed.), *Men and Violence. Gender, Honour and Rituals in Modern Europe and America*. Chicago: Ohio State University Press, 1998.

Spiller, P., Finn, J. and Boast, R. *A Legal History of New Zealand*. Wellington: Brookers, 1995.

Stokes, G. *The Politics of Identity in Australia*. Cambridge: Cambridge University Press, 1997.

Taylor, H. 'Rationing crime: the political economy of criminal statistics since the 1850s', *Economic History Review*, 61, 1998, pp. 569–90.

Taylor, I., Evans, K. and Fraser, P. *A Tale of Two Cities: Global Change, Local Feeling and Everyday Life in the North of England. A Study in Manchester and Sheffield*. London: Routledge, 1996.

Tidrick, K. *Empire and the English Character*. London: I. B. Tauris, 1992.

Toynbee, A. *A Study of History*, 12 vols, Vol. I. London: Penguin, 1935.

Walker, R. *Ka Whawhai Tonu Matou: Struggle Without End*. Auckland: Penguin Books, 1990.

Walton, J. K., Blinkhorn, M., Pooley, C., Tidswell, D. and Winstanley, M. J. 'Crime, migration and social change in North-West England and the Basque Country, c.1870–1930', *British Journal of Criminology*, 39, 1, 1999, pp. 90–112.

Ward, A. *The Show of Justice: Racial 'Amalgamation' in Nineteenth Century New Zealand*, 2nd edn. Auckland: Auckland University Press, 1995.

Weaver, J. C. *Crimes, Constables, and Courts: Order and Transgression in a Canadian City, 1816–1970*. Montreal/Kingston: McGill/Queens University Press, 1995.

Weisser, M. R. *Crime and Punishment in Early Modern Europe*. Brighton: Harvester, 1979.

White, P. *On Living in an Old Country. The National Past in Contemporary Britain*. London: Verso, 1985.

White, P. *A Journey Through Ruins. A Keyhole Portrait of British Postwar Life and Culture*. London: Paladin, 1992.

Whittaker, N. *Platform Souls. The Trainspotter as 20th Century Hero*. London: Indigo, 1995.

Wiener, M. 'The sad story of George Hall: adultery, murder, and the politics of mercy in mid-Victorian England', *Social History*, 24, 2, 1999.

Wiener, M. *The un-Englishness of Crimes of Passion*. Paper to the British Academy Comparative Histories of Crime Conference, Keele University, July, 2002a.

Wiener, M. *The Criminal Ideology of the Victorian Judiciary*. Paper to the British Criminology Society Conference 'Crossing Borders', Keele University, July 2002b.

Williams, C. *Being Beastly about the Germans: Police, Violence and Nationalism in mid-20th cent. Britain*. Paper to the British Academy Comparative Histories of Crime Conference, Keele University, July 2002.

Wood, J. 'Self-policing and the policing of the self: violence, protection and the civilizing bargain in Britain', *Crime, History and Societies*, forthcoming 2003.

Wrightson, K. 'Two concepts of order: justices, constables and jurymen in 17th century England', in Brewer, J. and Styles, J. (eds), *An Ungovernable People: The English and Their Law in the Seventeenth and Eighteenth Centuries*. London: Hutchinson, 1980.

Zehr, H. *Crime and the Development of Modern Society: Patterns of Criminality in Nineteenth-Century France and Germany*. London: Croom Helm, 1976.

Chapter 2

It's a small world after all? Reflections on violence in comparative perspectives

John Carter Wood

Violence almost inevitably evokes a comparative perspective. Whether on an individual or collective level, violence is compared across time (e.g. through legal precedents or narratives of a prior, pacific 'golden age' (Pearson, 1983: 3–11)) as well as space (e.g. as particular kinds of violence are perceived as non-native or nations are ranked by their 'quantity' of violence). It has also been claimed that comparative approaches are useful intellectual tools: 'violence is understood best when it is examined over a range of cultural settings, and in a full variety of social situations' (Riches, 1986: vii). Certainly, as the essays in this collection attest, historical violence studies are now developing in a distinctly comparative direction; however, 'comparative history' has many meanings and raises challenging questions. In addressing some – though by no means all – of these questions, I will explore some general conceptual issues in comparative violence history. First, I will consider a few disciplinary matters related to the study of violence. I shall also examine various kinds of 'boundaries': those that framed the experiences of historical subjects as well as those that historians impose in the course of their work. In particular, I will suggest the utility of looking at the 'mobility' and 'permeability' of 'cultures of violence'. Finally, I evaluate one potentially useful conceptual framework and point to two issues that comparative studies can helpfully illuminate – the 'narratives' and 'practices' of violence – while drawing attention to the ways that findings and theories can be borrowed and lent across disciplines and national boundaries.

Scales of analysis and the locations of violence

Numerous and diverse discourses have grown around the phenomenon of violence, tending to gather around the well-known poles of 'nature' and 'nurture'. The sources of violence are accordingly 'located' differently: within the individual's biology or psychology or among the social and cultural networks that surround him or her. Those methodologies interact with different scales of space, time and violence that influence the degree of contact (or conflict) among various disciplines. While the nature-or-nurture question is always present in any analysis of violence, it has particular relevance to those who work cross-culturally. First, both sorts of approaches make use of comparative perspectives. Second, once the boundary of the locality or nation is breached and the geographical scale of a historical inquiry increases, the commonalities in the subject under study may become more prominent. In comparative violence history, then, violence itself moves to the fore. As the parameters of social and cultural contingency and national specificity within which most historians work are stretched, history confronts other disciplines that frame the phenomenon of violence in very different ways.

Biological explanations of violent behaviour have been present since the nineteenth-century birth of evolutionary theory. Darwin, for example, argued that humankind's 'worst dispositions' were caused by reversion to a 'savage state, from which we are not removed by many generations' (Darwin, 1871: 79). Such 'naturalistic' views have gathered force with that field's continuing development (Wiener, 1990: 159–71; Lorenz, 1966; Weisfeld, 1994). The most trenchant and widely cited evolutionary arguments on human violence come from Martin Daly and Margot Wilson. They view homicide through the lens of evolutionary adaptation, concluding, for instance, that much male-on-male violence has its source in status striving that serves the interests of reproduction (Daly and Wilson, 1988: 163–86; Daly and Wilson, 1994: 268–9). Child abuse and infanticide are positively correlated with step-parenthood, not as adaptive behaviours, but rather due to a relative degree of decreased effort by non-genetic parents in the care of their young (Daly and Wilson, 1988: 83–93; Daly and Wilson, 1994: 270–1). Other Darwinian explanations relevant to aggression and violence have followed (Wrangham and Peterson, 1996; Turner, 1994; Pitchford, 2001), while arguments for the 'selfish gene' have gained a strong, if contentious, foothold (Dawkins, 1990). Evolutionary methodologies work on two scales simultaneously, locating the sources of violence in the minute level of genetics while making universal and global conclusions. Daly and Wilson, for example, are expressly comparative and wide ranging, using statistical studies from medieval England, modern US cities and tribal groups in Africa, the Americas and Asia (Daly and Wilson,

1988: 35, 147–8). While making some allowance for cultural impacts upon variability in violence rates, the emphasis in their approach is to show similarity across time and space (Daly and Wilson, 1988: 152–61, 284–91).

Psychology has also influenced interpretations of the phenomenon of violence and – to varying degrees – has tended toward universalising it. In some analyses, deeply imprinted structures in the human mind rather than particular forms of social interaction are the sources for a range of human behaviours, violence among them (Pinker, 1997; Beck, 2000). However, it is Freud who seems to have attracted the most interest among historians in looking at aggression and violence, perhaps due to a certain ambivalence within his analysis that is visible, for example, in his essay *Civilisation and Its Discontents*. On the one hand, he suggests the existence of psychological drives that would remain immune to radical trans-formations of social life: thus, aggression is an 'ineffaceable feature of human nature' (Freud, 1994: 42).[1] However, at the same time Freud leaves room for historical perspectives as to the ways that violence has interacted with different kinds of social organisation. In his view, the 'struggle between Eros and Death' – between love and aggression – has shaped the historical development of human civilisation, and 'the fateful question of the human species seems...to be whether and to what extent the cultural process developed in it will succeed in mastering the derangements of communal life caused by the human instinct of aggression and self-destruction' (Freud, 1994: 49, 70). Here, internal tendencies toward aggression are instinctual and eternal; only the success or failure of cultural defence mechanisms is contingent and changeable. Undoubtedly, historians have been able to make good use of Freudian insights (Gay, 1985; Gay, 1993; Gatrell, 1994: 236–41; Fergusson, 1998: 357–9). However, while the evolutionary chronology is vast, that of the psychological can be absent, lacking – even in the case of self-described 'psychohistory' – an approach that locates human psychological experiences within any particular kind of timescale. One psychological history reader makes this point clear: 'In our teaching of undergraduates, we have discovered that psychohistory is an ideal vehicle for introducing the timeless questions of human motivation in the past' (Cocks and Crosby, 1987: ix).

'Nature' and 'nurture' are, of course, shorthand terms, and most studies mix elements of both approaches (Daly and Wilson, 1988: 9). There are, furthermore, profound disagreements within psychology and evol-utionary biology. What I point to here is the interrelationship between these approaches and comparative violence history: although prone to using comparative data, they tend toward finding similarities in violent behaviour on a global and more-or-less timeless scale. Such broad geographical and chronological parameters can make meaningful comparisons difficult, and they leave little place for history, at least a history that assumes social relations, cultural patterns or local contingencies have more to offer than merely cataloguing symptoms of a universal human condition. As a discipline, historians interested in cross-cultural violence study will need to find ways of using – or alternatively challenging – these theories (Hunt, 1996). At the same time, the expansion of violence history in a comparative direction poses intriguing questions about its reliance upon models of discursive or social constructionism (D'Cruze, 2000: 18). For instance, Arnot recently registered her 'dissatisfaction' with the tools of social, cultural and economic explanation in dealing with her historical evidence on the practice of infanticide (Arnot, 2000: 63). As a result, she reaches to modern psychiatry and, using a comparative perspective, suggests a universal element in the experience of that kind of violence.[2] Such analyses point to the instabilities of disciplinary borders and the potential for fruitful borrowing across them. The boundaries between society and individual – and between the biological or psychological and the cultural – will be key aspects of understanding violence in a comparative perspective.

Making (and breaking) boundaries

It may be legitimately asked whether or not a nation-oriented violence history makes sense. I think it does, but other questions (and boundaries) are inevitable. What is being emphasised: the general issue of violence itself or its place within a particular national narrative? What phenomena were impacting on violence and vice versa, and to what extent were they cross-national? What boundaries did historical subjects themselves see as relevant to violence? What kinds of larger comparative frameworks are appropriate? As I suggested in the preceding section, once the scale of study is expanded, the focus shifts more decisively to the foregrounding of violence itself as the common denominator between two (or more) geographical or chronological territories, thus drawing history into more direct engagements with other disciplines. I will return to this theme in my final section, but I first want to consider some of the tensions between national and international perspectives on violence.

Even leaving aside the global biological and psychological arguments I have already discussed, social and cultural influences on violence – e.g. migration, capitalism, legal systems, religion and social theory – were international. State borders have rarely been successful at confining economic change, cultural transmission and the movements of people. For example, capitalism began to impact all European nations (at differing rates) at any time between the seventeenth and nineteenth centuries, depending on one's point of view. Concurrently, state building and class formation were international phenomena that reciprocally interacted with attitudes toward violence. Law forged links among those nations characterised by, say, Roman or common-law systems and, through imperialism, was exported globally. Religious belief and church actions influenced attitudes and the treatment of violence across national boundaries. Criminals were themselves highly mobile. The great social theorists – such as Marx, Durkheim, Weber, Freud, Elias or those of the Chicago School – combined detailed empirical work with transnational conclusions about human behaviour, a sociological inheritance that has greatly influenced the historiography of violence.

Criminology, even before the study of crime was given that name, was shaped by the Enlightenment's emphasis on the universality of reason and human understanding. Physical and social theories of crime and violence evolved internationally and were applied and compared globally. The resulting policies spread widely, from Beccaria's punishment theories to the American prison experiments that formed a key example-in-practice for European penologists (Emsley, 1987: 216–17). Wetzell has recently commented upon the development of European criminology, emphasising its cross-national character. For example, three medical explanations were most influential in the nineteenth century, those of the Austrian Franz Joseph Gall (phrenology), the Frenchman Etienne-Jean George ('homicidal monomania') and the Briton James Pritchard ('moral insanity') (Wetzell, 2000: 17). Social analyses were equally international: the 'moral topographies' of the 'dangerous classes' – focused upon the urban centres that were coming to dominate nineteenth-century Europe – were remarkably similar in their assumptions, methods and rhetoric. From 'moral statisticians' – such as Quételet, Guerry and Chadwick – to the 'moral topographers' – Frégier's study of Paris, Mayhew's investigation of London and Avé-Lallemant's inquiries into the *Gaunertum* (the German professional criminal class) – these various streams fed into a discipline that assumed the relevance of cross-cultural, comparative crime analysis. Thus, Wetzell concludes, 'the late nineteenth-century birth of criminology was in many respects a general western European phenomenon, taking place in Italy, France, Germany, and to a lesser extent Britain, among other countries' (Wetzell, 2000: 26–31).

At the same time, international phenomena were nationally, regionally and locally fragmented: the creation of violence as a social issue coincided with the expansion of nationalism and the erection of imagined boundaries that may not have fit the actual patterns of human behaviour either within or across them. The perception and depiction of national differences increased, a characteristic common to western capitalist societies that also contributed to reshaping attitudes toward violence and aggression (Sibley, 1984; Gay, 1993: 68). For example, although an international 'bourgeois experience' is at the heart of Peter Gay's study of aggression, 'others' were often defined by their nationality (Gay, 1993: 35–6). Many nineteenth-century British commentators applied the language of national identity to violence, finding numerous ways to compare and discuss the predilections of foreigners for violence: usually, though not always, these comparisons were favourable to Britain (Wood, 2001: 244–50; Gaskell, 1836: 256–57). Nationalist narratives of violence were not confined to the British (Broers, 2002). The interrelationship between violence and national identity presents a useful topic in its own right while at the same time emphasising that crime and the social discourses devoted to understanding violence have often been characterised by a tension between the national and transnational, tensions that can also be identified within the modern practice of violence history. Most histories of violence – including my own – have been done within the framework of either a locality (such as particular cities) or the nation state, a tendency visible in recent bibliographies (Johnson and Monkkonen, 1996; Spierenburg, 1998). However, a pioneering 'comparative' violence history was contained in Gurr's study of crime and civil strife in Britain, Sweden, Australia and India based upon statistics gleaned from their capital cities. He found common trends such as declining violence in the nineteenth and early twentieth centuries and rising violence from the 1930s and 1940s onward (Gurr, 1976: 57–64). Comparative or synthetic treatments have recently become more prevalent, based on the expansion of violence history in several countries and the use of common conceptual bases (Johnson and Monkkonen, 1996; Ruff, 2001). Nevertheless, as violence history has developed, so has its complexity, making definitive comparative judgements an even more daunting task.

The parameters of a larger field of comparison are themselves problematic. A signal example of 'European' violence history is Julius Ruff's recent study of violence in the early modern period. It may be questioned whether or not Ruff's work – despite its achievements – is, strictly speaking, comparative, as, methodologically, his effort is to assemble a generalised view of violence in Europe and emphasise commonalities rather than to systematically compare what was different and similar within it. Since there has been a great expansion in violence studies in several European countries (one, however, that has been uneven, as Ruff points out) there will be a great deal more effort toward establishing a common European violence history. That probable tendency is welcome, as cross-national comparisons have the potential to highlight international trends and uncover connections between violence and a variety of other social, cultural and economic issues. Nonetheless, the notion of 'Europe' is itself an unstable category, considering the dramatic differences among its various regions and cultures. Framing concepts such as 'the West' or 'Anglo-Saxon' (or less geographically rooted ones such as a trans-Atlantic 'middle-class culture') raise similar, and perhaps obvious, issues of definition (Bossy, 1983; Riches, 1986; Mitzman, 1987).

The relevance of the boundaries applied to violence history depends very much on the questions being asked. For instance, the assumption behind cross-national quantitative analysis appears to be that what is being measured are the 'amounts' of violence and that such 'levels' can be laid side by side. Such comparative, quantitative studies have been relatively rare, perhaps owing to the questioning to which violence statistics themselves have been subject. As debates around homicide statistics have suggested, particular cultural contexts, state administrative processes and often-complex legal nuances are inseparable from understanding the creation of violence statistics, and these are factors that have changed over time (Cockburn, 1991; Taylor, 1998; Archer, 1999). If violence statistics are highly questionable even within one national boundary, what does that suggest for the uncertainties of comparing two or more countries in order to come up with a meaningful quantitative result? For example, different criminal justice systems count and group crimes such as murder, attempted murder and manslaughter in very diverse ways (Daly and Wilson, 1988: 13; Boschi, 1994: 3). Nevertheless, having taken in all of the critiques of statistical studies, the accumulation of long-term and large-scale statistical comparisons have succeeded in shifting several emphases of violence studies, some of which are of great consequence for cross-national study. In particular, the overarching problem – taken on a 'western' or 'European' scale – is beginning to shift from explaining (and comparing) increasing violence over the last five centuries to exploring what now appears to have been a general decline in violent crime (Johnson and Monkkonen, 1996: 3–4). Several national studies confirm this general picture, pointing to one of the values of comparative quantitative study, but also raising several new questions.

Furthermore, partly in reaction to uncertainty about violence statistics, the 'linguistic turn' in violence studies has, by and large, sought to discern cultures of violence and has emphasised the difficulty of making easy cross-national quantitative comparisons. The imagined 'place' of violence, its ideological construction in any given society, and its mercurial instability across time have increasingly featured in historical inquiry (Cockburn, 1994; Amussen, 1995; Wiener, 1998). Here too, the tensions between national and cross-national perspectives are apparent, raising other questions about boundaries. Among these are the twin issues of what I call the 'mobility' and 'permeability' of cultures of violence. Cultures of violence were (and are) highly mobile, and through social interactions from trade to migration they cross national boundaries, bringing them into conflict and compromise with other mentalities. For instance, the international mobility of sailors and their transmission of culture was a dramatic feature of early-modern life (Rediker, 1987). Migrants brought many things with them, their attitudes toward and rituals of violence among them. As armies swept across Europe in various periods of its bloody past, the experience of violence crossed boundaries and influenced civilian life (Ruff, 2001: 44–72; Knafla, 2002). European imperialist nations exported their own national cultures abroad, including their legal systems and attitudes toward a wide range of behaviour, violence included. Such mobility interacted with the permeability of national and local boundaries, leading to exchange and mixture among cultures of violence. Mobility and permeability had a complicated geography; however, borderlands, seaports and towns and cities with large immigrant populations are promising locations in which to examine the exchanges among cultures of violence (Brooks, 2000). For example, in Liverpool, the Irish population was often seen to have particular fighting rituals and codes of violence and to have imported sectarian disputes and structures of community order different from those native to England (Neal, 1988; Archer, 2000: 44). Other international port towns, such as Amsterdam, saw the mixing of people from all over the world, who also brought with them the weapons and cultures of violence with which they were most familiar. Such mixing highlights the variances between and mobility of different violence customs, even while cultural permeability – along borders or within sites of economic and social interaction – raises questions about the very notion of a self-contained 'national' culture of violence. The imagination of nationhood is, furthermore, not always parallel to political borders: regional differences could be pronounced and 'national' conceptions of otherness could be applied internally. For instance, labourers in Lancashire were identified as being prone to brutal and 'un-English' forms of violence (Archer, 2000: 45–6). Corbin has pointed to the ways that community violence in France was influenced by a flexible nationalism: the victim of one late nineteenth-century lynching was described by the crowds that attacked and killed him as a 'Prussian' although he was French (Corbin, 1992: 67–77). Similarly, the position of the Irish as 'outsiders' within Britain meant that they were often subjected to violence that exceeded the boundaries applied in intra-community disputes among 'locals' (Conley, 1991: 53–8, 156–66; Wood, 2001: 339–55).

The development of violence as a social issue was structured by both an outward-looking sharing of conceptualisations and understandings as well as an inward-looking national identity. Similarly, contemporary violence history has applied various geographical scales and frameworks to understanding violence in the past. What I have hoped to highlight in this section is the need to interrogate the boundaries applied to violence while also suggesting that the mobile, permeable and changing boundaries of cultures of violence offer rich subjects for comparative violence history. There were not only several layers of such boundaries – local, regional, national, continental, ethnic or colonial – but these boundaries existed concurrently, overlapping and interacting with violence, its representation and its administration over time. It appears to me that these are issues that lend themselves to comparative violence history, in which potentially important points can be made about the interrelationship between violence and other forms of social, cultural and economic life.

Borrowing and lending

Thus far I have posed a number of questions as to the assumptions within all comparative violence history. What is being compared? How do we locate violence in terms of the individual and the social? On what temporal and geographical scales do we work, and what are their methodological consequences? What boundaries were imposed or assumed by the historical subjects we are investigating? What processes of inclusion and exclusion did violence serve in constructing national identities? Some progress has been made in examining those boundaries, and I will now suggest the developing methodologies and agendas for comparative, cross-national violence history.

That there is some universal, human element in violence is, I think, unmistakeable; however, this common inheritance is understood, enacted and lived in distinct, culturally specific ways that change across time. I suggest that the work of Norbert Elias – already common in national violence studies – presents a framework for negotiating this and other tensions and boundaries in violence history. For instance, Elias addresses the boundary between the individual and society, asserting the inability to separate the sphere of the 'individual' from that of the 'social' and suggesting that 'the structures of personality and of society evolve in an indissoluble interrelationship' (Elias, 1994: 88). The 'open personality' possesses 'relative autonomy' but is 'fundamentally oriented toward and dependent on other people throughout his life', forming the basis for a 'figuration', a social framework defined as 'a structure of mutually oriented and dependent people' (Elias, 1994: 213). By historicising Freud, a key part of Elias's work is the supposition of 'certain mental equipment' that locates the urge for violence within a deeply human 'affect structure' (Spierenburg, 1995: 21). But Elias distinguishes what he refers to as 'the natural raw material of drives, which indeed perhaps changes little throughout the whole history of mankind' from socially created (and thus more malleable) 'structures of control' (Elias, 1994: 487). The rate of change or state of development of this apparatus of 'affect control' is different in particular places and particular times; however, the 'civilising process' suggests a unified, human-scale mental structure, allowing room for the exploration of both difference and similarity, and emphasising the influence of historical development.[3] It also straddles the line between national and transnational perspectives: his key work is based upon French, German and English sources and explored the Europe-wide cultural changes unleashed by the Renaissance, the Enlightenment and state development. It approaches the questions of looking at behaviour both quantitatively and qualitatively, in ways that are helpful in the sense of looking at both change and continuity.

There are, of course, problems that inhere in Elias's theory, some of which refer to questions I raised earlier. One is the issue of scale: Elias's study of the civilising process was both 'long term' and based upon European or western sources. Its applicability to societies outside of these contexts has been little explored and the commonalities among European countries have been emphasised over differences (Spier, 1994; Goody and Goudsblom, 1997). Furthermore, like some biological or psychological theories, the emphasis on 'affect' as a source of violence can itself be critiqued by suggesting that it does not allow sufficient scope for other, cultural motivations for violence. Arguably, certain kinds of violence are generated by a particular cultural or social framework (whether related to deprivation, relative disappointment, patriarchy, distributions of power and so on), rather than originating in universal psychological impulses; and Elias's emphasis upon the repressive functions of culture can be questioned using the same methods applied by Foucault in his critique of the 'repressive hypothesis' on sexuality (Foucault, 1990). Despite these qualms, Elias's conceptual framework has proved its worth in the context of national studies (Dunning, Murphy and Waddington, 1992), and I suggest that because of its in-built negotiation of the boundaries to which I have pointed, it is particularly applicable and helpful in the context of comparative violence history.

The importance of culture in explaining violence points to two final conceptual issues. In preceding sections, I have mainly focused upon two uses of the term 'comparative': in measuring quantifiable phenomena across borders – however defined – or in tracing violence's movements and role in cultural exchange. There is, however, another type of comparative history that involves using particular conceptualisations from one region and seeing the extent to which they function in another (perhaps very different) area or time. This approach has long been a mainstay of anthropology, a pioneering field in comparative violence studies. In this context, I shall focus on the cultural issues of the 'narratives' and 'practices' of violence. For example, Nordstrom's recent ethnographic study of violence in Mozambique explores (in the context of civil war) some of the key conceptual issues facing scholars of violence. Locating her study within 'the human condition', Nordstrom emphasises that 'the encounter with violence is an extremely personal event':

> I have come to question traditional assumptions that people experience life in uniquely cultural-specific ways, that what happens to individuals in World War II Europe, in Bosnia, in Mozambique or in the Amazon Basin is fundamentally different and that these experiences are ultimately incommensurable, incomparable, unique. (Nordstrom, 1997: 4–6)

She goes on to suggest the necessity to balance difference and similarity, but a crucial theoretical point emerges: the relationship between experience and narrative. The actual experience of violence, like any other human experience, is notoriously difficult – if not impossible – to reconstruct in its entirety. What we have are stories: attempts to put experience into words, as Nordstrom recounts a conversation with a group of children in a village under attack:

> The narrative of the attack was not the actual experience of that violence, it was trying to find a meaningful way to deal with it. And this meaning, which changes over time, circumstance and speaker, is a cultural production. (Nordstrom, 1997: 21)

Here, her method connects the cross-cultural aims of anthropology to the interests of the linguistic turn. Nordstrom suggests that the experience of violence is universally human (which would seem to connect it to evolutionary biological and psychological approaches) and inaccessible; however, she delineates a useful emphasis in the comparative study of violence. Although all societies 'narrativise' violence, the specific contours of that process vary widely across not only cultures but also over time within a given geographical boundary. The 'different aspects of the same human being' identified by Elias (i.e. the individual and the social) can be seen as connected by the narrative structures of cultural mentalities that emerge out of and in turn shape social interaction (Elias, 1994: 201).

From historical and anthropological research, we know that the content and form of violence narratives are diverse and changeable. Such diversity does not represent simply superficial differences hiding a single 'truth' of violence, and because of the ubiquity of narratives of violence, there is much potential in looking at the ways that such narratives work in different contexts. Such analyses can, I believe, be usefully taken on as central concerns in comparative history. Violence narrativisation studies are diverse and growing, stretching across societies and disciplines. For instance, like Nordstrom, Das emphasises the narrative/violence connection, examining the articulation of grief through lamentation and mourning in the context of large-scale collective violence against women surrounding the birth of the Indian nation (Das, 1997). Das makes use of Indian literature, but also borrows elements from Wittgenstein's philosophy and classical Greek mourning rituals. Caton has examined the use of poetry to express, understand and shape violence during an instance of Yemeni tribal warfare in the early 1980s, and his analytical categories regarding violence are of wide relevance (Caton, 1999). Bourke has pointed to the importance of particular narratives of violence in shaping the combat experiences of soldiers from Britain, the United States and Australia (Bourke, 1999: 44–68), a phenomenon that has also been studied across a broader chronological and geographical span (McCarthy, 1994). There has been an increasing interest in the 'representations' of violence; however, I would suggest that narrative studies should go beyond the way violence was depicted: narratives are not only representations, they are also the foundations of mentalities – the ways that violence is understood – and mentalities (and therefore narratives) shape action.

The interrelationship between narrative and violence is suggested in another conclusion that can be drawn from previously conducted comparative work, both in history and anthropology. All societies have developed a variety of 'practices' of violence shaped by particular codes and belief systems that demarcate acceptable from unacceptable violence and constrain violence into limited, culturally legitimate forms. Such configurations point to other social tendencies: for instance, that men are particularly prone to developing ritualised forms of fighting seems one of the human universals to which Daly and Wilson point (Daly and Wilson, 1988: 163–86). Simply to give one example, duelling is a ritualised form of violence that has been subject to intensive and detailed historical study on various scales: national, class, continental and transcontinental. There is a substantial body of work on duelling as a European-wide phenomenon, emphasising the transnational mentalities of European elites (Kiernan, 1988; Spierenburg, 1998). However, while all elites performed duels, their structures have proven to be very distinct. For example, the *Mensur*, a duel conducted within the context of the German university system, was very different to the duels carried on by Englishmen or American southern gentlemen. Such rituals took various forms and had different longevities: although the aristocratic duel in Britain had faded by the early nineteenth century, American southern elites appear to have remained relatively less pacified, and the *Mensur* was a signal feature of German fraternity life into the twentieth century (Andrew, 1980; Gorn, 1985; Simpson, 1988; Greenberg, 1990; Gay, 1993: 9–14).

Cultures of honour are one example of the mixture of the global and culturally specific contexts of violence. Every culture has some element of ritual attached to violence and a set of codes that define what, where, when and how violence is legitimate. Community self-policing – whether in various forms of vigilantism, 'rough music' or community lynching – features on all of the inhabited continents. Violence within the family is an international phenomenon; however, every society shapes differently the limits and meanings of spousal conflict or child discipline. Thus narrative shapes practice, but practices of violence can also themselves be read in terms of the syntaxes of violence that they enact. What I have been suggesting is an approach to comparative violence history that effectively confronts – and balances – the issues of similarity and difference that seem to inhere in the phenomenon of violence. Certain arguments from the scientific community (themselves based on particular assumptions) apply a scale of analysis that is so broad that it cannot help but to discount cultural and social differences for biological or psychological universals. Viewed from high enough up, the world is indeed very small, and the distinguishing characteristics of the activity that takes place on it recede into the background. However, the emerging body of comparative historiography of violence, while emphasising certain general trends, has also illuminated that, with different assumptions and a smaller geographical and chronological scale, the diverse ways that violence is seen, is shaped and functions in any given society in any particular era have come to the fore. Nobody, after all, experiences life on an evolutionary timescale, or as a global phenomenon. I would suggest that while violence history needs to interact with these other disciplines, its approach and scale are closer to the ways that life is experienced and can usefully show that, in terms of violence, the world is both small, and unimaginably vast.

Notes

1. Freud goes on to note an 'eagerly denied' 'bit of truth': 'that men are not gentle, friendly creatures wishing for love, who simply defend themselves if they are attacked, but that a powerful measure of desire for aggression has to be reckoned as part of their instinctual endowment' (1994: 40). He continues: 'Culture has to call up every possible reinforcement in order to erect barriers against the aggressive instincts of men and hold their manifestations in check by reaction-formations in men's minds' (1994: 40). Critiquing communist faith in redistribution of property as a road to limiting social violence, Freud argues that even the radical removal of property distinctions would not eliminate the instinct of aggression: 'This instinct did not arise as the result of property; it reigned almost supreme in primitive times when possessions were still extremely scanty; it shows itself already in the nursery when possessions have hardly grown out of their original anal shape; it is at the bottom of all the relations of affection and love between human beings – possibly with the single exception of a mother to her male child' (1994: 41–2).

2. 'There is a wealth of evidence in psychological literature from many countries from many generations and from across the socio-economic spectrum that unconscious defence mechanisms are universally used by people as coping strategies. Accepting that there is a limit beyond which human beings cannot be reconstructed does not somehow invalidate the historical enterprise, rather it enriches the understanding that can be reached from historical enquiry. If there is a certain unity between ourselves and actors in the past, there is also an immense diversity in the many ways in which what we share has been shaped and mediated by historical conditions and the very cultures and societies that people construct. Arguably, history is the task of understanding the rich interplay between that unity and diversity' (Arnot, 2000: 64).

3. 'The behaviour patterns of our society, imprinted on the individual from early childhood as a kind of second nature and kept alert in him by a powerful and increasingly strictly organized social control, are to be explained … not in terms of general, ahistorical human purposes, but as something which has evolved from the totality of Western history, from the specific forms of behaviour that develop in its course and the forces of integration which transform and propagate them. These patterns, like the whole control of our behaviour, like the structure of our psychological functions in general, are many-layered: in their formation and reproduction emotional impulses play their part no less than rational ones, drives and affects no less than ego functions' (Elias, 1994: 518).

References

Amussen, S. 'Punishment, discipline and power: the social meanings of violence in early modern England', *Journal of British Studies*, 34, 1, 1995, pp. 1–34.

Andrew, D. 'The code of honor and its critics: the opposition to duelling in England, 1700–1850', *Social History*, 5, 1980, pp. 409–34.

Archer, J. ' "The violence we have lost"? Body counts, historians and interpersonal violence in England', *Memoria y Civilización*, 2, 1999, pp. 171–90.

Archer, J. ' "Men behaving badly"?: Masculinity and the uses of violence, 1850–1900', in D'Cruze, S. (ed.), *Everyday Violence in Britain, 1850–1950: Gender and Class*. London: Longman, 2000, pp. 41–54.

Arnot, M. 'Understanding women committing newborn child murder in Victorian England', in D'Cruze, S. (ed.), *Everyday Violence in Britain, 1850–1950: Gender and Class*. London: Longman, 2000, pp. 55–69.

Beck, A. *Prisoners of Hate: The Cognitive Basis of Anger, Hostility, and Violence*. New York: Harper Perennial, 2000.

Boschi, D. *The Pattern and Incidence of Homicide in Rome, 1841–1914*, paper read at the IAHCCJ roundtable, Paris, 3–4 June 1994.

Bossy, J. (ed.) *Disputes and Settlements: Law and Human Relations in the West*. Cambridge: Cambridge University Press, 1983.

Bourke, J. *An Intimate History of Killing: Face-to-Face Killing in Twentieth-Century Warfare*. London: Granta Books, 1999.

Broers, M. 'War and crime in Napoleonic Italy, 1800–1814: regeneration, imperialism and resistance', in Knafla, L. (ed.), *Policing and War in Europe*, Criminal Justice History, vol. 16. Westport, CT: Greenwood Press, 2002, pp. 21–52.

Brooks, J. 'Served well by plunder: *La Gran Ladronería* and producers of history astride the Río Grande', *American Quarterly*, 52, 1, 2000, pp. 23–58.

Caton, S. *'Anger Be Now Thy Song': The Anthropology of an Event*, Occasional Papers of the School of Social Science, Harvard University, No. 5, 1999.

Cockburn, J. 'Patterns of violence in English society: homicide in Kent, 1560–1985', *Past and Present*, 130, 1991, pp. 70–106.

Cockburn, J. 'Punishment and brutalization in the English Enlightenment', *Law and History Review*, 12, 1, 1994, pp. 155–79.

Cocks, G. and Crosby, T. (eds) *Psycho/history: Readings in the Method of Psychology, Psychoanalysis, and History*. London: Yale University Press, 1987.

Conley, C. *The Unwritten Law: Criminal Justice in Victorian Kent*. New York: Oxford University Press, 1991.

Corbin, A. *The Village of Cannibals: Rage and Murder in France, 1870*, trans. A. Goldhammer. Cambridge, MA: Harvard University Press, 1992.

Daly, M. and Wilson, M. *Homicide*. New York: Aldine de Gruyter, 1988.

Daly, M. and Wilson, M. 'Evolutionary psychology of male violence', in Archer, J. (ed.), *Male Violence*. London: Routledge, 1994, pp. 253–88.

Darwin, C. *The Descent of Man and Selection in Relation to Sex*, vol. 1. London, 1871.

Das, V. 'Language and the body: transactions on the construction of pain', in Kleinman, A., Das, V. and Lock, M. (eds), *Social Suffering*. Berkeley, CA: University of California Press, 1997, pp. 67–91.

Dawkins, R. *The Selfish Gene*. Oxford: Oxford University Press, 1990.

D'Cruze, S. 'Unguarded passions: violence, history and the everyday', in

D'Cruze, S. (ed.), *Everyday Violence in Britain, 1850–1950: Gender and Class*. London: Longman, 2000, pp. 1–24.

Dunning, E., Murphy, P. and Waddington, I. *Violence in the British Civilising Process*, Leicester University Discussion Papers in Sociology No. S92/2, July 1992.

Elias, N. *The Civilizing Process: The History of Manners and State Formation and Civilization*, trans. E. Jephcott. Oxford: Blackwell, 1994.

Emsley, C. *Crime and Society in England, 1750–1900*. Harlow: Longman, 1987.

Fergusson, N. *The Pity of War*. London: Allen Lane, 1998.

Foucault, M. *The History of Sexuality, Volume I: An Introduction*, trans. R. Hurley. New York: Vintage Books, 1990.

Freud, S. *Civilization and Its Discontents*. Mineola, NY: Dover Press, 1994.

Gaskell, P. *Artisans and Machinery*. London, 1836.

Gatrell, V. *The Hanging Tree: Execution and the English People, 1770–1868*. Oxford: Oxford University Press, 1994.

Gay, P. *Freud for Historians*. Oxford: Oxford University Press, 1985.

Gay, P. *The Cultivation of Hatred: The Bourgeois Experience, Victoria to Freud, Vol. 2*. New York: W. W. Norton, 1993.

Goody J. and Goudsblom, J. 'Goody versus Goudsblom: *Pour ou Contre* Norbert Elias?', *Polis*, 7, 1999–2000, http://www.sciencespobordeaux.fr/polis/vol7ns/article6.html.

Gorn, E. ' "Gouge and bite, pull hair and scratch": the social significance of fighting in the Southern Backcountry', *American Historical Review*, 90, 1985, pp. 18–43.

Greenberg, K. 'The nose, the lie and the duel in the antebellum South', *American Historical Review*, 95, 1990, pp. 57–74.

Gurr, T. *Rogues, Rebels and Reformers: A Political History of Urban Crime and Conflict*. Beverly Hills: Sage Publications, 1976.

Hunt, L. *Psychoanalysis, the Self, and Historical Interpretation*, paper presented at History and the Limits of Interpretation, A Symposium, Rice University, 15–17 March 1996, available at http://www.ruf.rice.edu/~culture/papers/Hunt.html.

Johnson, E. and Monkkonen, E. (eds) *The Civilization of Crime*. Urbana, IL: University of Illinois Press, 1996.

Kiernan, V. *The Duel in European History: Honour and the Reign of Aristocracy*. Oxford: Oxford University Press, 1988.

Knafla L. (ed.) *Policing and War in Europe*. Westport, CT: Greenwood Press, 2002.

Lorenz, K. *On Aggression*, trans. M. Latzke. London: Methuen, 1966.

McCarthy, B. 'Warrior values: a socio-historical survey', in Archer, J. (ed.). *Male Violence*. London: Routledge, 1994, pp. 105–20.

Mitzman, A. 'The civilizing offensive: mentalities, high culture and individual psyches', *Journal of Social History*, 20, 1987, pp. 663–87.

Neal, F. *Sectarian Violence: The Liverpool Experience, 1819–1914*. Manchester: Manchester University Press, 1988.

Nordstrom, C. *A Different Kind of War Story*. Philadelphia: University of Pennsylvania Press, 1997.

Pearson, G. *Hooligan: A History of Respectable Fears*. London: MacMillan Education Limited, 1983.

Pinker, S. *How the Mind Works,* New York: W. W. Norton, 1997.

Pitchford, I. 'The origins of violence: is psychopathy an adaptation?' *Human Nature Review,* 1, 2001, pp. 28–36.

Rediker, M. *Between the Devil and the Deep Blue Sea: Merchant Seamen, Pirates, and the Anglo-American Maritime World, 1700–1750*. Cambridge: Cambridge University Press, 1987.

Riches, D. (ed.) *The Anthropology of Violence*. Oxford: Basil Blackwell, 1986.

Ruff, J. *Violence in Early Modern Europe, 1500–1800*. Cambridge: Cambridge University Press, 2001.

Sibley, D. *Geographies of Exclusion: Society and Difference in the West*. London: Routledge, 1984.

Simpson, A. 'Dandelions on the field of honor: dueling, the middle classes and the law in nineteenth-century England', *Criminal Justice History*, 9, 1988, pp. 101–50.

Spier, F. *Norbert Elias's Theory of Civilizing Processes Again Under Discussion: An Exploration of the Sociology of Regimes*, paper for the 13th World Conference of Sociology, Bielefeld, Germany, 18–23 July 1994, available at http://www.usyd.edu.au/su/social/elias/confpap/regimes.html.

Spierenburg, P. 'Elias and the history of crime and criminal justice: a brief evaluation', *IAHCCJ Bulletin*, 20, 1995, pp. 17–30.

Spierenburg, P. (ed.) *Men and Violence: Gender, Honor and Rituals in Modern Europe and America*. Columbus: Ohio State University Press, 1998.

Taylor, H. 'Rationing crime: the political economy of criminal statistics since the 1850s', *Economic History Review*, 51, 3, 1998, pp. 569–90.

Turner, A. 'Genetic and hormonal influences on male violence', in Archer, J. (ed.), *Male Violence*. London: Routledge, 1994, pp. 233–52.

Weisfeld, G. 'Aggression and dominance in the social world of boys' in Archer, J. (ed.), *Male Violence*. London: Routledge, 1994, pp. 42–69.

Wetzell, R. *Inventing the Criminal: A History of German Criminology, 1880–1914*. Chapel Hill, NC: The University of North Carolina Press, 2000.

Wiener, M. *Reconstructing the Criminal: Culture, Law and Policy in England, 1830–1914*. Cambridge: Cambridge University Press, 1990.

Wiener, M. 'The Victorian criminalization of men', in Spierenburg, P. (ed.), *Men and Violence: Gender, Honor and Rituals in Modern Europe and America*. Columbus: Ohio State University Press, 1998, pp. 197–212.

Wood, J. *'The Shadow of Our Refinement': Violence, Custom and the Civilizing Process in Nineteenth-Century England*, PhD dissertation, University of Maryland, College Park, 2001.

Wrangham, R. and Peterson, D. *Demonic Males: Apes and the Origins of Human Violence*. New York: Houghton Mifflin, 1996.

Chapter 3

Moral panics and violent street crime 1750–2000: a comparative perspective

Peter King

Historians and criminologists have used the concept of moral panics, first fully developed by Jock Young and Stanley Cohen in the early 1970s, in a wide variety of ways (Cohen, 1972; Young, 1971). Indeed it could be argued that the notion of 'moral panics' has been overused. It has been applied to everything from soccer violence to social security 'scroungers', from crack addict crime to child abuse, from mobile phone theft to the murder of children by children. In the process it has entered mainstream discussions of crime and has become heavily diluted as a result (Thompson, 1998). The idea that a moral panic is a discrete event or cycle of events with a beginning and an end, which follows a process and has a product, has often been lost. The term has been very frequently applied to more diffuse or recurring events, such as fears about new-age travellers or 'depraved youth' (Muncie, 1999: 8). Alternatively it has often been trivialised by those who have used it in relation to ephemeral news themes – such as attacks by rottweilers on innocent pedestrians. It has also been marginalised by several criminologists for a number of rather different reasons, being seen by some as a polemical rather than an analytical concept, associated with cynical 'debunking for political ends' (Waddington, 1986: 258; Goode and Ben-Yehuda, 1994: 51) and by others as characterised by 'a degree of inadequacy' (Sparks, 1995: 54).

For all these reasons the possible explanatory power and question-raising potential of the concept of moral panic is in danger of being undermined. This, I want to argue, would be a considerable loss. By focusing here on one of the most frequently recurring forms of moral panic – those that centre on violent street crimes – this chapter aims to explore how the comparative historical analysis of different types of moral panic can offer new and important insights into the usefulness of this particular concept. This species of moral panic has, it will be argued, its own developmental curve – its own lifecycle pattern. Media-created crime waves and moral panics about violent street crime can be traced as far back as the eighteenth century, if not further. More important, despite vast social, economic and cultural changes, there are interesting continuities in the ways such panics develop, create policing and penal initiatives, and then quickly fade away into the background.

Violent street crime forms a very useful focus for a case study of the concept of moral panic for several reasons. First, a number of detailed historical analyses of particular panics are available spanning three centuries and two continents (King, 1987; Davis, 1980; Hall *et al.*, 1978; Fishman, 1981a). Secondly, while the importance of other crimes has waxed and waned in the public consciousness, robbery with violence has continued to be regarded as among the most serious of all crimes throughout the period being studied here (Beattie, 1986; King, 2000; Philips, 1977; Pratt, 1980). As Geoffrey Pearson rightly pointed out in his more general study of the history of respectable fears in his book *Hooligan*, 'The case of street robbery is particularly interesting because this is commonly the most sensitive area for registering public concern about crime' (Pearson, 1983; Pratt, 1980: 5). Thirdly, studies of media output suggest that violent crimes, and especially violent street crimes, are a central thread in crime reporting (Beckett and Sasson, 2000: 78). They also suggest that such items are more likely to be thoroughly read than those relating to other kinds of news, and that the amount of crime in different readers' papers can affect their level of anxiety about this issue (Roshier, 1973: 31–3: Williams and Dickinson, 1993). Twentieth-century studies conducted at many different times and in many different places suggest, moreover, that violent crimes are massively over-represented in television news programmes and in almost all newspapers. This is the pattern not only in British and North American newspapers, but also in those published in other parts of Europe as well as in Africa (Marsh, 1991: 72–5; Reiner, 2002: 383–5). Finally, Waddington's much publicised critique of the concept of moral panics which argued that 'it is time to abandon the term' (Waddington, 1986: 258) was based on a very critical analysis of only one study of a violent crime-related moral panic (Hall *et al.*, 1978). By showing that the 1972–3 study he disparaged is part of a much broader historical pattern which Waddington took no account of, this article also hopes to re-evaluate both that critique and the influential volume, *Policing the Crisis*, that was its target. By closer scrutiny of historical work on four specific moral panics focusing on violent crime (in 1765, 1862, 1972 and 1976) this chapter will argue that a common six-stage pattern is followed in each case, and that the recurrence of that pattern across such vastly different periods raises important questions about the role, nature and importance of moral panics as well as offering an opportunity to re-evaluate current critiques of the concept. What is that pattern?

The pattern of moral panic

The pattern of moral panic that manifested itself on all these occasions stretching across 250 years went roughly as follows:

- An initial act or acts of violent street crime provoked the media to turn their attention to that theme.

- The media then exaggerated the threat posed by this particular form of crime – for example, by referring to 'many' violent street crimes when evidence existed for only one or two, and by creating negative and fearful stereotypes of the typical offender (folk devils).

- By making the public, the police and the authorities increasingly aware of a new crime threat, the media increase the amount of such crime reported.

- The extent of the violent street crime is then vastly overestimated by the media, the public and the authorities.

- New heavier control and punishment measures are introduced by the police, the courts and sometimes the legislature.

- After a couple of months or so the panic begins to die away as the actions of the authorities calm initial fears, the media grow tired of the story and readers lose interest.

In order to ascertain the degree to which these four moral panics followed this common lifecycle pattern, a brief survey of each is now necessary.

London 1862

One of the best historical studies of this type of moral panic is Jenifer Davis's work on the 1862 garotting panic (Davis, 1980). In 1862, against a background of growing debate about crime and penal policy, one event set off a wave of newspaper reporting. On 17 July Hugh Pilkington MP was accosted late at night after leaving the Commons. He was choked and struck on the head by one malefactor while another relieved him of his watch. In contemporary parlance he was garotted. The press immediately began to fan the flames of panic. Two days later, without referring to any specific individuals, *The Spectator* reported that 'Highway robbery is becoming an institution in London and roads like the Bayswater road are as unsafe as Naples.' Two days further on *The Observer* talked of 'The wholesale highway robberies that are every day committed.' The press quickly built up a picture of the garotters as 'folk devils' – as threatening, violent, unfeeling and deeply dangerous. They were described as 'degenerate, coarse, brutal ruffians', as 'a race of hardened villains', as 'a species of … profound enemies of the human race' or as 'an irredeemable criminal class'. It is clear that in the second half of 1862 the ways the public, the police, the courts and Parliament reacted to this wave of reporting further amplified the threat and indeed may have effectively created it.

Minor events were turned into garotting incidents. Some crimes were literally created by the panic. One unfortunate man walking home on a foggy night thought someone was following him and feared he was about to be mugged. He therefore turned round and attacked his pursuer who was in fact innocently walking home the same way. His attack was then reported as a dangerous mugging. The police created further panic. They increased plainclothes patrols between 10 p.m. and 2 a.m. They set up special observation initiatives, they arrested many more men as 'suspicious characters and reputed thieves', and they used the panic for their own purposes, expanding their definition of garotting with strategic elasticity. In one court case, for example, they described a pub brawl as a garotting because they wanted these particular thieves taken off the streets. This tendency to deliberately make crimes more serious than they actually were can be seen in the case of John Boney Redwood. The policemen arresting him for stealing £2 'imagined' also seeing him knocking his very drunken victim down. Redwood could see the consequences coming. 'I know there have been a great many garotte robberies about,' he remarked, 'and now you have me I suppose I must suffer for it.' He did. He got ten years penal servitude rather than a few weeks in gaol.

Magistrates added to the escalation process by tending to redefine minor crimes, such as pick-pocketing, as garottings and therefore sending them on to the major courts. The result was inevitably a rise in reported violent street robberies that in turn fuelled further panic. The metropolitan returns reveal that an average of 32.5 robberies with violence per year occurred in 1860–1. By contrast, the 1862 figure rose threefold to 97. However, all of that increase came after 17 July. Up to that date only 15 cases had been reported. Thus the moral panic was not caused by an increase in garottings. Rather the rapid increase in the number of garottings recorded was caused by the moral panic.

This 'crime wave' not only produced an immediate increase in crime control measures – more policing, the redefining of minor crimes as more serious, tougher sentencing in the courts – it may also have helped produce a number of important legislative changes. In the immediate aftermath an Act was passed which temporarily reversed the long-term movement away from corporal punishment by reintroducing flogging along with imprisonment for garotting and all robbery with violence. A year later stricter sentencing policies were introduced in a further Act – a journey towards greater severity continued in the 1865 Prisons Act and the Habitual Criminals Act of 1869. The panic allowed the advocates of longer sentences, of tougher prison regimes and of less freedom for those allowed out on parole under the 'ticket of leave' system (not to mention those who advocated a return to flogging) to mobilise public opinion and get all these policies through. These moral entrepreneurs had successfully ridden on the back of a media-created crime wave and got the changes they wanted. The panic reached its peak in November and, following the trial of 23 alleged garotters at the Old Bailey during that month, it then gradually faded in intensity. However, although there is some debate between historians about this issue, its consequences on penal policy may have been far reaching (Bartrip, 1981; Davis, 1980). How similar was the panic that occurred a hundred years earlier in the provincial Essex town of Colchester?

Colchester 1765

The newspapers were extremely well developed by the 1860s but even in the eighteenth century, when provincial newspapers were usually weekly four-page productions, it is clear that they could start similar crime waves. In the Colchester area in 1765, for example, an almost identical sequence of events took place (King, 1987). In the mid-1760s the two local newspapers – the *Chelmsford Chronicle* and the *Ipswich Journal* – usually reported only a few robberies a year. However, in November 1765 this suddenly changed as the *Chelmsford Chronicle* in particular published a huge rash of reports on crime in Colchester and the heath lands surrounding it (see Figure 3.1). 'Scarce a night passes without a robbery being attempted either in the town or in its neighbourhood,' the *Chronicle* reported. The key figures, the 'folk devils', that the reports focused on were a gang of footpad robbers wearing white smocks (or 'foot banditti' as they were termed). The notion that 'a large gang of desperate robbers have taken their rendezvous

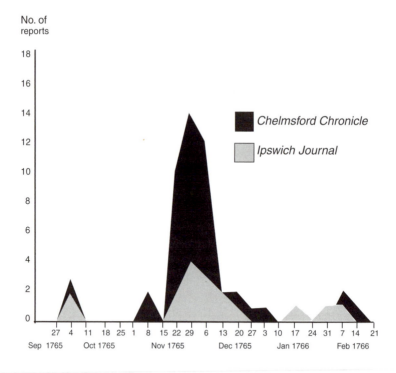

Figure 3.1 Reports relating to crime in the Colchester area 1765–66; *Chelmsford Chronicle* and *Ipswich Journal* compared. Includes both unsolved crimes and counter-measures.

around Colchester' and were perpetrating various robberies, atrocities and rescues was central to this wave of reporting.

The public was frightened. Many were reported to be arming themselves. Farmers began travelling to market only in large groups. Subscriptions were raised to fund large rewards for the arrest of the robbers. The Colchester authorities reacted by introducing a number of measures. In these pre-police days there was no professional body ready at hand, but the authorities offered rewards, employed a horse patrol, formed a prosecution association, set up information networks using the local innkeepers, increased the street lighting in Colchester and used parish constables and watchmen to arrest a considerable number of suspects (including several innocent migrants who made the mistake of travelling in white smocks). The number of petty thieves prosecuted in the borough court also rose, and the court's magistrates started to use their power to transport minor property offenders – a power they had previously ignored in favour of the time-honoured punishment of whipping. The Colchester crime wave quickly came to an end after a burst of reports of countermeasures by the authorities, the arrest and trial of one offender, and the publication of reports that the rest of 'the gang' had dispersed. In all it lasted about two months and centred once again around the early winter month of November when the nights rapidly grow longer.

Deeper investigation reveals that the panic was almost certainly initiated by the *Chelmsford Chronicle*, which was very keen to develop this crime theme (King, 1987). At the beginning of the panic the printer promised to help apprehend 'these enemies and pests to society' by printing any accounts of local robberies that were sent to him. He kept his promise, publishing more crime reports in the next edition than would normally have appeared in nearly a year. It was no accident that the *Chronicle* was keen to turn this crime theme into a crime wave. It was in the middle of a life and death circulation war with the old established Ipswich paper and Colchester, the area's largest town (which stood halfway between Chelmsford and Ipswich), was the vital territory where it needed to increase its readership. It is no surprise therefore that most of the alarming reports were printed only in the *Chronicle*. The Chelmsford paper – only a year old at this point – survived and went on to be Essex's main newspaper, but this may have been little comfort to the next generation of larcenists who were convicted at the Colchester borough sessions. Since the court never returned to its previous milder sentencing policies after the panic, they were now at considerable risk of being transported.

New York 1976

A remarkably similar pattern can be found in America 200 years later. If the common patterns seen in both 1765 and 1862 are impressive the continuities implied by Fishman's work on the New York crime wave of 1976 are even more interesting (Fishman, 1981a). In mid October the city's three daily newspapers and five local TV stations reported a surge of robberies directed at the elderly. Reporters conducted long interviews with elderly victims and amplified the threat by following up in detail almost every crime that could possibly fall into this category. A 'folk devil' was quickly established – black or Hispanic youths with previous criminal records. The NYPD put much greater resources into its Senior Citizens Robbery Unit following up cases more thoroughly than ever before. Community meetings, reported in detail in the newspapers, advised the elderly on how to avoid becoming victims. The panic escalated featuring on national news as well as local. The New York legislature immediately began to put forward legislation designed to crack down on this type of crime. Juvenile offenders' records were to be made available before sentencing, 16 to 19 year-olds attacking the elderly were to be denied juvenile status, and prison sentences were to be mandatory for offenders who committed crimes of violence against old people. This legislation was never passed, however, because in early December the New York crime wave disappeared almost as suddenly as it had come (see Figure 3.2), making it easy for the Governor to quietly veto the proposals nine months later. Like its counterpart 210 years earlier, this New York crime wave had lasted about seven to eight weeks, had centred on the month of November and had disappeared almost as quickly as it came.

Britain 1972

Across the Atlantic four years earlier the British moral panic which Stuart Hall *et al.* (1978) made the subject of a book-length study in *Policing the Crisis* also began with an elderly victim. In this case, however, the widespread reporting of a London robbery in which an elderly widower was stabbed to death led to a more general focus on violent street crime which was fanned by the national newspapers' importation of the

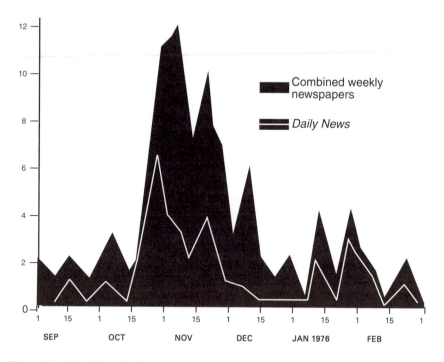

Figure 3.2   The New York crime wave of muggings against the elderly.

American term 'mugging'. Full of sensational and fearful associations already developed across the Atlantic, mugging was portrayed as a frightening new strain of crime. These crimes of violence were immediately described by the media as 'escalating' and by October a flood of mugging reports was filling up the national newspapers. The stereotypical offender was also quickly established as young, usually black and brought up in big cities characterised as being very near to social breakdown. The police and the local authorities immediately set up, or escalated, several types of counter-initiative. Special anti-mugging squads and patrols were formed. The police presence in key areas, such as the public parks, was increased and the minor petty larcenies discovered by those manning these initiatives were frequently labelled as muggings. Perceptions that a widespread wave of muggings was being experienced led to public demands for heavier punishments, which were soon put into practice. The judiciary declared war on the muggers handing out deterrent sentences involving long terms in prison. The panic peaked in late September, October and early November but then (except for a brief revival following a very heavy sentencing decision six months later) it rapidly subsided. Once again a moral panic focusing on violent street crime had peaked for about two months in late autumn/early winter and then declined following the same cycle of newsworthiness as that found in our other three examples.

Similarities: a common lifecycle?

These four moral panics may have used different labels – foot banditti, garotters, muggers and suchlike – but the similarities between them are quite remarkable. Timing and duration are the two most obvious examples of this. If we concentrate on the earliest and latest of the panics (i.e. Colchester in 1765 and New York in 1976) about which we have detailed figures rather than mere monthly totals (Figures 3.1 and 3.2), it is immediately clear that both arose at exactly the same time of year. They also both lasted for almost exactly the same time period – seven to eight weeks. The detailed information in Figures 3.1 and 3.2 also indicates other similarities. A sharp initial rise was followed by a relatively long tail in both places, although in Colchester the tail tapered away slightly faster, probably because the editor of the *Chelmsford Chronicle* felt increasingly unhappy about reporting the subject (King, 1987: 441). The overall shape of the curve was also very similar in Colchester and New York except that in 1976 a presidential election caused a brief dip in reporting half way through. More important, perhaps, in both cases one newspaper started the panic and the other local media then followed – some more enthusiastically than others. In Colchester it was, of course, the *Chelmsford Chronicle*. In New York the crime wave began in the third week of October in *The Daily News* and it took about a week before the other newspapers and the television station that Fishman monitored took up the theme.

It is also very noticeable that the emphasis of the reporting shifted in both cases as the crime wave moved through its lifecycle. In New York *The Daily News* headlines during the first week emphasised 'the problem' citing incident after incident of crimes against the elderly. By week three, however, the balance of stories in the New York media had changed in nature. Increased emphasis was now being placed on 'what was being done about the problem' by the police, the legislators and the public authorities. In Colchester the same thing happened. In the first two weeks the newspapers were dominated by the problem – by reports of robberies in and around Colchester. By weeks three and four, however, there were many more reports about counter-measures than there were about robberies (King, 1987: 444, Fig. 2).

The degree of parellelism between Colchester in 1765 and New York in 1976 seen in Figure 3.1 and 3.2, and in all these aspects of both moral panics, is quite remarkable because they occurred in such entirely different contexts. Colchester had around 10,000 inhabitants. New York had millions. Colchester had no paid full-time police force worth mentioning. New York had the huge NYPD. Colchester's locally based circulating media were two weekly four-page newspapers. New York had many daily newspapers, television and radio stations – indeed a vast phalanx of media news outlets. Colchester was a fairly typical early modern town. New York was a huge city emblematic of late modernity. Why were the patterns so similar? This is a complex question and we need many more case studies and a more international sample to answer it. However, a number of preliminary thoughts can perhaps be offered at this point.

Understanding the continuities

The reasons for these continuities in patterns of moral panics about violent crime across such a huge time period are partly to do with the particular characteristics of violent crime as opposed to other forms of deviance. For example, violent street crime motivated by gain is a fairly consistent and visible part of most societies across time. There is, therefore, nearly always a pool of available incidents to make crime themes from. That is to say, the supply side of the equation is sorted. Crime waves about violent street crimes are unlikely to be starved out of existence by a lack of incidents on which to feed. Equally, moral panics tend to focus more easily on the kinds of crime committed by underdogs rather than those committed by 'top' dogs, many of which are highly covert operations. Thus it is much more likely that societies will have recurrent moral panics about violent street crime than about corporate crime (although the naked corruption of those who run corporate America has recently caused something of a panic of its own).

Another important characteristic is, of course, that violent street crime very easily raises great anxiety among almost all sections of the population. In the vast majority of societies almost everyone feels vulnerable to robbery in the street. Moreover, because most robberies can easily escalate into serious injury or murder, because few can avoid crossing public spaces where they may become victims, and because violent street crime can happen 'out of the blue', its anxiety-provoking properties tend to reach the parts of society that other forms of deviance can rarely reach. This means that the definitions of threat or crisis produced in moral panics about violent street crime are much less likely to be opposed than those on which many other types of panic are based. During moral panics about such issues as child abuse, raves, date rape or drugs the level of threat is often hotly debated, and may even be entirely negated by substantial proportions of the population. For example, moral panics about certain types of drug use often induce a strong oppositional voice because significant social groups maintain strongly that these activities pose no real threat to society. With violent street crime, however, the oppositional voice is usually weak and relatively unorganised, and arguments tend to be confined to smaller issues such as whether or not press reporting is out of all proportion to the 'real' threat posed.

The relatively high fear factor attached to violent street crime may also help to explain the very specific seasonal pattern exhibited by all the four moral panics surveyed here. It was not just the 1765 and 1976 panics that peaked at the same time of year. The 1862 and 1972 crime waves also followed comparable paths peaking in October/November. Moreover recent research on news stories about violent crime in the USA in 1993 has indicated that there was a sudden threefold increase in newspaper and television reporting of this type of crime in the late autumn and early winter of that year (Beckett and Sasson, 2000). Not all moral panics about violent street crime necessarily occur at this time of year, but it is interesting that all of the four discussed here occurred at the precise point in the year when the nights are rapidly drawing in and people are becoming aware of how dark the streets can be. Modern research indicates that fear of violent street crime is highly seasonal. A study done in two British cities in 1999–2000 indicated that, while only 20 per cent of respondents were worried that they might become victims of mugging between April and June, nearly twice that proportion (36 per cent) were worried about this possibility between October and December (Semmens, Dillane and Ditton, 2002: 803). It seems unlikely that fear of crime was any less seasonal in earlier periods when street lighting and police cover was even more inadequate or non-existent.

Why did both the 1765 and 1976 panics last for only about two months? One possible explanation may be that violent street crime is not a type of crime that creates longer lasting cycles of deviance amplification. This tends to make its lifespan shorter and more predictable. In many situations, such as the moral panics over drug-taking and over the activities of the 'mods and rockers' in the 1960s, media coverage may well encourage those doing the feared behaviour to increase or prolong that behaviour. The polarisation of the mods and rockers, for example, appears to have developed mainly after media reporting of it had begun. Equally, once drug-taking of certain types has been denounced by the media, by parents and by other authority figures, it may become increasingly attractive to the young as a means of expressing their own cultural identity. By contrast, violent street robbers usually want to avoid, rather than play up to, media coverage. In most situations there are virtually no social, recreational or psychological payoffs for them in attracting the attention of the authorities. Surveillance does not therefore amplify this kind of deviance directly, although it may well increase the level of it that is reported. Violent street thieves will usually be dispersed by surveillance and the threat of arrest rather than being encouraged to congregate or amplify their overt deviant activity.

More generally, there are at least two fairly obvious reasons why moral panics about a number of issues, and more especially about violent street crime, may have such a limited lifespan. Firstly, although the authorities may use moral panics for their own ends, it is not usually in their material, social or political interests to let panics about violent street crime continue for too long. Business can be affected. Faith in the police may be eroded if they do not bring the problem under control once new resources have been given to them. More generally failure to be seen to be controlling violent street crime after a certain time becomes increasingly embarrassing for the ruling elite, and in democratic societies this can be electorally damaging. The authorities therefore have every reason to ensure that news about the measures taken to combat the problem is soon available, since this will often calm the public down and thus begin to reverse the spiral of anxiety that began the panic in the first place.

Secondly, it would not necessarily be practical to prolong moral panics like these, even if it was desirable. As Goode and Ben-Yehuda have pointed out 'the degree of hostility generated during a moral panic tends to be fairly limited temporally; the fever pitch that characterises a society during the moral panic … is not typically sustainable over a long stretch of time' (1994: 39). Issues such as panics about violent street crime have their own cycles of newsworthiness, to use Hall's phrase (Hall *et al.*, 1978: 74). Newspaper readers and the consumers of television and radio news programmes grow tired of such themes fairly quickly and new ones are therefore needed. After a couple of months it will often, therefore, be in the interests of the media as well as the authorities to move on, or at least to de-escalate the level of coverage. Both the 1862 and the 1972 moral panics lasted much longer than two months, but in both years the core period during which the newspapers were full of stories about violent street crimes was, like the 1765 and 1976 crime waves, very clearly restricted to about two months. After that period the issue still appeared fairly regularly, and in 1973, for example, the handing out of extremely heavy sentences against offenders arrested during the panic caused a considerable resurgence of interest in the media for a while. However, in none of these four cases did the media find it possible and/or desirable to sustain exceptionally high reporting levels beyond this initial two-month period. In the wake of the initial period of intense panic, the issue may remain a secondary and useful crime theme, referred to at appropriate moments and still very much part of the collective memory. As such it may still be called up fairly effectively by moral entrepreneurs and reactionary penal reformers as a potent part of their case for new laws, sentencing practices and penal regimes. However, the cycle of extreme anxiety characteristic of a full blown moral panic was clearly not sustained in any of these four violent street crime-related panics beyond at the most two or three months.

The creation of moral panics

A study of these four moral panics may also provide useful ways of exploring the genesis of this type of event. The role of the media's institutional need to create news that will catch the public's imagination should never be underestimated in this context. However sophisticated or unsophisticated the news media were at any particular moment, those who ran these enterprises could not help but be aware that crime stories presented as isolated and unrelated items tend to be less attractive, less interesting and less thought-provoking to readers/viewers than those that are organised into crime themes. Such themes can, of course, provide the basis for a moral panic and indeed the initiators of both the 1765 and 1976 panics were, it appears, key media workers searching for newsworthy themes.

Fishman's studies are particularly relevant because he and his research workers were able to sit in one of the local television stations as observers (Fishman, 1981: 1981b). They watched as the editor assembled the daily news programme, decided what the major stories were to be and assigned resources such as reporters and camera crews to those stories. In the process the development of a moral panic unfolded before their eyes. As they watched the television editors choose which themes to go for each day, they noted that the editors were swamped by crime news, almost all of it sent by the NYPD 'police wire'. Faced by the issue of how to make these routine reports of robberies, suicides and corner shop stick-ups into 'news', their answer was, whenever possible, to develop a specific crime theme and then pursue it. This was what occurred when a group of violent crimes against the elderly happened to coincide on one day. The editor sent reporters out having decided that this would make a good theme. The reporters focused on any relevant incidents and followed them up with in-depth reporting of the potential threat posed by this type of crime. This rapid increase in the reporting of crimes against the elderly then forced (or enabled) the police and the authorities to react, thus reinforcing in the public mind the reality of the threat. This crime theme quickly became a perceived crime wave; indeed the 1976 New York research provides a wonderful study of the anatomy of a wave of crime reporting which quickly became a moral panic about the particular kind of crime it focused on. However, despite the dissipated and relatively unorganised nature of newspaper reporting in the eighteenth century, something fairly similar evidently happened in Colchester 210 years earlier. Here the printer/editor was looking for a theme to sell his newspaper and lacking any reporters (budgets were too tight to pay for them in the eighteenth century), he did the next best thing – he initiated a sense of panic, asked readers to send in reports and then proceeded to publish them all, however wild. The following week the authorities duly reacted and the Colchester crime wave was in motion.

This does not mean, of course, that all these moral panics were created solely, or even mainly, by the press, and it is as we reflect on some of the other potential forces behind these movements that some of the discontinuities in these patterns of moral panic emerge more clearly. From their differing points of view and on the basis of different levels of primary research, the historians/criminologists who have investigated these four moral panics have come to very different conclusions about the primary forces that lay behind them. Some have stressed the role of moral entrepreneurs and critics of current penal practices (Davis, 1980). Others have seen specific moral panics and the related activities of the authorities as a broader means by which the ruling elite coped with a general 'crisis of hegemony' in the British state (Hall *et al.*, 1978). The detailed debates that have surrounded these suggestions (Sindall, 1990; Waddington, 1986; Bartrip, 1981) cannot be reviewed here, but the panics discussed in this chapter do indicate that while the mid-nineteenth century may have been an especially fruitful time for moral entrepreneurs and campaigning groups, these are not necessarily as central as some writers have suggested to the timing of the moral panic process (Goode and Ben-Yehuda, 1994: 141–2). The presence of such groups is not a necessary condition for the creation of a moral panic, although they may play a considerable role in the dynamics of such events.

Of all the potential relationships and groups that could be involved – the public, the police, the politicians, the media, the moral entrepreneurs, the courts, the law-makers, the law-breakers – the research on twentieth-century moral panics centring on violent street crime suggests that a key role, and perhaps the central role, was played by the symbiotic relationship between the media and the policing authorities (and to some extent the courts). Once fairly sophisticated professional policing bodies are well established, much of the initial dynamism that creates this kind of crime wave comes from the way the media feed, and feed off the information provided by, the policing agencies and the authorities' policing initiatives (Fishman, 1981b; Hall *et al.*, 1978). The centrality of this relationship is less obvious in earlier periods. In all of the four panics discussed here, the newspapers (and later the television and radio news) played a key role in creating a crime wave dynamic on the basis of relatively minor sets of individual acts. However, in 1765 and even to some extent in 1862 the police/press relationship was less central. In the twentieth century, by contrast, things were very different. In New York in the 1970s the media were willingly fed by the Senior Citizens Robbery Unit and by the highly selective police press wire (Fishman, 1981b), and Hall *et al.*, argue for a similar loop in Britain in the same decade. The police 'do not simply respond to moral panics. They form part of the circle out of which moral panics develop … they also, advertently or inadvertently, amplify the deviancy they seem so absolutely committed to controlling' (Hall *et al.*, 1978: 52). Policing measures, some of which were in place before the panic began, clearly increased the number of cases receiving publicity in 1972 and 1976, but in 1862, and more particularly in 1765, the authorities' policing initiatives were mainly reactions to, rather than part of the initial dynamic of, the crime wave.

There were also other discontinuities among the factors that created these four outbreaks. It has been argued, for example, that it is difficult to see the British moral panic in the early 1970s, analysed in *Policing the Crisis*, as a completely disproportionate reaction, because violent street crime may indeed have been rapidly growing in intensity in the period immediately prior to the wave of reporting in the newspapers (Waddington, 1986). A real rise in levels of law-breaking may also have played some role in 1862, but in 1765 and 1976 the evidence for this is very thin indeed. In 1976 the violent perpetrators of New York may have turned their attention en masse towards the elderly for those seven weeks and then returned to their old habits. Equally in the Colchester area there may have been a real influx of violent foot banditti unprecedented in the history of the town for those few weeks in 1765, despite the authorities' almost complete failure to identify any of them. Both these scenarios seem extremely unlikely, however, and the 1972 panic (on which Waddington based his general critique of the concept of moral panic) is probably the only one of the four in which the reaction of the press cannot be assumed to have been highly disproportional. It would certainly be very difficult to see the events of 1765 and 1976 as measured responses to real outbreaks of more intensive law-breaking activity. Waddington's lack of a comparative historical perspective may therefore have misled him into being too dismissive of the notion of moral panic.

This is not to argue, of course, that moral panics never have any grounding in real increases in deviant activity, although, in the case of most of those centring on generalised fears about violent street robbery, it does not seem unduly 'polemic' to argue that the real basis of these spiralling fears was extremely flimsy. Equally, however, it could be argued that the analysis presented here does not support the assertion made by Hall *et al.*, (1978: 186, 221) that moral panics are 'one of the forms of appearance of a more deep seated historical crisis' which 'have signalled, time and time again in the past, periods of profound social upheaval, of economic crisis and historical rupture.' Historians and sociologists are adept at finding a crisis when their analysis needs one and 1972 and 1862 can, at a pinch, be made to fit the model. However, there are precious few signs of historical rupture in 1976 and 1765. There was an election going on in 1976 but there are no signs of a specific social crisis in New York at that time. Equally, while 1765 was a postwar year and peacetime years did witness heightened anxiety about crime in the eighteenth century (Hay, 1982; King, 2002), this does not explain why similar panics did not occur in Colchester in more troubled peacetime years after 1765. Moral panics may or may not express, or coincide with, the widespread and free-floating anxieties which often arise in periods of social crisis or rapid social change, but these are not necessary conditions for the development of moral panics about violent street crime.

Conclusion

It would be unwise to criticise previous work too deeply on the basis of four case studies alone. These four are clearly not the only occasions when full-blown moral panics about violent crime have occurred (Beckett and Sasson, 2000: 87), and other panics about violent street crime which have yet to be analysed (or even uncovered) may have followed very different trajectories – although this seems fairly improbable. What then can we conclude on the basis of this comparative study? Despite the differences just outlined, the tremendous similarities between these four panics remains the core impression created by this brief survey across nearly 250 years. Not only did they all follow much the same six stages, they also had much the same core effects. Although these moral panics came in different sizes – local, city-wide, national – they each created heightened levels of public alarm which generated support for repressive changes at various levels of the criminal justice system. These included changes in policing practices, in the way crimes were defined by victims, in the sentencing policies of the courts, in prison regimes and in various aspects of legislative practices in relation to crime and justice. The depth of the long-term institutional sediment these four panics left behind varied immensely. Some of the changes they created were deep and long lasting while others were ephemeral, but they all tended in the same direction – towards greater severity.

By studying one specific type of moral panic this chapter has questioned a number of the assumptions sometimes made in recent work on moral panics. For example, both Waddington's critique of the concept and Hall et al.'s insistence on linking moral panics to periods of historical rupture seem less tenable in the light of this long-term comparative analysis. Equally Goode and Ben-Yehuda's suggestion (1994) that moral panics 'do not ... go through specific predetermined stages, with a beginning, a middle and a predictable end' clearly needs qualification in the light of this study. In addition, the tendency of much of the literature to assume that (witch-hunts excepted) moral panics are essentially a feature of modernity, and in particular of late modernity, clearly requires further thought (Thompson, 1998: 11; Sparks, 1995). Eighteenth-century historians have long argued that the concept is equally applicable to their period (Hay, 1982; King, 2000; Rawlings, 1999) and the immense con-tinuities between the pattern of events in Colchester in 1765 and those in New York 210 years later suggest that it is very unhelpful to see these kinds of moral panics as simply outgrowths of the modernisation process. In their volume on moral panics Goode and Ben-Yehuda (1994) recently asked, 'Are the dynamics of the moral panic different during different historical time periods, or different from one society to another?' The only effective way to answer this question is to unpack the ragbag of moral panics into different groupings and, having created a typology, to investigate comparatively the lifecycle patterns of each type of panic.

This chapter has been an attempt to begin that process. Much work remains to be done and many more moral panics have, no doubt, yet to be discovered, created or fully analysed. However, on the basis of this early foray into the field it seems clear that, in the English-speaking West at least, there are tremendous similarities across the last two and a half centuries in the patterns of activity created by, and the lifecycles of, moral panics about violent street crime. Within those patterns two more specific aspects stand out. First, more often than not the role of the media, and/or of the symbiotic relationship between the media and the police, is so central to both the rise and fall of this type of moral panic that the law-breakers themselves appear as mere bit players in most of these dramas. Second, the lack of any link between two and possibly three of these moral panics and any sense of general 'crisis' or 'historical rupture' suggests that they may best be seen not as expressions of 'fundamental contradictions in social relations', but rather as the outcomes of specific conjunctions of law-breaking events, policing needs and knee-jerk reactions by the authorities, and, most important of all, the all-embracing institutional and entre-preneurial needs of the various media to make news as well as to report it.

References

Bartrip, P. 'Public opinion and law enforcement: the ticket-of-leave scares in Mid-Victorian Britain', in Bailey, V. (ed.), *Policing and Punishment in Nineteenth Century Britain*. London: Croom Helm, 1981.

Beattie, J. *Crime and the Courts in England 1660–1800*. Oxford: Clarendon, 1986.

Beckett, K. and Sasson, T. *The Politics of Injustice: Crime and Punishment in America*. Thousand Oaks, CA: Pine Forge Press, 2000.

Cohen, S. *Folk Devils and Moral Panics. The Creation of the Mods and Rockers*. London: MacGibbon and Key, 1972.

Davis, J. 'The London garotting panic of 1862: a moral panic and the creation of a criminal class in mid-Victorian England' in Gatrell, V. *et al.* (eds), *Crime and the Law. The Social History of Crime in Western Europe since 1500*. London: Europa, 1980.

Fishman, M. 'Crime waves as ideology', in Cohen, S. and Young, J. (eds), *The Manufacture of News: Deviance, Social Problems and the Mass Media*. London: Constable, 1981a.

Fishman, M. 'Police news. Constructing an image of crime', *Urban Life*, 9, 4, 1981b: pp. 371–94.

Goode, E. and Ben-Yehuda, N. *Moral Panics. The Social Construction of Deviance.* Oxford: Blackwell, 1994.

Hall, S. *et al.* (eds) *Policing the Crisis: Mugging, the State and Law and Order.* London: Macmillan, 1978.

Hay, D. 'War, dearth and theft in the eighteenth century: the record of the English courts', *Past and Present* , 95, 1982, pp. 117–60.

King, P. 'Newspaper reporting, prosecution practice and perceptions of urban crime: the Colchester crime wave of 1765', *Continuity and Change,* 2, 1987, pp. 423–454.

King, P. *Crime, Justice and Discretion in England 1740–1820.* Oxford: Oxford University Press, 2000.

King, P. 'War as a judicial resource. Press gangs and prosecution rates 1740–1830', in Landua, N. (ed.), *Law, Crime and English Society 1660–1830.* Cambridge: Cambridge University Press, 2002.

Marsh, H. 'A comparative analysis of crime coverage in newspapers in the United States and other countries from 1960–1989: a review of the literature', *Journal of Criminal Justice,* 19, 1, 1991, pp. 67–80.

Muncie, J. *Youth and Crime. A Critical Introduction.* London: Sage, 1999.

Pearson, G. *Hooligan. A History of Respectable Fears.* London: Macmillan, 1983.

Philips, D. *Crime and Authority in Victorian England: The Black Country 1835–60.* London: Croom Helm, 1977.

Pratt, M. *Mugging as a Social Problem.* London: Routledge, 1980.

Rawlings, P. *Crime and Power. A History of Criminal Justice 1688–1998.* London: Longman, 1999.

Reiner, R. 'Media made criminality. The representation of crime in the mass media', in Maguire, M., Morgan, R. and Reiner, R. (eds), *The Oxford Handbook of Criminology.* Oxford: Oxford University Press, 2002.

Roshier, B. 'The selection of crime news by the press', in Cohen, S. and Young, J. (eds), *The Manufacture of News. Deviance, Social Problems and the Mass Media.* London: Constable, 1973.

Semmens, N., Dillane, J. and Ditton, J. 'Preliminary findings on seasonality and the fear of crime', *British Journal of Criminology,* 42, 2002, pp. 798–806.

Sindall, R. *Street Violence in the Nineteenth Century.* Leicester: Leicester University Press, 1990.

Sparks, R. 'Entertaining the crisis: television and moral enterprise' in Kidd-Hewitt, D. and Osborne, R. (eds), *Crime and the Media. The Post-modern Spectacle.* London: Pluto, 1995.

Thompson, K. *Moral Panics.* London: Routledge, 1998.

Waddington, P. 'Mugging as a moral panic: a question of proportion', *British Journal of Sociology,* 37, 2, 1986, pp. 245–59.

Williams, P. and Dickinson, J. 'Fear of crime: read all about it? The relationship between newspaper crime reporting and fear of crime', *British Journal of Criminology,* 33, 1, 1993, pp. 33–56.

Young, J. *The Drugtakers.* London: Paladin, 1971.

Chapter 4

'The great murder mystery' or explaining declining homicide rates

Maria Kaspersson[1]

Despite what might be believed from reading media reports on violence in general and lethal violence in particular, the rate of homicide has decreased over time. Depending on the time frame used, this decline is more or less dramatic. When compared in the longest possible terms – medieval and early modern times – the decline is not only dramatic, but also sudden. Depending on how frequencies are estimated, in the seventeenth century the homicide rate fell as much as to a hundredth of its previous level! The frequency has thereafter remained relatively stable since the eighteenth century. It is this 'mysterious' decline I would like to explore here.

For the purpose of my research (Kaspersson, 2000a) I compared homicide and infanticide over three periods of time, covering in all 400 years. In each of these periods, I studied the changes in the prevalence of homicide (its frequency) and its pattern (form). Depending on changes in legislation (1608 and 1734) and other factors like the two world wars, the periods chosen were 1576–1608, 1720–65 and 1920–39. Collectively these time zones covered periods when homicide was *the most* and *the least* prevalent in Sweden (von Hofer, 1985). Given the availability of recorded evidence reaching back to the fifteenth century, Stockholm was chosen as the geographical region for the purpose of study.

Homicide was chosen since it is perhaps the crime most amenable to study over time. Homicide has always been considered serious and brought to court, and there is reason to believe it is also a crime that is difficult to hide, which means that a large percentage of all homicides committed will be discovered (Gurr, 1981; Beattie, 1986; Cockburn, 1991). At the same time, changes in the legal definition matter less, since it is the outcome – the victim's death – that counts. Other forms of violence have varied much more in legal definition (with a wider range of violent acts being considered criminal today), which is why they could not as easily be compared over time (Österberg, 1996).

The approach is not without its difficulties and limitations, however. Defining what constitutes homicide is problematic (Spierenburg, 1996). For example, infanticide has typically been excluded on the basis that it is a phenomenon that deserves its own distinctive form of analysis (Jansson, 1998) and few such analyses have been attempted within Sweden (Jakobsson and Jakobsson, 1990; Lövkrona, 1999). I consequently adopted a definition of homicide which included *all* types of killing that were and are considered to be criminal. This meant that three principal forms of lethal violence were studied – murder, manslaughter[2] and infanticide.

Another problem in comparing different time periods, even within a homogenous area such as Stockholm, are the varying characteristics of practices of recording cases of lethal violence. The principal form of data utilised is court material collated from the Stockholm district courts. Between the sixteenth and eighteenth centuries the courts coded homicide by the number of victims. In the twentieth century this had changed to the number of indicted offenders. To overcome this limitation references were also made to national vital statistics (cause of death) compiled between the eighteenth and twentieth centuries (SCB, 1925–42; SCB, 1969[3]) to provide an independent comparative data source to complement the court records used.

The choice of homicide in a long-term perspective is justified by existing research on crime in the early modern period, which indicates that the frequency of homicide decreased significantly between 1500 and 1800 across European societies. This decrease is expressed both in the *frequency* of homicide based on estimated population figures (Beattie, 1974; Gurr, 1981; Cockburn, 1991; Österberg, 1996) and in decreased *percentage* of the total of registered crimes (Sharpe, 1984; Beattie, 1986; Johnson and Monkkonen, 1996).

In this chapter I want to concentrate less on the empirical findings and more on how continuities and discontinuities can be accounted for. The main focus will be on how changes in frequency and form over time can be explained and various factors and theories will consequently be considered. Another objective is to test the explanatory power of these theories which have sought to explain variations in the rate of homicide.

Empirical findings

A summary of the findings from the study of patterns and frequencies in homicide in Stockholm between the sixteenth and twentieth centuries (Kaspersson, 2000a) is presented below to provide a background to the discussion on continuities, discontinuities and explanations that will follow. Over the last 400 years the Swedish society has changed dramatically. From a small-scale, local, agrarian society, it has now become a highly industrialised, modern and bureaucratic state. When considering the question of homicide and how it has changed, both continuities and discontinuities were found.

The principal *continuity* is that people have tended to kill in much the same way over time, and often from the same motives and in the same places. Death typically results from male anger aroused in a context where one or more parties to a particular dispute have sustained a provocation. The provocation would typically have been generated by an insult to a person's honour, by non-payment of a debt, by alcoholic intoxication or by a desire for violence for its own sake. The same kind of people, typically men drawn from lower socio-economic positions, are also over-represented in the population of offenders, even if the middle classes had some statistically significant representation in the sixteenth century.

However, what is most apparent from the research findings are the *discontinuities* revealed in patterns of homicide over time. The dramatic decrease in the frequency of homicide between the sixteenth and eighteenth centuries is without doubt the most significant of these (see Figure 4.1), especially the rapid decline during the seventeenth century and its relative stability thereafter.

Tendencies towards the 'privatisation' of homicide also bear note here. From a pattern of homicide in the sixteenth century which was principally based upon men killing other men in public places, we moved by the twentieth century to a society in which homicide has become increasingly confined to the private sphere. Relatively speaking, a larger percentage of men and women are now involved in killing family members than was apparent in earlier epochs. Another important discontinuity is the 'rise and fall' of infanticide (see Figures 4.2 and 4.3) and suicidal murders,[4] which were conceived as serious social issues in the eighteenth century, but which have more or less disappeared since then from the public agenda.

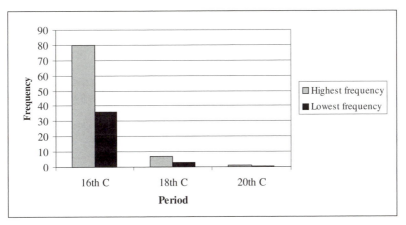

Figure 4.1   Highest and lowest estimated frequency of homicide per 100,000 inhabitants.

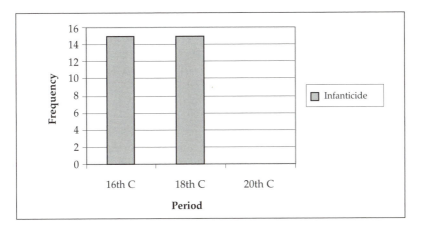

Figure 4.2   Frequency of infanticide per 100,000 inhabitants.

Explaining the continuities – masculinity and violence

The most evident continuity in the study is that most forms of homicide, with the important exception of infanticide, were committed by men and principally against other men of a similar socio-economic position. Even if fewer men over time became involved in committing homicide, it is still evident that it is principally a male activity and is linked with the way that masculinity is established in western societies more generally. This confirms the facts we already know, namely that violence is typically male,

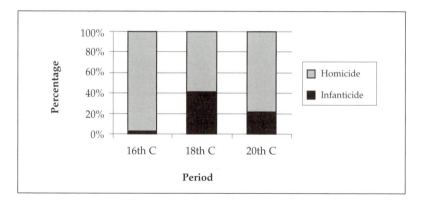

Figure 4.3   Distribution of homicide (murder and manslaughter) and infanticide.

violence is associated with the way masculinity is constructed within the gender order, and cultures of violence are specifically evident in the working classes (Wolfgang, 1958; Messerschmidt, 1993; Liliequist, 1999).

Male homicide can be explained in terms of masculinity, honour, social class and resources (Daly and Wilson, 1988; Polk, 1994). Honour and masculinity are things men have to defend in order to maintain status in other men's eyes. If you come from a culture (usually underclass) where violence is used as a response to different kinds of attacks, you are more likely to respond with violence yourself. Physical toughness and violence are means by which the underclass male can assert his masculinity and defend himself against challenges from other males. This culture of masculinity often equates power with violence. Conflicts between working-class life and the image of power make some men adopt a more aggressive masculinity.

There are compelling economic reasons why working-class as opposed to upper-class males resort to violence in defence of their honour. Polk (1994) suggests that males further up the social ladder have other options to gain and defend their masculinity. They have reputation, status and economic resources and therefore less need to resort to physical prowess to subdue competition or control the female partner. A male who is well integrated into a role of economic success is able to ground his masculinity in behaviours that do not involve physical confrontation and violence. Fewer of these options are available to working-class men, who then might deploy violence instead.

Within some working-class segments, there are situations where violence can be viewed as a 'cultural expectation' (Wolfgang, 1958). This encourages violent behaviour and emphasises masculine honour and physical prowess. Victim precipitation and alcohol use are other important factors. These ideas fit Wolfgang and Ferracuti's (1968) concept of 'subcultures of violence'. These subcultures provide scripts to guide masculine action. They set the stage for violence and create conditions under which males feel impelled towards violence. An insult to a man's honour in a public house, for example, consequently provides a typical 'stage setting' for violence.

Explaining the discontinuities

In order to explain the changing patterns within homicide a range of different theories were examined. These will be used to derive hypotheses that might help explain the decline in homicide, specifically from the sixteenth to the eighteenth centuries, when the drop was most notable. They will then be tested against the empirical findings of the homicide study.

Time-specific forms of homicide

Can the decline in homicide be explained as a consequence of time-specific forms of homicide that were once prevalent, but which have disappeared over time? Examples of time-specific homicides include those committed by soldiers in the sixteenth century (Liliequist, 1999), infanticide (Lövkrona, 1999; Kaspersson, 2000b) and suicidal murders (Jansson, 1998; Kaspersson, 2001) perpetrated mainly in the seventeenth and eighteenth centuries. Evidence indicates that the 'disappearance' of these time-specific kinds of homicide has contributed to its lower frequency, but they can only explain part of the decline and do not answer why the decrease was sharpest in the seventeenth century.

The advances in medical and forensic knowledge

To test this variable two related hypotheses were formulated:

1. Did increased medical and forensic knowledge lead to a decrease in the frequency of homicide as a consequence of victims having their injuries treated more successfully?

2. Did the development of medical forensic science lead to a decline in registered homicide because it would lead to a greater accuracy in recording practices? Were cases that once would unquestionably have been considered homicide not so labelled, as the cause of death was more clearly distinguished?

Support for both of these hypotheses can be found. Improvement in medical procedures certainly led to a decline in fatalities, as injuries sustained were more successfully treated in later periods (Renander, 1962; Sharpe, 1981; Stone, 1983; Cockburn, 1991). Likewise, improvements in forensic science certainly meant that fewer cases came to be classified as homicide between the sixteenth century and the eighteenth centuries (Fisher-Homberger, 1983). Infanticide cases and the importance of proving the cause of death were important factors in the development of forensic medicine (Crawford, 1994; Harley, 1994; Jackson, 1996). In the sixteenth century the death of a victim was typically considered to be connected with an originating act of violence, while in the eighteenth century causes of death were more carefully classified and distinguished. They were now registered as non-homicide related deaths occasioned by, for example, accidents or disease (Kaspersson, 2000a). What is interesting with regard to explaining the noted decline in homicide in the seventeenth century is that the first hypothesis can explain decline in general, but not the sustained decline through this period. The latter does go some way to explaining the abrupt fall in the frequency of homicide in this century, with the introduction of internal autopsies in the seventeenth century, even if, again, not all of the decline can be explained.

Decline in readiness to use violence

This factor explains the decline in the rate and frequency of homicide by asserting that the perpetrators (men) who might once have become implicated in lethal violence in the past, no longer did so to the same extent as Swedish society evolved and developed over time. This hypothesis is derived from Elias' (1978, 1982) theory of the civilising process and Bourdieu's (1966) work on the sentiment of honour. The former will be discussed in more detail below.

Can the decline in homicide be explained by reference to the changing ways in which the threats to someone's honour are interpreted over time? The decline in lethal violence might be explained by the fact that what was once registered as a threat, which would demand or provoke a violent response, was no longer considered by individuals to carry the same degree of provocation or to demand the same kind of response. People's capacity to become insulted decreased, in effect, as society became more civilised (Jarrick and Söderberg, 1993, 1994) and individualised (Jansson, 1998). By looking at changes in how honour was conceived it would appear that concepts of honour have changed over time. Where violence was considered a socially acceptable way to resolve a slight against someone's honour in the sixteenth century (Furuhagen, 1996; Liliequist, 1999), by the eighteenth century this had changed and other forms of conflict resolution were used more frequently. Increased recourse to the courts in libel cases illustrates this (Andersson, 1998; Jarrick and Söderberg, 1998). At the same time, honour changed from being collective and related to one's belonging to a certain group, to being individual and related to the individual person (Jansson, 1998). Honour slights therefore became less provoking over time as they did not challenge your honour in connection to the group to which you belonged or wanted to belong. Where once seen a challenge would demand a violent act, an attack on individual honour would not demand the same level of retaliation.

Explaining the violence that remains

Following the period of greatest decline in the late seventeenth century, rates of homicide stabilised around a more continuous level (von Hofer, 1985; Lilja, 1995). This occurred despite the fact that society itself underwent a number of significant changes (Högberg, 1981). What then explains this stabilisation and the lack of further major decline?

The homicide frequency in Sweden reached its lowest ever in the 1920s and 1930s. Thereafter the frequency has increased again, but to rates far below those of the early modern period (von Hofer, 1985). One way to explain this phenomenon is to consider homicide in the interwar period as a *residual* (Kaspersson, 2000a). By residual I mean violence that no changes in society, changed behaviour or medical practices can affect. It is the kind of violence that, to echo Durkheim (1894/1964), a particular society, defined by certain structural forms, cannot get rid of without having to change radically and fundamentally to become, in other words, other than it is. One way of testing the residual hypothesis is (a) to see whether the kinds of homicide that occurred in the twentieth century also occurred in the sixteenth and eighteenth centuries; or (b) to identify kinds of homicide that were present in earlier centuries but which no longer occur today.

To take the case of (a), then, there are some forms of homicide that do remain more or less constant over time. Public brawls between men, often alcohol intoxicated, in public places is one example (Lenke, 1990; Polk, 1999). They are strangers or acquaintances, and since alcohol disinhibits, these men are more easily provoked. As long as people drink in public places, some fights will always result in death. Also, in societies where masculinity remains associated with violence as a means to define manhood, violence would appear to remain a constant, even allowing for the development of 'civilising processes' that make people more reluctant to use violence, and improved medical care that saves more lives of wounded persons.

The case of *domestic homicide* is another form of homicide that has occurred in all periods, but to a different extent (Sharpe, 1981; Cockburn, 1991; Spierenburg, 1996). Domestic homicide is a killing directed at partners or other members of the close family and is also more unaffected by other forms of social change than other kinds of homicide. One way of demonstrating this is by comparing the *percentages* and *frequencies* of domestic homicide in relation to other kinds of homicide over time. The *frequency* of domestic homicide decreased from the sixteenth century onwards (Figure 4.4), but its *percentage* of all homicides together increased over the same time (Figure 4.5). The *level* of domestic homicide consequently was higher in the sixteenth century than in later periods, but *relatively* speaking it constituted a much smaller part.

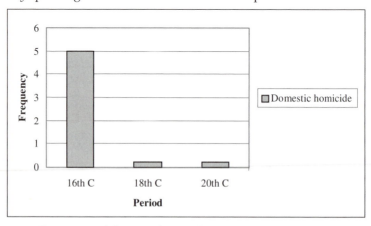

Figure 4.4   Frequency of domestic homicide per 100,000 inhabitants.

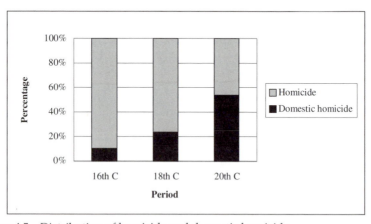

Figure 4.5   Distribution of homicide and domestic homicide.

The most likely explanation to this phenomenon is that it is not domestic homicide that has changed so much over time, but rather that other kinds of homicide disappeared instead, e.g. duels and honour-related fights. From this the conclusion can be drawn that domestic homicide is a kind of homicide that is more enduring over time than other kinds, a residual. The characteristics that make it possible would appear to be culturally embedded in ways that have not changed (Kühlhorn, 1984; Lundgren, 1990; Hydén, 1992). It is a consequence, perhaps, of the ways in which the gender order locates women in relation to men within a domestic sphere characterised by asymmetries in power relations. It is also a crime committed in places where the effects of such asymmetries are much more difficult to control.

With regard to (b), however, it is evident that a number of forms of homicide that were evident in the past have disappeared, precisely because of these civilised developments along with a number of other social changes. Infanticide and suicidal killings are no longer big issues in the modern state. Women, for example, now have less reason to kill their illegitimate children as cultural changes have lessened the stigma a woman who gives birth out of wedlock would suffer (Ulbricht, 1988; Kaspersson, 2000b). Simultaneously, women in Sweden who do not want babies are now provided with other options such as contraceptives and abortion (Jakobsson and Jakobsson, 1990), but this is not a general feature, since these are not available for all, e.g. Irish and Muslim women. Suicidal murders disappeared as a combination of a lessened taboo against suicide and the decriminalisation of suicide attempts (Jansson, 1998). More importantly, the abolition of the death penalty in 1921 – after having been imposed more and more rarely since the eighteenth century – meant this was not a crime that would 'pay off' any more (Kaspersson, 2001).

Homicide and social theory – rethinking the relation

One finding that became evident in the attempt to explain the changing form of homicide is that many forms of criminological and sociological theory do not appear to be particularly helpful in explaining the object of analysis. Typically, the reason why most failed is that, far from predicting, or indeed explaining, a *decline* in homicide, they predict instead the precise opposite, its *increase*. Also, some theories are static rather than dynamic, which is why for example control theory is difficult to apply to explain change (Furuhagen, 1996), even if historians have adapted it for this purpose (e.g. Österberg, 1991).

Anomie and conflict

Anomie and conflict theories associated with Durkheim and Marxism illustrate the point of predicted increases when in reality a decrease took place. In the case of Durkheimian approaches to the study of crime, the growth of a more anomic society accompanying the 'forced division' of labour would suggest that violent crime such as homicide would increase. This would occur, hypothetically, because the class of people subject to the anomic processes brought about by modernisation would increase in size (Durkheim, 1893/1933; Merton, 1957). Instead, what this study suggests is that if homicide can be associated with anomie expressed by, or within, a particular group, then it was far more prevalent in the early modern period and decreased thereafter over time (Ylikangas, 1976).

The case of the soldiers in the sixteenth century illustrates this well. They were over-represented in homicide cases in relation to their percentage of the population as a whole. They were young men, used to violence and trained in the use of weapons. As a group they shared a common set of values, which placed a strong emphasis on honour, manliness and action (Ylikangas, 1976; Liliequist, 1999). At the same time, they were often in conflict with the local population, causing tensions and violence as a result of the soldiers' marginalised and excluded position in society. This group would arguably be considered 'anomic' in Durkheimian terms. As the modern state developed, however, this group was successfully incorporated into society.

The stress placed in conflict theory on the criminogenic tendencies that accompany industrialisation and urbanisation also tend to suggest that crimes such as homicide would increase (Marx and Engels, 1970). The reason for this would be that the dislocation that accompanies the development of capitalist class-divided societies acts to construct an urban underclass whose mode of existence is orientated towards criminality (Hay, 1971; Thompson, 1975; Chapman, 1980). What the study indicates, however, is that the development of an industrial, urbanised society did not lead to more homicide, but to much less. The explanatory power of conflict theory in respect of the case of this category of violent crime is thus limited in its reach. It *can* explain violent protest and the development of new ways of regulating working-class life. It *cannot* explain the changing rate in homicide. On the other hand, this study does not deal with the time after the Second World War, which would also need to be considered.

The civilising process

The one theory that does appear to have the greatest explanatory potential would be the theory of the civilising process, developed by Elias (1978,

1982) and more recently by theorists such as Spierenburg (1996, 1998), Söderberg (1990a, 1990b) and Jarrick and Söderberg (1993, 1994). This approach helps to explain the changing patterns in homicide and accounts for the development of the external and internal conditions that over time would lead to a decrease in the expression of forms of lethal violence. These conditions were, among others, the growth of alternative forms of conflict resolution, changing conceptions of honour and the growth of social norms that became over time more antagonistic to violence. The other positive feature is that it accommodates these developments within a framework of state development that possesses considerable ex-planatory power. What this approach suggests, then, is that to understand the changing rate of homicide, and in particular its decline, we do need to examine how this offence is related to the development of a centralised state and to the evolution of civilising processes more generally.

Where this approach is weaker is in explaining the sharp decrease in the seventeenth century. As a theory, the idea of a civilising process is typically one that predicts the formation of a polite society and of individuals governed by increasing levels of self-control as a product of changes that reach back over a number of centuries. The rapid decline in homicide, however, and its stabilisation thereafter must be seen to present facts that would tend to refute this argument, since significant change occurred within a short concentrated period of time. This does not entail that the theory is fatally compromised, rather that it is presented by an anomaly that requires further consideration. Unfortunately, the time periods studied here did not include a detailed study of homicide in the seventeenth century. The other weakness of the civilising process as a theory is that while it can explain *some* significant factors responsible for the changing patterns in homicide, it does not explain them *all*.

Routine activity theory

One approach which can help explain the anomaly posed by a significant decline in homicide while society remained relatively stable, and which, I will suggest, is not incompatible with the Eliasian approach, is routine activity theory. This approach, by Cohen and Felson (1979), was originally developed to explain the *increase* in direct contact crimes (e.g. violence) in the postwar period, even if no larger changes in the structural conditions that motivate crime had taken place. If one applies this theory in the reverse way, i.e. to explain the *decrease* in homicide in the early modern period, it proves to be useful.

When applied to the subject of homicide, observed changes in its fre-quency can be explained by changes in the distribution of likely offenders, suitable targets (victims) and capable guardians. For example, the changing concepts of honour that occurred over time affected the behaviour of offenders, victims and guardians. As people became less sensitive to slights of one's honour, the number of likely offenders, just as with the number of suitable targets, declined. The changes over time in social control can also be seen as having affected the prevalence of capable guardians or the willingness in people to act like capable guardians. As violence was decreasingly seen as an acceptable solution in honour conflicts, it is possible that more people tried to prevent the use of violence in such situations. What we then need to study is what changes in likely offenders, victims and guardians took place in the seventeenth century to see if an answer can be found.

Conclusion

What this study of homicide poses for theory in general, and criminological theory in particular, is that homicide is an offence category whose changing nature is not explainable by reference to many of the existing approaches. Many theories appear to predict a rise in homicide when in fact it fell over time, and dramatically over a very short time period. Even the approaches that could explain it are limited. At the inception of my research I tried to prove historical, sociological and criminological theory, but paradoxically ended up testing their limits, thereby raising several new questions for theory as well as demonstrating the need for future research.

Maybe the difficulties in explaining the decline in homicide over time are due partly to the relative narrowness of the phenomenon. Homicides might be too few in number, too limited a phenomenon, to be able to shed light on fundamental changes in society. It is possible that homicide has to be put in a wider context of human behaviour, where other forms of violence are considered as well, to be able to give a fuller picture and meaning.

Homicide also demands to be regarded within a gender perspective. It seems that men always have been 'macho', but perhaps much more so in the sixteenth century than later on. It is, then, of interest to highlight the concept of masculinity over time, its changes and the causes for these (Messerschmidt, 1993). It is also necessary to connect masculinity to the civilising process to see if it is a part of it, or maybe a parallel process.

The seventeenth century seemed to be crucial in the decline in homicide. This study did not include it, but maybe a detailed study could help answer the questions *when* the decline took place, and maybe even contribute explanations to *why* it took place and *how quickly*. It is also worthwhile to investigate what impact the many wars, especially the Thirty Years War (1618–48), had on homicide. A tentative hypothesis (Boes, 1996; Österberg, 1996) could be that soldiers returning from war were so tired of violence they felt an acute reluctance to perform it at the same time as women and children remaining at home developed a more peaceful way of life.

Notes

1. An earlier version of this paper was presented at the Comparative Histories of Crime Conference in Keele, 16 July 2002. I would like to thank all those who have given me feedback and comments on it.
2. In the sixteenth-century study involuntary manslaughter was included, but made up for not more than 7 per cent. They were included as it was difficult to separate voluntary from involuntary killings from the court's description of the cases.
3. SCB (Swedish Census Bureau), 'Cause of Death Statistics for Stockholm', published yearly (with back lag) 1925–42; 'Historical Statistics for Sweden. Part 1. Population, 1720–1967' (based on registers of births and deaths), published 1969. For publishers see the references.
4. By a suicidal murder is meant the killing of someone, preferably a child, in order to be sentenced to death. This was to avoid committing a socially unaccepted and taboo suicide.

References

Andersson, H. 'Androm till varnagel ...' Det tidigmoderna Stockholms folkliga rättskultur i ett komparativt perspektiv, Stockholm Studies in Economic History No. 28. Stockholm: Almqvist & Wiksell International, 1998.

Beattie, J. 'The criminality of women in eighteenth-century England', Journal of Social History, 8, 1974, pp. 80–116.

Beattie, J. Crime and the Courts in England 1660–1800. Oxford: Clarendon Press, 1986.

Boes, M. 'The treatment of juvenile delinquents in early modern Germany: a case study', Continuity and Change, 11, 1996, pp. 43–60.

Bourdieu, P. 'The sentiment of honour in Kabyle society', in Peristany, J. (ed.), Honour and Shame. The Values of Mediterranean Society. Chicago: University of Chicago Press, 1966.

Chapman, T. 'Crime in eighteenth-century England: E. P. Thompson and the conflict theory of crime', Criminal Justice History. An International Journal, 1, 1980, pp. 139–55.

Cockburn, J. S. 'Patterns of violence in English society: homicide in Kent', Past & Present, 130, 1991, pp. 70–106.

Cohen, L. E. and Felson, M. 'Social change and crime rate trends: a routine activity approach', *American Sociological Review*, 44, 1979, pp. 588–608.

Crawford, C. 'Legalizing medicine: early modern legal systems and the growth of medico-legal knowledge', in Clark, M. and Crawford, C. (eds), *Legal Medicine in History*. Cambridge: Cambridge University Press, 1994.

Daly, M. and Wilson, M. *Homicide*. New York: Aldine de Gruyter, 1988.

Durkheim, É. *The Division of Labour in Society*. New York: Bobbs-Merrill, 1893/1933.

Durkheim, É. *The Rules of Sociological Method*. New York: Free Press, 1894/1964.

Elias, N. *The Civilizing Process*, Vol. 1, *The History of Manners*. Oxford: Basil Blackwell, 1978.

Elias, N. *The Civilizing Process*, Vol. 2, *State Formation and Civilization*. Oxford: Basil Blackwell, 1982.

Fischer-Homberger, E. *Medizin vor gericht. Gerichtsmedizin von der Renaissance bis zur Aufklärung*. Bern: Verlag Hans Huber, 1983.

Furuhagen, B. *Berusade bönder och bråkiga båtsmän. Social kontroll vid sockenstämmor och ting under 1700-talet*. Stockholm: Brutus Östlings Bokförlag Symposium, 1996.

Gurr, T. R. 'Historical trends in violent crime: a critical review of the evidence', *Crime and Justice. An Annual Review of Research*, 3, 1981, pp. 295–353.

Harley, D. 'The scope of legal medicine in Lancashire and Cheshire, 1660–1760', in Clark, M. and Crawford, C. (eds), *Legal Medicine in History*. Cambridge: Cambridge University Press, 1994.

Hay, D. 'Property, authority and the criminal law', in Hay, D., Linebaugh, P. and Thompson, E. P. (eds), *Albion's Fatal Tree. Crime and Society in Eighteenth-Century England*. London: Allen Lane, 1971.

von Hofer, H. *Brott och straff i Sverige. Historisk kriminalstatistik 1750–1984*, Urval 18. Stockholm: SCB, 1985.

Högberg, S. *Stockholms historia del 1*. Stockholm: Bonnier Fakta, 1981.

Hydén, M. *Woman Battering as Marital Act. The Construction of a Violent Marriage*, Stockholm Studies in Social Work No. 7, Stockholm, 1992.

Jackson, M. *New-born Child Murder. Women, Illegitimacy and the Courts in Eighteenth-Century England*. Manchester: Manchester University Press, 1996.

Jakobsson, S. and Jakobsson, S. W. *Orons och förtivlans gärningar. Ogifta kvinnors vånda för havandeskaps och barnsbörds skull, Stockholm 1887–1901*. Stockholm: Tidens förlag, 1990.

Jansson, A. *From Swords to Sorrow. Homicide and Suicide in Early Modern Stockholm*, Stockholm Studies in Economic History No. 30. Stockholm: Almqvist & Wiksell International, 1998.

Jarrick, A. and Söderberg, J. 'Spontaneous processes of civilization. The Swedish case', *Etnologia Europaea*, 23, 1993, pp. 5–26.

Jarrick, A. and Söderberg, J. 'Inledning' and 'Namnskick och individualisering i Stockholm under 1700-talet', in Jarrick, A. and Söderberg, J. (eds), *Människovärdet och makten. Om civileringsprocessen i Stockholm 1600–1850*, Stockholmsmonografier 188. Uppsala: Stockholmia Förlag, 1994.

Jarrick, A. and Söderberg, J. *Odygd och vanära. Folk och brott i gamla Stockholm*. Stockholm: Rabén Prisma, 1998.

Johnson, E. A. and Monkkonen, E. H. 'Introduction', in Johnson, E. A. and Monkkonen, E. H. (eds), *The Civilization of Crime. Violence in Town and Country since the Middle Ages.* Urbana, IL and Chicago: University of Illinois Press, 1996.

Kaspersson, M. 'Dödligt våld i Stockholm på 1500-, 1700- och 1900-talen', doctoral thesis, 4, Stockholm University, 2000a.

Kaspersson, M. *Infanticide in Stockholm in the Eighteenth Century,* paper presented at the British Society of Criminology Conference, Leicester, July 2000b.

Kaspersson, M. *Liberation by Murder. Suicidal Killings in Stockholm in the Eighteenth Century,* paper presented at the International Conference of the History of Violence, Liverpool, July 2001.

Kühlhorn, E. *Den svenska våldsbrottsligheten,* BRÅ Rapport 1984: 1. Stockholm: Allmänna förlaget, 1984.

Lenke, L. *Alcohol and Criminal Violence. Time Series Analysis in a Comparative Perspective.* Stockholm: Almqvist & Wiksell International, 1990.

Liliequist, J. 'Violence, honour and manliness in early modern Northern Sweden', in Lappalainen, M. and Hirvonen, P. (eds), *Crime Control in Europe from the Past to the Present.* Helsinki: Hakapaino, 1999.

Lilja, S. 'Stockholms befolkningsutveckling före 1800: problem, metoder och förklaringar', *Historisk Tidskrift,* 155, 1995, pp. 304–37.

Lövkrona, I. *Annika Larsdotter barnamörderska. Kön, makt och sexualitet i 1700-talets Sverige.* Lund: Historiska media, 1999.

Lundgren, E. *Gud och alla andra karlar: en bok om kvinnomisshandlare.* Stockholm: Natur och Kultur, 1990.

Marx, K. and Engels, F. *The Communist Manifesto.* Harmondsworth: Penguin, 1970.

Merton, R. *Social Theory and Social Structure.* New York: Free Press, 1957.

Messerschmidt, J. *Masculinities and Crime. Critique and Reconceptualization of Theory.* Lanham, MD: Rowman & Littlefield, 1993.

Österberg, E. 'Brott och social kontroll i Sverige från medeltid till stormaktstid. Godtycke och grymhet – eller sunt förnuft och statskontroll?', *Historisk Tidskrift,* 70, 1991, pp. 150–65.

Österberg, E. 'Criminality, social control, and the early modern state: evidence and interpretations in Scandinavian historiography', in Johnson, E. A. and Monkkonen, E. H. (eds), *The Civilization of Crime. Violence in Town and Country since the Middle Ages.* Urbana, IL and Chicago: University of Illinois Press, 1996.

Polk, K. *When Men Kill. Scenarios of Masculine Violence.* Cambridge: Cambridge University Press, 1994.

Polk, K. 'Males and Honor Contest Violence', *Homicide Studies,* 3, 1999, pp. 6–29.

Renander, A. *Kortfattad lärobok i medicinens historia.* Uppsala: Almqvist & Wiksell.

SCB (Swedish Census Bureau) (1925–42) *Dödsorsaker. Folkmängden och dess förändringar.* Stockholm: Sveriges Offentliga Statistik, 1962.

SCB (Swedish Census Bureau) *Historisk kriminalstatistik för Sverige. Del 1. Befolkning. 1720–1967.* Stockholm: Allmänna förlaget, 1969.

Sharpe, J. 'Domestic homicide in early modern England', *Historical Journal,* 24, 1981, pp. 29–48.

Sharpe, J. *Crime in Early Modern England 1550–1750.* London: Longman, 1984.

Söderberg, J. 'En fråga om civilisering. Brottmål och tvister i svenska häradsrätter 1540–1660', *Historisk Tidskrift*, 110, 1990a, pp. 229–58.

Söderberg, J. 'Elias och civilsationen', *Historisk Tidskrift*, 110, 1990b, pp. 577–83.

Spierenburg, P. 'Long-term trends in homicide: theoretical reflections and Dutch evidence, fifteenth to twentieth centuries', in Johnson, E. A. and Monkkonen, E. A. (eds), *The Civilization of Crime. Violence in Town and Country since the Middle Ages*. Urbana, IL and Chicago: University of Illinois Press, 1996.

Spierenburg, P. 'Masculinity, violence and honor: an introduction' and 'Knife fighting and popular codes of honor in early modern Amsterdam', in Spierenburg, P. (ed.), *Men and Violence. Gender, Honor, and Rituals in Modern Europe and America*. Columbus, OH: Ohio State University Press, 1998.

Stone, L. 'Interpersonal violence in English society 1300–1980', *Past and Present*, 101, 1983, pp. 22–33.

Thompson, E. P. *Whigs and Hunters. The Origins of the Black Act*. London: Allen Lane, 1975.

Ulbricht, O. 'Infanticide in eighteenth-century Germany', in Evans, R. J. (ed.), *The German Underworld. Deviants and Outcasts in German History*. London and New York: Routledge, 1988, pp. 108–40.

Wolfgang, M. *Patterns in Criminal Homicide*. Philadelphia: University of Pennsylvania, 1958.

Wolfgang, M. and Ferracuti, F. *The Subculture of Violence: Toward an Integrated Theory in Criminology*. Beverly Hills, CA: Sage, 1968.

Ylikangas, H. 'Major fluctuations in crimes of violence in Finland. A historical analysis', *Scandinavian Journal of History*, 1, 1976, pp. 81–103.

Chapter 5

Strangers, mobilisation and the production of weak ties: railway traffic and violence in nineteenth-century South-West Germany

Susanne Karstedt

During the nineteenth century and until the mid-twentieth century recorded interpersonal violence shows a clear decline. This well-established[1] feature of violent crime (see Eisner, 2001), however, has been debated within two competing frameworks of interpretation. The 'Foucauldian gaze' on modernising societies focused on how the deeply uprooted population and society in a period of industrial upheaval and conflict was 'disciplined', and consequently on how the criminal justice system and related institutions tightened their grip of control over the unruly and disorderly crowds, the young and women. The Eliasian perspective in contrast stressed an overall process of 'civilization' that started in early modern times. The 'civilisation process' was slowly but consistently substituting external disciplining forces by mechanisms of individual self-control. An important though somehow neglected feature of the Eliasian perspective are the seminal changes of the 'interrelatedness' of society – the relationships and interactions that form the fabric of every day life – and how these engendered a change of cultural patterns and mentalities in the population, and impacted on the patterns of deviance and conformity.

However, both explanations of the decline of interpersonal violence overestimate the role of discipline and neglect how the process of modernisation and 'mobilisation' (Deutsch, 1961) engendered a new way of life for the population that in itself produced incentives for conformity:

rising real wages that gave new prospects and hope to families; opportunities of education and social mobility; work in factories instead of labouring the farmland; the attractions of life in cities in contrast to rural areas; housing, pensions and medical aid that improved the lot of the working classes and helped to close the divide of society and attenuate social inequality.[2] Obviously, life in cities and working in factories enforced new mentalities that were perhaps less shaped by discipline 'from above' than by adaptation to and embracing a new way of life 'from below'. Notwithstanding the uprooting of traditional social bonds and industrial and political conflict, the disintegrative forces during the process of modernisation might well have been balanced or even over-come by the formation of new types of bonds that were more preventive than conducive to interpersonal violence.[3]

This essay seeks to examine how new social bonds and links were developed by the first 'traffic revolution' that was brought about by the railways in the nineteenth century. The extraordinary increase of railway travel and the development of mass transport could have added to the disruptive forces of modernisation. However, simultaneously, 'travel is a process of both transport and communication' (Deutsch, 1956: 156), and thus railway travel forged new bonds within a 'society of strangers' and contributed to communication and interaction. As such it can be taken as an indicator of such new links and bonds developing in society, and its impact on trends of interpersonal violence can be explored. The study is based on empirical data from Württemberg, then a kingdom and part of the *Deutsche Reich* and today one of the states of federal Germany in the south-west of the country, that cover the second half of the nineteenth century.

The great traffic revolution and changing mentalities

The impact of railway travel on the economy and social structure, on social interaction and relationships, and consequently on mentalities can hardly be underrated. In order to get an impression of what contemporaries witnessed and expected, we might start in the present and consider the impact of globalisation and new communication technologies on the time-space dimension of our daily life – distances are vanishing, virtual realities emerging, and the unification of human society into a 'global village' seems to be imminent – just to name the most common expectations and predictions for a radical change of traditional experiences of time, space and place. The 'great traffic revolution' that the railways set off in the first half of the nineteenth century came with no less great expectations for a radical change of the time-space dimension of life and its consequences for society.

Contemporaries of the railway revolution experienced the shrinking of the world in a very similar way. They were conscious of the dialectics of this process. The extremely fast development of the rail network and rail traffic engendered simultaneously an extension and a reduction of space. The reduction in time of travelling resulted directly in an extension of distances travelled and space that could be travelled. However, for the eyewitnesses the world did not shrink to become a 'global village', but the nation converged in the 'metropolis'. Vice versa, this process appears to be an infinite extension of the metropolis until it has integrated even the most distant parts of the country into its area (Schievelbusch, 1986: 30).[4] The assumption that globalisation will engender a radical shift in social behaviour and mentality, or even in the modal character of our times, is as valid for the revolutionary change that railway traffic set off more than 150 years ago. The new technology was a decisive factor in the Industrial Revolution, and it had a major role in the ensemble of factors that changed the fabric of social life forever (Fishlow, 1966; Hawke, 1970; Faith, 1990; Wolf, 1992).

Contemporaries envisioned the radical change of social life that the railways engendered in surprisingly similar ways to present expectations about globalisation and the impact of the IT revolution. For the Saint-Siminonists, the new transport technology would function as a powerful force for a more egalitarian society and promote democracy, peace and progress. It would bring people closer together, not only in space, but in social space. Class differences would disappear in the train compartment, and the new technology would contribute more than anything else to social equality. Constantin Pecqueur expressed these hopes of emancipation and egalitarianism as early as 1839:

> The communal journeys on trains … inspire, to a great degree the sentiments and habits of equality and liberty. By causing all classes of society to travel together and juxtaposing them into a kind of living mosaic … the railroads quite prodigiously advance the reign of truly fraternal social relations and do more for the sentiments of equality than … the tribunes of democracy. To thus foreshorten for everyone the distances that separate localities from each other, is to equally diminish the distances that separate men from one another. (Schievelbusch, 1986: 70–1)

Georg Simmel, in contrast, stressed the disruptive forces of the travel revolution. About 60 years later he noted that railway traffic and public transport contributed more to the disorientation of social behaviour and perceptions:

> Before the appearance of omnibuses, railroads and street cars in the nineteenth century, men were not in a situation where for periods of minutes or hours they could or must look at each other without talking to one another. Modern social life increases in ever growing degree the rule of mere visual impression which always character- ises the preponderant part of all sense relationships between man and man, and must place social attitudes and feelings upon an entirely changed basis. The greater perplexity which characterises the person who only sees, as contrasted with the one who only hears, brings us the problems of emotions of modern life (*Lebensgefuehl*): the lack of orientation in the collective life, the sense of utter lone- someness, and the feeling that the individual is surrounded on all sides by closed doors. (Simmel, in Park and Burgess, 1969: 360–1)

Both authors mark the extreme positions which were to dominate the contemporary *tableau* of discourse: integration and anonymisation, centralisation of the nation state and the segregation of regions, regional impoverishment and economic and social progress. Wilhelm Heinrich Riehl, one of the first to invent and apply methods of social ethnography to contemporary society in the mid-nineteenth century, summed up what he had found during his travels through the rural south of Germany (mainly by foot), talking to people of all social strata: 'We are measuring the country on a new scale. Countries become larger and the world smaller. The people have come closer together. This has created a different country, and different people [*Dadurch ist ein anderes Land, sind andere Leute geworden*], (Riehl, 1861: 63, 72, trans. SK).

The superstition that grew up around the start of railway traffic is a telling expression of the fears and hopes of a population confronted with the unimaginable revolution of traffic as it had been known hitherto. In some regions in South Germany, it was common talk that the railways would disappear as quickly as they had appeared. Their time would be measured according to 'the time that the devil grants those who have signed away their souls to him in exchange for worldly pleasures'. In another region people told that at each station when the trains stopped, one passenger had gone missing, 'who was taken away by the devil for his remuneration' (Riehl, 1861: 62–4). Obviously, this 'rural myth' expressed the fear of anonymity, and of long-distance travelling in such anonymous contexts as the railways established.[5] Riehl comments on this:

The people are suspicious of the radical change of our total civilization [*unserer gesamten Gesittung*] and our society, which should be engendered sooner or later by the new transport system; in particular the farmer feels that he cannot remain the 'traditional farmer' by the side of the new railway. (In these tales) the people's worries are expressed that modern transport not only shapes a new country, but a new people. However, every one fears to become someone different, and those who want to rob us of our characteristic way of life appear to be more a specter from hell than a good spirit. (Riehl, 1861: 64–5, trans. SK).

These tales and Riehl's sensitive reports both mirror the extremely rapid development of the railway network, which had already achieved its highest density ever by the last quarter of the nineteenth century. However, the population seems to have soon put the initial fears and suspicions aside, and embraced the new transport technology (see the indicators of passenger transport shown in Figures 5.1 to 5.3).

All social classes were affected by the decisive changes of their time-space paths. The railways were the first technology that had an immediate and equal impact on the lives of the total population, it was the first *mass-*

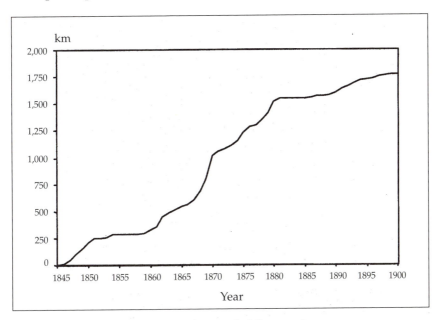

Figure 5.1   Development of the rail network (kilometres).

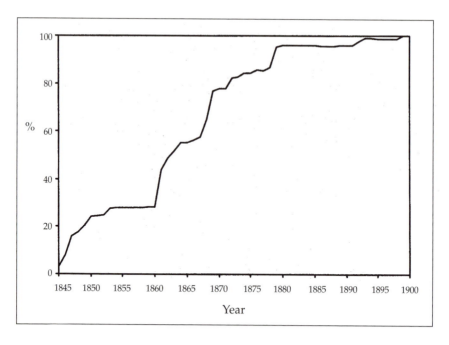

Figure 5.2   Access to rail network (proportion of the population with direct access).

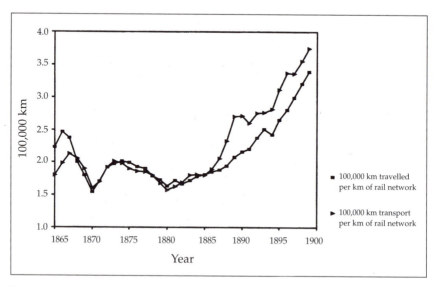

Figure 5.3   Volume of usage by travelling public and for transport of goods.

impact technology. Similar to the change in the rhythm of social life (Thompson, 1980), the new pattern of territoriality had an impact on modern mentality. Both processes came hand in hand. The new transport technology required and produced a precision of the time of travelling hitherto unknown: trains were running on timetables given in minutes. Rural and urban regions became connected to an unknown extent both in terms of transport of goods and passengers. Consequently, rural and more traditional patterns of life came into direct confrontation with modern patterns of factory work and mass consumption. The ability of the population to travel short as well as long distances to their place of work changed the daily, weekly and annual rhythms of the life of large parts of the population. Families were brought closer together through the soon affordable means of rail transport, yet simultaneously became more distanced from each other through the daily, weakly or seasonal travel to work. The new technology of mass transport brought a large and ever increasing number of travellers onto the road who met as strangers at stations and in train compartments but who nonetheless had to develop transient but considerate and polite relationships. Notwithstanding the fact that classes travelled as much apart as they were in other realms of society (and the hopes of the Saint-Simonists did not come immediately true), they mixed at stations and on platforms more than ever before. The public space had been extended on an extraordinary scale.

Transport, mentalities and violence: strangers and the development of weak ties

The contrast between integration and disintegration, between relatedness and isolation has informed research on violence since the nineteenth century, historical as well as contemporary. Did the structural and cultural changes that encompass both modernisation and 'social mobilization' (Deutsch, 1961) mainly engender processes of disintegration that increased the level of violence, or did new forms of solidarity, communication and moral patterns emerge that reduced the level of violence during the otherwise tumultuous process of industrialisation? What precisely are the contributions of railway transport to such changes in habits and mentalities, and how are these related to interpersonal violence?

Modern railway traffic enlarged the public sphere and public space while intricately linking these with the relative intimacy of usage in passenger transport. It created an environment that simultaneously increased anonymisation and individuation/isolation as it created new forms of integration. The use of the new means of transport came with decisive demands and requirements for behavioural patterns, and the role of the traveller was redefined in several of its dimensions. Travelling on railways made it necessary to engage with strangers for a shorter or longer time span in distanced relationships, free of conflict and other disturbances. Social distance had to be retained even in the smallest space; however, consideration of others was required. This applied analogously to behaviour at stations and waiting rooms. The role of the traveller became more and implicitly egalitarian. The technical and organisational conditions of rail travel created an environment that in principle levelled out social differences and inequality, and mixed the classes despite considerable efforts to reproduce the lines of social stratification while travelling.[6]

Railway traffic opened up new opportunities of mobilisation. People could leave their traditional space of social control, even for short periods. The anonymity of the traveller's role provided relief from the conventional normative pressures; however, it required simultaneously a high amount of normative and instrumental self-control, acceptance of others and restraint when joining them on the trains. However transient these relationships were, they required a certain amount of generalised trust in others from passengers as well as from transporters of goods like farmers and businessmen.

Consequently, railway traffic in part shifted the balance of strong and 'weak ties' (Granovetter, 1973) as it had been shaped by traditional society, but mainly produced new ties and additional social capital for the modernising society in several ways. It produced stronger ties and contributed to existing ones and social relationships by bringing people closer together, and it produced new connections and ties in private and business life. In sum, railway traffic in terms of transport and communication increased the general level of social capital by producing both types of ties or social capital: strong ties within groups, and weak ties between strangers, the latter in particular engendering the development of tolerance and a 'benevolent disinterest' in others (Hirschmann, 1988).

What was the impact of such changes in the quality and quantity of social capital on the levels of violence? The perspective informed by the theory of the civilisation process would focus on the normative and instrumental self-control to which rail traffic contributed, and which decreased the level of violence. The development of railway traffic and public transport increased the amount of situations that require a large extent of self-control, and on the other hand provided a context in which such personal dispositions could be acquired. If such situational requirements increase at a faster pace than such dispositions can be developed, the violence-reducing impact might be eclipsed for a short time. This will in particular happen at the beginning of railway travel and in times of its exponential growth.

The mobilisation of the population by rail travel increased the amount of 'weak ties' in societies. Consequently rail transport contributed to the rapid development of selective, on-the-spot, 'objective' and rational, contractual and non-emotional types of social relationships, and the thorough 'modernisation' of social relationships. The strength of such weak ties is embedded in their limitations, and in their transient and anonymous character. Such behavioural patterns – though potentially conducive to minor conflicts – at the same time make it easier to handle conflicts and reduce their intensity. They give rise to cultural patterns of generalised trust within a population (see Karstedt, 2002), and establish relationships that are less prone to intense interpersonal and group conflicts than the stronger ties in traditional societies.[7]

Mass transport on railways contributed to the change in the core parameters of social control in modernising societies. By creating a vast new type of public space it reduced the level of informal control of behaviour. Within the spatial and technological ensemble of railway traffic informal controls were thinned out, and the space for more formal controls was considerably enlarged. Rail transport with its mixing of strangers and classes in small spaces created situations in which violent conflicts could emerge more frequently. Consequently, rail traffic might have directly created opportunities for interpersonal violence, mainly among strangers. Simultaneously, the decrease of informal controls in the public space that mass transport had created should have engendered an increased willingness of the public to invoke formal authorities and to mobilise more formal controls (Black, 1976).[8]

Consequently, rail transport should have changed the level of violence and the mentalities related to it in two directions. It might have directly increased less severe forms of interpersonal aggression and brought a higher amount of these to the attention of authorities, while it more indirectly influenced habits and mentalities that reduced the more severe types of interpersonal violence. But during which period did such changes take place and start to make themselves felt in the everyday life of the population? It can be argued that the impact on social life was most intense at the onset of railway development. However, the inertia of social patterns and relations should not be underrated. The balance to be reached between situational requirements of railway travelling and the development of collective and personal disposition needed time and adjustment. Therefore it can be reasonably assumed that the thorough change of these patterns took off only after railways became a means of mass transport and were used for travelling on a large scale by the majority of the population. Accordingly, the point of 'take-off' would be located in this period, and an increasing and in particular cumulative and balanced impact on social patterns should be assumed for the period when railways as a means of mass transport were fully established.

Rail transport and violence in Württemberg in the nineteenth century

Data

Contemporary as well as historical research on changes of mentalities and habits and their impact on violent behaviour is burdened with considerable difficulties. Indicators for such changes mainly consist of structural indicators that can only be theoretically linked to such changes. Literacy and education as well as urbanisation have been used as 'classic' indicators of the increase of self-control, or the 'objectification' (Simmel) of relationships. Rail travel being a process of both transport and communication can be rated as a particularly suitable indicator of the increase of new types of relationships and bonds, communication and mentalities in the population. It has been used among other indicators of communication to measure the increase of relatedness within and between countries (Deutsch, 1956). More recently, comparative cross-national studies of violence conducted at the World Bank have used several indicators of communication (like telephones in households) to measure the amount of social capital in societies, and its impact on levels of violence (Lederman, Loayza and Menendez, 1999). Railway traffic in addition is an indicator for which an 'impact period' can be clearly defined, and is thus of particular advantage in determining the period in which the change in cultural patterns, mentalities and habits took place or at least 'took off'. However, it is only one in the ensemble of several factors that brought such changes about, and its impact needs to be controlled for these factors.

The state of Württemberg and its specific pathway toward modernity during the second half of the nineteenth century allows for a relative isolation of the impact of rail transport among the ensemble of modernising factors. Württemberg was a latecomer among the German states in industrialising its economy. Industrialisation only started in the last quarter of the nineteenth century, and until then it was characterised by a rural and small tradesmen economy. Urbanisation started in the last two decades of the century, and only in the late 1880s did Stuttgart become and remain until 1900 the only major city with more than 100,000 inhabitants, while the second largest city Nuremberg never grew beyond

40,000 inhabitants. Until the end of the century, Württemberg remained an emigration country, and did not experience any substantial influx of immigrants. However, Württemberg started building a railway network as early as 1845 and extended it rapidly so that the population was provided with an extraordinarily dense rail network during the last quarter of the century. As a result, the impact of the transport revolution brought about by railway traffic on modern mentality can be analysed in the main independently from and unbiased by other factors of the process of modernization. The fact, that it took less than 30 years to establish a full rail network that connected the total population allows to specify the period quite exactly for which we assume a decisive impact on be-havioural patterns.[9]

The problems of quantitative historical research on interpersonal violence are considerable (see Eisner, 2001; Godfrey, 2003; Godfrey, Emsley and Dunstall, this volume). Like most of such research on nineteenth-century violence this study relies on official statistics of conviction rates, which adds a particular problem to the general one's of the validity of such statistics. Any change of mentality and attitudes toward interpersonal violence should have affected the criminal justice system likewise, and the decisions of judges and prosecutors.[10] The Crime Statistics of Germany (*Krimnalstatistik des Deutschen Reiches*) cover violent crime from 1882 to 1900 for different types of interpersonal violence. Three types of violent crime are analysed covering this period after the unified Penal Code was introduced in 1871:[11] murder and homicide, common assault and grievous bodily harm/aggravated assault. These are calculated as rates per 100,000 of the over 18-year-old population to control for population growth. In order to check for a change of attitudes within the criminal justice system, murder and homicide (*Mord und Totschlag*) were included in one category to account for judges' tendencies to favour convictions for homicides in order to avoid the death penalty (Johnson, 1995: 128–30). For common assault and grievous bodily harm (*leichte und schwere/gefährliche Körperverletzung*) it was checked if less tolerant attitudes toward violence had caused a substitution of the minor offence for the more severe one (and vice versa) (Gillis, 1996: 69). The results showed a marginally non-significant but positive effect, so that it can be excluded that an increase in the convictions for grievous bodily harm resulted from shifting minor forms (and vice versa), but in contrast, it has to be assumed that both forms varied concomitantly.[12] The interpretation of the results is embedded in the wider framework of this study by contrasting them with the impact of mobilisation on crime in the pre-industrial and pre-railway society.

The development of rail transport in Württemberg

Württemberg was an economic latecomer among the German states, and the gap between its economic development and that of other German states increased continuously after 1870. Until the end of the century it was still dominated by a rural economy. Consequently, urbanisation was slow, partially due to the typical structure of the economy comprising a majority of small and medium-sized though highly specialised businesses, which has been preserved until today and is one of the backbones of the present German economy. Württemberg had only 14 communities with more than 10,000 inhabitants, and only one with more than 100,000 at the end of the century. In 1900, only 20 per cent of the population lived in cities with more than 10,000 inhabitants, which hardly featured the characteristics of modern urban life.

Given this backward economic situation, the early and fast extension of the rail network is quite surprising.[13] It was mainly fuelled by demands for transport from other German states and considerable competition among the South German states, and soon proved to be a valuable investment (Riehl, 1861: 65). The first railroad was opened in 1845. As soon as 1860 the total rail network had a length of 326 kilometres; one-third of the counties and at about half a million of the inhabitants (30 per cent) were connected. The extent of linkages within the network was still low at this time, but linkages increased at a rapid pace until 1880. By this time the rail network was established as it remained until the end of the century. Between 1860 and 1880 the rail network was extended to a total length of 1,555 km (1,817 km in 1900 (see Figure 5.1)). In 1880, all counties and cities were connected by railroads, and 95 per cent of its citizens (see Figure 5.2). The network – measured by the number of junctions – increased tenfold. By 1880, Württemberg had achieved within 20 years a modern system of mass transport for passengers and goods.

The development of the transport of goods and passengers followed these lines. Between 1860 and 1880 the amount of goods transported increased sixfold, and again threefold until the end of the century. Already in 1860, 3 million passengers were transported and travelled a total of 80 million kilometres. Until 1880, both indicators (number of passengers and amount of travel) increased threefold, and again during the last two decades of the century. The intensity of use by passengers and for transport of goods (numbers of passengers and tons of goods/travel by passengers and of goods per kilometres of rail network available) decreased slightly during the period from 1860 to 1880 when the network was extended at a fast pace so that supply grew faster than demand. During the last two decades of the century, the considerable increase in the intensity of use for passenger travel and the transport of goods indicates that the public used the new transport technology, now fully in place, to an ever increasing extent (see Figure 5.3). In sum, the data suggest that the 'take-off' point for the changes of mentality and social patterns can be located in the late 1860s, but certainly started to gain momentum and increased its impact in the decade before and after 1880.

Notwithstanding the fact that Württemberg was a transit and export country (of agricultural goods), the railroads were used to a much higher proportion for passenger travel. There were little signs of other, mostly slow macro-structural changes that could have engendered cultural modernisation, consequently the development of railroad traffic should have had a more important role in such changes than in other regions and countries.

Development of crime in Württemberg

The Crime Statistics (*Kriminalstatistik*) of the *Deutsche Reich* show that during the last two decades of the nineteenth century Württemberg differed considerably from the development in property and violent crimes in Germany in general and in its single regions and states. Between 1883 and 1902 Württemberg had a conviction rate for all crimes below that of Germany, and the gap only decreased by the end of the century from 15 per cent to 10 per cent. During the first decade after the turn of the century, total conviction rates had reached the level of Germany, which corresponds to an increase in convictions in Württemberg of about 35 per cent. For theft and aggravated theft (which includes burglary) the rates of conviction are significantly below those of Germany as a whole, the large and economically advanced states like Prussia, Bavaria and Saxony, and the large cities like Hamburg and Bremen. In contrast, Württemberg had higher rates of in particular aggravated forms of violence that exceeded those of Prussia and Saxony as well as those of the large cities Hamburg, Bremen and Berlin.[14] Between 1880 and 1900 the development of crime mainly follows the pattern for Germany as a whole. As in Germany and its regions conviction rates for simple theft decreased from about the late 1880s, while the rates for aggravated theft remained at the same levels. The position of Württemberg within the German states taken together shows that it had not fully developed the typical modernised structure of criminality with high rates of theft and lower and decreasing rates of violence compared to other more advanced regions and states. Figures 5.4 and 5.5 show that the rates for murder and homicide varied considerably during the period, while grievous bodily harm/aggravated assault increased during the period, and no change in convictions for common assaults is to be seen.

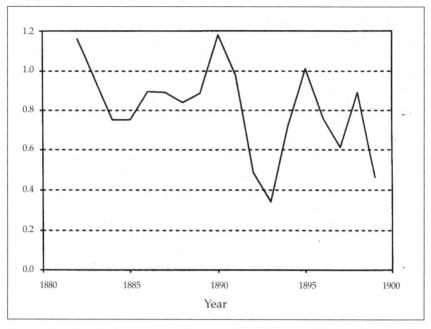

Figure 5.4 Convictions for murder and homicide per 100,000 of criminally responsible population (age 18 and over) 1882–99.

Modelling the impact of railway transport on violent crime

All types of violent crime were analysed, grievous bodily harm and aggravated assault being combined into one indicator of more severe violence. Two indicators of the development of the rail network, the intensity of usage for passenger travel and transport of goods (Figure 5.3) are included as independent variables. Since the rail network was fully established by 1880, both are the best indicators of the mobility of the population, the mobilisation of everyday life and within the economy. The impact of other modernisation and economic factors was controlled by including urbanisation and indicators of economic growth and activity in the regression equations. These indicate the change of behavioural patterns and habits that are related with violence. Urbanisation was used as a proxy for these changes, and was defined as the proportion of the population living in cities with a population of 10,000 and more, assuming that the changes in habits and mentality developed in larger cities.[15] Two other indicators controlled for economic prosperity and development. For Württemberg the development of building capital (stock and net investment) is well documented for the whole period due to the obligatory

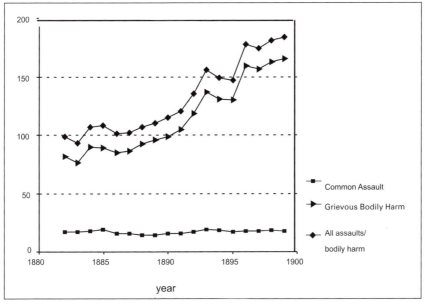

Figure 5.5 Convictions for assaults for 100,000 of criminally responsible population (age 18 and over).

fire insurance that included all buildings (Loreth, 1974). They are used as proxies for a measure of the Gross Domestic Product and the general economic development as well as the economy's cyclical development (see Table 5.1).

Table 5.1 shows the results of multivariate time series regression models (Prais-Winsten, GLS estimates) for the different violent crimes: murder and homicide, all assaults and grievous bodily harm. For common assault no model could be calculated that sufficiently fulfilled statistical requirements. From the two indicators of mobility passenger travel was included because it fulfilled model requirements regarding correlation with the control factors. For all types of violent crime a significant impact of the increase of passenger travel is found that is negative for murder and homicide, but positive for assaults. The models do not show a significant effect of urbanisation. This is in line with results of McHale and Johnson (1976a, 1976b; Johnson, 1995) who found no significant correlation for Prussia for 1885 and 1990 (but see Thome, 2002). However, the fact that the impact of urbanisation on murder and homicides reaches significance at the 0.05 level and is positive for both other types suggests a disintegrative impact of urbanisation. The period covers the beginning of urbanisation in Württemberg, which Zehr (1976) has found to be generally more strongly

Table 5.1 Usage of rail network by the public and violent crime (convictions per 100,000 of the criminally responsible population of 18 years and over) 1882–1900 (*Prais-Winsten; GLS*)

	Model 1: Murder and homicide		Model 2: All assaults/ bodily harm		Model 3: Grievous bodily harm/ aggravated assaults	
	[b]	[β]	[b]	[β]	[b]	[β]
Usage of rail network by passengers	−2.39	−0.38 **	105.4	0.74 **	89.84	0.53 **
Building net investment	0.67	0.46 **	−26.04	−0.85 **	−21.65	−0.73 **
Urbanisation	0.73	0.58 *	3.65	0.07 (ns)	8.11	0.16 (ns)
	(−0.57)		(−67.54)		(−91.45)	
N	18		18		18	
R² (adjusted)	0.46		0.78		0.78	
Durbin-Watson	1.49		1.52		1.53	

** significant at 0.01 level; * significant at 0.05 level.

related to interpersonal violent crime than later phases of urbanisation. For the indicator of economic development a different impact is found for murder/homicide and assaults. In correspondence with Johnson's (1995) and Thome's results (2002), assaults increase during economic crises and vary with the scale of social and political conflicts during such crises. Murder and homicide in contrast decrease during economic crises, a result, which lends itself to an interpretation in terms of anomic tendencies. According to Durkheim (1983) these increase during periods of economic growth while economic crises lessen anomic pressures.

Weak ties and the shift of interpersonal violence

The models show that the development of mass transport played a role in the changes in habits and mentalities that are related to interpersonal violence, albeit in different directions, and thus contributed to what can be termed a shift in violent behaviour during the process of modernisation. The production of 'weak ties' in society, that related strangers and encouraged self-control in conflicts, reduced very severe conflicts and respective situations as they emerged in strongly bonded communities, and consequently reduced the most severe and lethal forms of inter-personal violence. On the other hand, the results for assaults/grievous bodily harm suggest that weak ties and more anonymous situations in the enlarged public space might have been favourable to inducing less severe conflicts and the minor forms of interpersonal violence. It is not clear if an increase in the number of situations that caused such conflicts was responsible, or an increase in the willingness of the public to invoke the authorities because of the lack of informal controls in public space. The fact that both types of minor violent offences are affected by mass transport of persons in the same way supports the hypotheses that the transport revolution had an increasing and not an inhibiting impact on the less severe forms of violent conflicts.

The study covers the period when the rail network was fully developed and could unfold its impact on modern civilisation. Its results can be contrasted with the impact of pre-industrial mobility on crime – both property and violent crime – between 1834 and 1851, and the impact of rail transport on property crime between 1880 and 1900. Situating this study within such a framework will help to determine more precisely the modernising impact of rail transport, and the role of opportunity struc-tures during its development (Karstedt, 1999). Pre-industrial mobility was measured in terms of mobility between communities in Württemberg, which mainly consisted of labour migration between villages and cities.[16] Inner-state mobility did not have an independent impact either on property or on violent crime, but both were strongly affected by the rural food crises that coincided with labour migration.[17] Pre-industrial mobility in the rural economy of Württemberg neither contributed to anonymi-sation nor to 'individuation', and thus did not change the fabric of social life in a way that it could have affected patterns of violent behaviour.

In contrast to the impact of the usage of the rail network on inter-personal violent crime, no such effect could be determined for property crimes, either for passenger travel or for the transport of goods. Just as during the first half of the century, property crimes were affected by economic crises; however, the indicator of economic wealth (stock of building capital) had a negative (though non-significant) impact on property crimes. This suggests that during this period better economic conditions did not then produce the enhanced opportunities for property crimes as occurred later in the twentieth century. In addition, even if railway travel contributed and provided such new opportunities (indicated by the positive though non-significant effect), the impact is negligible and the population did not take advantage of such op-portunities on the scale they were provided. All the results taken together support the argument that indeed the development of mass transport changed the patterns of relatedness within society, and the moral fabric in which violent conflicts were embedded.

The first transport revolution contributed obviously in a formative way to the changes in mentalities and habits of violent behaviour. The gains in terms of individual autonomy, 'objectivation' and rationalisation of social relationships and of mechanisms of self-control made a de-escalation of severe conflicts mainly in more intimate relationships possible. However, the new modes of behaviour that it brought about in public space increased the potential for those types of conflicts that are expressed in less severe interpersonal violence. Mass transport on railways contributed enormously to mobility, and subsequently to anonymity and the volatility of social contacts, thus increasing the amount of conflict situations, and favouring their albeit small-scale escalation, notwithstanding a potential increase in self-control. The enlargement of public space contributed to the invoking of the authorities and their involvement in personal conflicts that could not be solved within personal and relatively stable networks of relationships. The increasing demands on self-control in interactions with strangers might have sensitised people and increased their readiness to report. The production of weak ties by the new mass transport technology simultaneously unleashed integrative and disintegrative forces in society, and consequently impacted on different types of violence in different ways.

Notes

1. This perspective has not been uncontested by historians (see, for example, Godfrey, 2003).
2. See for a more contemporary and cross-sectional analysis Wagatsuma and de Vos (1984), where they describe the mentality of a working-class neighbourhood in rapidly industrialising postwar Japan, and the role of hope and prospects in securing conformity even under dire circumstances.
3. For a discussion of this Durkheimian perspective from a cross-sectional and cross-national perspective see Karstedt (2001).
4. This of course mirrors the concomitant process of sprawling urbanisation; however, there seems to be a telling difference between the image of the 'global village' and that of the 'metropolis'.
5. The 'urban myths' that emerge and are spread on the World Wide Web are an analogous feature of the IT revolution.
6. This led to the paradoxical situation that women travellers in the USA – because they were not allowed to travel together with men – initially had to share their compartments with African-Americans until this 'situation' was resolved by segregation policies (Young Welke, 1992).

7. Durkheim had observed such a pattern in his comparison of rural and urban homicide rates. He argued that it was the strong ties in the traditional rural areas that contributed to the intensity of social conflicts and eventually their higher rates of lethal interpersonal violence (1983: 419).

8. Only a minority of German railways were operated as private enterprises, and at the end of the nineteenth century they were mainly run by the Federal State. The personnel were civil servants who represented the authority of the state to the travellers. They used to exert their authority until the end of the twentieth century, when the German railways were privatised, and the personnel were retrained as service providers.

9. Two other reasons make Württemberg a suitable region for historical research on crime and modernity. It had an elaborate system of annual statistics and economic accounting as early as 1813, including statistics of decisions (only sporadically) and convictions by higher and lower courts, that allows for more precise calculations of the relevant indicators than normally available for that period. Between 1815 and 1900, its territory did not change, a situation quite exceptional for historical research in Germany.

10. Even if the efficiency of the police had increased in Germany at the end of the nineteenth century, the courts might have counteracted this tendency; the number and proportion of those who were acquitted increased. Generally, sentencing became milder, while more and increasingly less severe offences were prosecuted. However, whether this situation was caused by a change in the practice of the courts or by an actual increase in such offences is indeterminable (Thome, 2002; Johnson, 1995).

11. Uniform Crime Statistics are only available after 1880. However, statistics for thefts were available from 1872.

12. See Thome (2002) for the same period (1883–1902) in Germany.

13. However, Württemberg had a positive balance of capital and the extension of the rail network was mainly paid for by its own stock of capital.

14. According to Thome (2002), during this period the South-West of Germany ranked third in its rates of grievous bodily harm, the South-East and East being the top two.

15. This definition follows Zehr (1976) and defines urbanisation at the higher end of the scale. Usually, a much lower index of 2,000 inhabitants is used (Braudel, 1988; Tilly, 1986; Gillis, 1996).

16. These studies cover the period from 1834 to 1851; however, the interrupted time series for theft and in particular assault ('insults') and murder/homicide allow only for partial correlations and models based on a small number of years.

17. Economic prosperity and crises were measured in terms of the mean price of corn.

References

Black, D. *The Behavior of Law*. New York: Academic Press, 1976.

Braudel, F. *The Identity of France: History and Environment*. London: Collins, 1988.

Deutsch, K. 'International communication: the media and flows', *Public Opinion Quarterly*, 20, 2, 1956, pp.143–60.

Deutsch, K. 'Social mobilization and political development', *American Political Science Review*, 55, 3, 1961, pp. 493–514.

Dunstall, G. *Frontier and/or Cultural Fragment? Interpretations of Violence in Colonial New Zealand*, paper to 'Comparative Histories of Crime' conference, Keele University, July 2002.

Durkheim, E. *Der Selbstmord*. Frankfurt: Suhrkamp, 1983.

Eisner, M. 'Modernisation, self-control and lethal violence. The long-term dynamics of European homicide rates in theoretical perspective', *British Journal of Criminology*, 1, 4, 2001, pp. 618–38.

Faith, N. *The World the Railways Made*. London: Bodley Head, 1990.

Fishlow, A. *Railroads and the Transformation of the Ante-Bellum Economy*. Cambridge, MA: Harvard University Press, 1966.

Gillis, A. R. 'Urbanization, sociohistorical context, and crime', in Hagan, J., Gillis, A. R. and Brownfield, D. (eds), *Criminological Controversies. A Methodological Primer*. Boulder, CO: Westview, 1996, pp. 47–74.

Godfrey, B. (2003) 'Counting and accounting for the decline in non-lethal violence in England, Australia, and New Zealand, 1880–1920', *British Journal of Criminology*, 43, 2, 2003, pp. 340–53.

Granovetter, M. 'The strength of weak ties', *American Journal of Sociology*, 78, 4, 1973, pp. 1360–80.

Hawke, G. *Railways and Economic Growth in England and Wales, 1840–1870*. Oxford: Clarendon Press, 1970.

Hirschmann, A. *Engagement und Enttäuschung*. Frankfurt: Suhrkamp, 1988.

Johnson, E. *Urbanization and Crime. Germany 1871–1914*. Cambridge: Cambridge University Press, 1995.

Karstedt, S. 'Modernisierung, Verkehr und Kriminalität. Eine Studie zur kulturellen Modernisierung', manuscript, University of Bielefeld, 1999.

Karstedt, S. 'Die moralische Störke schwacher Bindungen. Individualismus und Gewalt im Kulturvergleich', *Monatsschrift für Kriminologie und Strafrechtsreform*, 84, 3, 2001, pp. 226–43.

Karstedt, S. *The Production of Trust in Modern Societies: A Cross-national Study of Social and Cultural Factors*, paper to Conference of the International Institute of Sociology, Krakow, 2002.

Kriminalstatistik für das Jahr 1902. Tabellenwerk. Statistik des Deutschen Reiches. Bearbeitet vorm Kaiserlichen Statistischen Amt. Bd. 155. (1904) Berlin: von Puttkammer & Mühlbrecht.

Kriminalstatistik für das Jahr 1904. Tabellenwerk. Statistik des Deutschen Reiches. Bearbeitet vorm Kaiserlichen Statistischen Amt. Bd. 169. (1906) Berlin: von Puttkammer & Mühlbrecht.

Lederman, D., Loayza, N. and Menendez, A. *Violent Crime: Does Social Capital Matter?* Washington: World Bank, 1999.

Loreth, H. *Das Wachstum der württembergischen Wirtschaft von 1818–1918. Jahrbücher für Statistik und Landeskunde von Baden-Württemberg,* 1. Heft. Stuttgart: Kohlhammer, 1974.

McHale, V. and Johnson, E. 'Urbanization, industrialization and crime in imperial Germany: Part I', *Social Science History*, 1, 1, 1976a, pp. 45–78.

McHale, V. and Johnson, E. 'Urbanization, industrialization and crime in imperial Germany: Part II', *Social Science History*, 1, 3, 1976b, pp. 225–40.

Riehl, W. *Land und Leute. Naturgeschichte des Volkes als Grundlage einer deutschen Social-Politik,* Bd. 1. 5. Verbesserte Aufl. Stuttgart: Cotta, 1861.

Schievelbusch, W. *The Railway Journey. The Industrialization and Peception of Time and Space in the 19th Century.* Leamington Spa: Berg, 1986.

Simmel, G. *Soziologie.* Berlin: Duncker & Humblot, 1908/1968.

Simmel, G. 'The natural forms of communication: sociology of the senses: visual interaction', in Park, R. and Burgess, E. (eds), *Introduction to the Science of Sociology Including the Original Index to Basic Sociological Concepts.* Chicago and London: University of Chicago Press, 1969, pp. 356–65.

Statistisches Handbuch für das Königreich Württemberg. 1900. Stuttgart: Kohlhammer.

Thome, H. 'Kriminalität im Deutschen Kaiserreich, 1883–1902. Eine sozialökologische Analyse', *Geschichte und Gesellschaft*, 28, 4, 2002, pp. 519–53.

Thompson, E. P. 'Zeit, Arbeitsdisziplin und Industriekapitalismus', in Thompson, E. P., *Plebejische Kultur und moralische Ökonomie. Aufsätze zur englischen Sozialgeschichte des 18. und 19. Jahrhunderts,* ed. D. Groh. Frankfurt: Ullstein, 1980, pp. 34–65.

Tilly, C. *The Contentious French.* Cambridge, MA: Belknap, 1986.

Wagatsuma, H. and de Vos, G. *Heritage of Endurance: Family Patterns and Delinquency Formation in Urban Japan.* Berkeley, CA: University of California Press, 1984.

Wolf, W. *Eisenbahn und Autowahn. Personen- und Gütertransport auf Schienen und Strasse. Geschichte, Bilanz, Perspektiven.* Hamburg: Rasch & Röring, 1992.

Württembergische Jahrbücher für Statistik und Landeskunde. Vol. 1813–1899. Stuttgart: Cotta/ Kohlhammer.

Young Welke, B. *'All the Women Are White; All the Blacks Are Men', or Are They? Law and Segregation in Common Carriers 1855–1914,* American Bar Foundation Working Paper No. 9215. Chicago: American Bar Foundation, 1992.

Zehr, H. *Crime and the Development of Modern Society. Patterns of Criminality in Nineteenth Century Germany and France.* London: Croom Helm, 1976.

Chapter 6

'Inventing' the juvenile delinquent in nineteenth-century Europe

Heather Shore[1]

The idea that the juvenile delinquent was legislated or 'invented' into existence in Britain during the nineteenth century has become a central paradigm in histories of crime. Thus the nineteenth century has largely retained its central place in the historical narrative of the somewhat sporadic reform of the criminal justice system. Moreover, while formal state mechanisms for juvenile justice were often not put into place until the early twentieth century, these systems were building upon a set of institutions and practices that were firmly rooted in the developments of the nineteenth. In the 1970s, the bare, Whiggish, histories of early juvenile justice were to be re-adorned through the work of Susan Magarey (1978) and Margaret May (1973). Taking a more socio-historical approach, this work suggested more complex ways of reading the interplay of factors which contributed to the serpentine processes at work during the early nineteenth century. Since then, further research has extended the chronologies of Magarey and May, and in particular focused on the pivotal importance of the 1810s, in the move towards a more formal system of juvenile justice (King and Noel, 1993; King, 1998; Rush, 1992; Shore, 1999). While it is important to recognise that this was a 'formalisation' rather than a 'creation' of a system, and in doing so to acknowledge the continuities between modern and pre-modern representations of delinquent and disorderly youth, the aim of this chapter is to reaffirm the importance of a nineteenth-century chronology by considering this history as part of a broader and longer set of historical processes. The flood of recent historical work has made it clear that simple teleological approaches to the history of juvenile delinquency will no longer suffice. Geoffrey Pearson's classic text on hooliganism identified a series of 'moral panics' about youth and violence (1983). Pearson argued that successive generations of Britons voiced similar fears about social breakdown and moral degeneration, their fearful rhetoric embodied in the form of the hooligan, the garotter and the juvenile delinquent. Thus the primary purpose of this chapter is to explore this 'chronology' in a comparative analysis of British and European juvenile delinquency, but also in relation to both pre-modern and post-nineteenth-century developments. In doing so, it will trace the contours of a new historiography which has emerged in the last decade, and which takes a more antithetical approach to the established discussions of juvenile delinquency by thinking about the nineteenth century as a series of pivotal 'moments' in the long evolution of European juvenile justice.

It is possible to argue that juvenile delinquency emerged as a distinct social problem once it came to be named in new ways through juvenile-specific legislation; once it came to be managed in new ways within juvenile-specific institutions by specialised staff; and once the families of deprived and disorderly children came to be subject to new forms of external intervention and regulation. These processes can be read as intrinsically modern in the sense that all three 'belong' to the nineteenth century and that all three signified the rise of new forms of social management which required a wider reorganisation of the relationships between the state, civil institutions and citizens. Persuasive as this chronology might be, however, it is necessarily complicated by the fact that the very same three developments can be identified in the two centuries prior to the nineteenth. Early modern European societies legislated for deprived and disorderly youths, set up institutions to reform them and tried to enforce parental responsibility for them. In 1849, Thomas Beggs urged the education of young delinquents; failure to do so could only lead to 'deteriorated men and women, each generation lower in scale than that which has preceded it' (1849: 51–2). Yet in the sixteenth-century text, *Oeconomia Christiana* (1530) Justus Menius warned parents, 'Your children will become wanton and scorn you and when they are grown they will be *wild and malicious*, harmful people, who also scorn government' (Harrington, 1998: 22). In the twentieth century, when biological and hereditary explanations for crime predominated, concerns about abnormal families and miscegenation in the case of mixed-race relationships reflected the continuing linkages made between the juvenile delinquent and broader social corruption (Cox, 2002; Fishman, 2002). Nevertheless, it was during the nineteenth century that the main forms of juvenile justice were established across Europe.

Legal processes and language

Legal distinctions between adults and children can be identified in various forms of social legislation enacted in and before the nineteenth century. Thus acts and statutes defining the rules of inheritance, apprenticeship and parental responsibility can be traced throughout the early modern period. Moreover, it would be unwise to overlook the power of early modern orders and proclamations, many of which stipulated restrictions on or regulation of delinquent youth. Age-related definitions of the juvenile delinquent, particularly in the context of law, have also historically been subject to discretion and negotiation. In early modern Spain the age of criminal liability was set at 14, although the age at which females could be accused of sexual misconduct was 12 (Nilan, forthcoming). In Britain the formulation of *doli incapax* (literally translated as 'incapable of [doing] harm'), allowed that children between the ages of 7 and 14 were presumed to be incapable of criminal intent; the prosecution's task was to undermine this presumption. Hence, in early seventeenth-century England, Dalton, in *The Countrey Justice* (1618), held that:

> An infant of eight yeares of age, or above, may commit homicide, and shall be hanged for it, viz. If it may appeare (by hyding of the person slaine, by excusing it, or by any other act) that he had knowledge of good and evill, and of the perill and danger of that offence ... But an infant of such tender yeares, as that he hath no discretion or intelligence, if he kill a man, this is no felonie in him. (Sanders, 1970: 11)

The specific age boundaries of *doli incapax* did vary over time, for example the age was amended to 8 in 1933 and 10 in 1963 (Gelsthorpe and Morris, 1994: 949–5). In France, Belgium, and several other continental states under the Napoleonic Code (1810), minors found guilty aged under 16 had to have been found to have *discernment*, thus to have knowledge of their wrong-doing (Christiaens, 1999: 10; Nilan, 1997: 81). In fact, criminal children were subject to specific legislation as early as the late eighteenth and early nineteenth centuries. In France, the Penal Codes of 1791 and 1810 had made the 'minority plea' a formal element of French law: juveniles (under 16) 'were exempt from the death penalty and other harsh or degrading punishments' (Nilan, 1997: 82; Berlanstein, 1979: 532). In the

Netherlands, in 1809, the codification of criminal law known as the Crimineel Wetboek was introduced which contained separate articles on children. This was replaced in 1811 by the Napoleonic Code. Moreover, Susan Magarey has convincingly argued that the cluster of Acts passed in Britain in the 1820s, aimed at policing vagrancy and malicious trespass, were in part designed to control delinquent children (1978: 20–2; Shore, 1999: 30–2).

What is remarkable here is the relative continuity in the range of formal measures to deal with social, and particularly youthful, disorder. While no one can deny the rush of legislative response to juvenile crime that was a feature of the later nineteenth and the twentieth centuries, these Acts might be more usefully regarded as a progression from such earlier measures. Arguably these acts formalised processes which had been in place, albeit often informally, for centuries. Indeed, Natalie Zemon Davis has identified 'an international movement for welfare reform in Europe in the decades after 1520' (1987: 24). However, there is little doubt that from the mid-nineteenth century onwards the use of a specific terminology became more pronounced. The Juvenile Offenders Act of 1847 in Britain, the 1896 Child Welfare Act in Norway, the 1902 Swedish Reformatory Acts, the 1912 Act establishing the Tribunal for Infants and Adolescents in France, and the Belgium Child Protection Act of 1912 all explicitly described this new legal subject and defined clear processes of reform (Christiaens, 1999; Kumlien, 1997; Alaimo, 1992). These Acts, perhaps for the first time, adopted the 'new' vocabulary of juvenile delinquency that had been formulated in the discursive process of the early decades of the nineteenth century. A stronger linguistic delineation of juvenile de-linquency thus aided the move from a more informal system to a more formal system of regulation, in which state responses were to dominate. However, this shift should not be overstated. Public and private sector measures frequently coexisted both in the pre-modern and modern period. That the state and philanthropic measures were not mutually exclusive can be seen in the case of institutional provision. The British Industrial and Reformatory School Acts of the 1850s and 1860s, the French Law of 1850 which proposed 'reformation of juvenile offenders by agricultural labour' and the new Dutch Penal Code of 1886 were all, to a degree, extending standardising state regulation to a philanthropic sector which was already well established (Radzinowicz and Hood, 1990: 159; Berlanstein, 1979: 531; Leonards, 2002: 116).

While there are significant continuities with the early modern period; it also clear that, in the move towards a separate juvenile justice system, the wheels turned exceedingly slowly. This raises a number of questions. Should the rise of separate juvenile justice systems be necessarily read as a sign of progress? Did the decline of older institutions like apprenticeship undermine existing forms of social support for adolescent youths? How far did a changing vocabulary promote a separate discourse, and thereby engender this judicial separation? Griffiths has remarked that nineteenth-century discourses of delinquency can seem very familiar to a historian of 'disorderly youth', 'idle apprentices' and 'saucie wenches' in the earlier period (Griffiths, 2002: 26, 30). Yet the emergence of new terminologies are key to understanding such continuities and discontinuities. In her investigation of the linguistic constructions of the child criminal in late eighteenth- and early nineteenth-century France, Nilan (1997) has argued that the romantic view of childhood was fundamentally ambivalent and that the greater emphasis on emotion and irrational impulses led to a stronger reconfiguration of the child as 'other'. Thus children who failed to conform to the romantic model became perhaps more inexplicably deviant than previously. According to Nilan, this model of innocent childhood re-emphasised the abnormality and deviance of the criminal child in opposition to the normal child (1997: 83–4). What this suggests is that the coincidence of new legal structures that enabled developments in legislation, a reformulation of youth and childhood, and a move towards the sometimes punitive reformatory systems to be found in many European countries during the nineteenth century may be significant. Thus it is likely that powerful class-based dichotomies were increasingly shaping the treatment of the juvenile offender. Consequently, the difference between hardened and corrupted working-class child and the innocent and pure middle-class child found its echo in the language of penality. Thus the discourses of reform and the reformulation of criminal justice increasingly focused upon the 'hardened', the 'incorrigible', the 'dangerous' juvenile offender – persistent juvenile offenders became an emblem for social breakdown and domestic instability.

In the twentieth century the language of delinquency again arguably shifted to reflect a new language of welfare, which has certain interesting early modern echoes. In Britain, for example, the more specific 'juvenile delinquent' was to some extent, replaced by the more generic and less judgemental 'neglected child'. While 'care and protection' had been implicit in previous legislation, the 1908 Children Act (and its successors in 1933 and 1948) took major steps to protect vulnerable children. This Act both extended the range of reasons for which a child (under 14) could be brought to court, and also blurred the distinction between the 'incorrigible' child and the child 'in danger'. Although this neo-welfarism had its earlier antecedents and its clear punitive sides, it does seem to have marked a broadening of the category 'juvenile delinquent' to the point where the category began to lose something of the specificity which it had carried since the mid-nineteenth century (Hendrick, 1994: 124). In summary, there is a clear divide between historians of the pre-nineteenth century who tend to focus on 'disorderly youths', and historians of the post-nineteenth century who have tended to focus on 'juvenile delinquents'. This divide is not based simply on the preferences of different scholarly camps, but, to a large extent, on the distinct (legal) languages used by contemporaries in each period and by the fact that the legal treatment of *all* children, as opposed to disorderly children, was fundamentally altered by far-reaching legal reforms of the early nineteenth century.

While legal language and definitions might have played with the distinctions between 'good' and 'bad' children, and 'disorderly' or 'delinquent' children, further distinctions were made between male and female juvenile offenders (Cox, 2003; Cain, 1989; Fishman, 1997: 96; Koeppel, 1987; Mahood, 1995; Shore, 1999). In Ancien Régime France the age of criminal liability for girls was 12, as opposed to 14 for boys. According to Shulamith Shahar (1990: 267), this was based on medieval beliefs that girls reached sexual maturity at an earlier age than boys. In Spain, consequently, girls were deemed to be culpable of sexual immorality from the age of twelve. In Britain gendered distinctions were more implicit than explicit. Both Cale (1993) and Mahood (1995), in work on nineteenth-century England and Scotland have commented on the differentiation inherent in discourses on juvenile crime between boy thieves and girl prostitutes. Similarly in interwar Norway of the twentieth century, the operation of after-care and probation services differed significantly between girls and boys. Thus reform schools for girls were preoccupied with prostitution and illegitimacy, and consequently models of after-care (Andresen, 2002). Perhaps unsurprisingly, early modern commentators on delinquency mouthed a very similar rhetoric. The sexuality of female youths was often more closely monitored than that of males, and further enabled in a range of institutions which offered gender specific arrangements (Griffiths, 1996: 29–30). The Toribios in eighteenth-century Seville was primarily associated with boys and young men. While sexual morality was a key concern, similar 'wayward' or 'disorderly' girls were sent to religious institutions (Tikoff, 2002: 67–8). In early modern Tuscany, refuges for wayward women took girls who had 'fallen into trouble'. In Tuscany charitable institutions did provide shelter for pauper girls, but differentiated between 'honest' girls and female 'deviants' (Cohen, 1992: 116). In 1758, the magistrate John Fielding established the House of Refuge for Orphan Girls in London. In his plan for the asylum Fielding emphasised the familiar construction of female juvenile sexuality, 'deserted Boys were Thieves from Necessity, their Sisters are Whores from the same Cause; and, having the same Education with their wretched Brothers, generally join the Thief to the Prostitute' (Fielding, 1758). Arguably, the equation between female juvenile offending and prostitution was confirmed and formalised in modern legislative and institutional responses (Kersten, 1989). In the late nineteenth- and early twentieth-century reformatories, as in early modern institutions, it is clear that in many cases girls were sent there for different reasons to the boys. As Andresen (2002), Cox (1997; 2003) and Harvey (1995) have pointed out in their respective studies of Norway, England and Germany, the majority of girls in reform schools were suspected of sexual activity and immorality, or were felt to be in danger of sexual corruption.

Institutions

The emergence of child-specific institutions has been seen as one of the key features of the nineteenth-century development of juvenile justice. By the twentieth century most European countries had some form of state reformatory programme made up of a range of institutions. However, European institutional initiatives to deal with the disorderly young date back at least to the fifteenth century. Criminal children, paupers, orphans and foundlings were catered for by a variety of local initiatives, mostly managed by religious charities or more secular civic agencies. For example, the Rasphuis (Saw House) established in Amsterdam in the seventeenth century, had wards for wayward youths (Spierenburg, 1991: 25–6), as did the Hôpital Général in eighteenth century Paris (Capul, 1989: 170–1). The Toribios was established in Seville in 1725 as an asylum for poor boys, but was regarded as a 'correctional' institution almost from its inception (Tikoff, 2002). Nevertheless, despite clear evidence for institutional provision in the early modern period and particularly in eighteenth-century European urban centres (Cavallo, 1989; Farge, 1993: 68–71; Innes, 1987; Radzinowicz and Hood, 1990: 133–5), the phase of institutional building associated with the early nineteenth century is still considered by many to be a watershed in the management of delinquency. Thus Hugh Cunningham argues that from the 1830s, 'there was an intensified phase of institution-building, catering for children of all kinds thought to be in need' (1995: 146). The early nineteenth century seems to be distinct in two major respects: in terms of the growth of a wider public debate about juveniles and the purpose of juvenile institutions, and in terms of the new ability and willingness of increasingly consolidated nation states to become involved in such projects. The result was a comprehensive programme of building and redevelopment.

Certainly, the innovative nature of these 'new' institutions can be overstated, given that they often incorporated early modern elements. Many, if not most, retained charitable management, large amounts of charitable funding and old-style discretionary admissions policies. Many, too, looked back to an idealised rural past and in this sense consciously used these institutions as a way of stemming a 'modern' urban industrial tide. Pioneering projects such as the Colonies Agricole at Mettray in France (Driver, 1990; Jablonka, 2000; Radzinowicz and Hood, 1990; Dekker, 1990) and the Rauhe Haus near Hamburg, and their British successors, the Philanthropic Society school in Redhill, Surrey, and the Hackney Wick Academy on the borders of London (Shore, 1999: 94–114, 132–147), tried to evoke an old rural society that, contemporaries felt, was increasingly under attack. This model proved highly influential and continued to shape European juvenile institutions, at least for boys, well into the twentieth century.

If, as the previous section suggested, European courts' treatment of juveniles narrowed somewhat from the early nineteenth century, European institutions' treatment of juveniles arguably widened. Increasingly, children deemed to be 'at risk', as well as those who had already committed crimes, were incorporated within the expanding welfare-punishment nexus. In the Netherlands, a specialised youth prison was opened in Rotterdam under article 66 of the Code Pénal. Subsequently, from 1857, special reformatories were opened for children who had not actually been convicted but were felt to be in need of moral reformation (the equivalent of the British industrial schools). Thus the House for Progress and Education (roughly translated) was opened for boys in Alkmaar, and in 1859 a similar institution for girls was opened in Montfoort (Leonards, 1990: 150). In Belgium, as Christiaens (2002: 92) has shown, an institution which had been founded in the 1840s as a Penitentiary House for Young Delinquents, had, by the 1890s, been renamed and become a Welfare School. In Britain, the incorporation of 'at risk' children into the state system was formalised in legislation. An Industrial Schools Amending Act of 1861 redefined the 'vagrant child' as 'almost any child under fourteen found begging, receiving alms, of no settled abode or means of subsistence or one who frequented criminal company' (Springhall, 1986: 167; Stack, 1994). A further Consolidating Act of 1866 widened the net even further by including orphans, children of criminal parents, and children whose parents were undergoing penal servitude. By the 1860s, delinquent, semi-delinquent and non-delinquent children were admitted to the industrial schools without previous imprisonment (Stack, 1994: 64–5). This broadening of definitions of delinquency was neither smooth nor seamless, however. It was the subject of much debate among many agencies in many arenas across Europe as Chris Leonards' (2002) work on nineteenth-century Penal Congresses has shown. The questions at hand were as difficult then as they are today: should children who had actually committed crimes be treated in the same ways as that of those who might go on to commit crimes? Was there any meaningful difference between the 'experienced' and the 'innocent', between children in trouble and children in need?

If nineteenth-century reformers sought to transform traditional charitable juvenile institutions by standardising their organisation and broadening their admissions, twentieth century reforms sought to transform them further by keeping broad admission criteria but by using them much more as a last resort. In the early twentieth century, these institutions came under considerable attack across Europe. Spaces that had been seen as safe for children were now widely cast as placing children in danger. In Britain, a 1913 government committee produced a damning report on industrial and reformatory schools, complaining of treatment that was harsh, old fashioned and unproductive (Smith, 1990: 126–7; Bailey, 1987: 47–57). In this sense, the early twentieth century does seem to occupy a particular place in the history of European states' ever-proliferating efforts to discipline, punish and care for their young citizens. Of course, those young citizens and their families played a key role in this broad history of governmentality themselves, and certainly not just as 'docile bodies', which, as the final section shows, should not be overlooked.

Families

The home environments and family relationships were, and remain, central to discourses of juvenile delinquency. The proper upbringing of children and the proper duties of parents were common subjects in medieval and early modern advice books, catechism and tracts (Cunningham, 1995: 41–78). The idea that children were moving beyond authority and stability, variously defined, was common to many of these fears. On the one hand, the rise of 'new' urban commercial pleasures, from coffee houses to video arcades, have been repeatedly identified as a recurring source of young people's rejection of established social order (Roberts, 2002), although, on the other, the disempowering of 'old' authorities, from apprentice masters to priests to teachers to parents, have been too. As Griffiths (2002: 31–2) has argued, much of the 'invention' debate has rested on the behaviour of a new generation of 'masterless' youths apparently created by the decline of apprenticeship and increase in urban migration in large areas of Europe in the late eighteenth and early nineteenth centuries. A long literature on European age-relations has argued that these developments caused very significant changes to the life-cycle experience of youths and their families, some of which resulted in both an actual and a feared increase in delinquency (King, 1998: 137–51; Mitterauer, 1992: 1–34; Springhall, 1986: 13).

Another fear expressed across discussions of delinquency in different periods is that of systematic generational decline. In short, the delinquent children of the day would be the corruptive parents of tomorrow. In mid-nineteenth century Britain, Mary Carpenter wrote of both the short- and long-term costs of delinquency: 'These young beings continue to herd in their dens of iniquity, to swarm in our streets, to levy a costly maintenance on the honest and industrious, to rise up to be the parents of a degraded progeny of pauper children' (Carpenter, 1851: 2). A century later, as Cox (2002) has shown, similar frenzied concerns continued to be raised about delinquent and neglected children in general, and perhaps in particular about 'mixed race' and black migrant children. The terminology may have changed since Carpenter's day, heightened by variants of social Darwinism, but the sentiment was clearly recognisable.

Parents themselves, though, were also blamed for causing their children's delinquency. In 1816, the *Report of the Committee for Investigating the Alarming Increase of Juvenile Delinquency in the Metropolis*, named 'The improper conduct of parents' as one of the principal causes of juvenile crime in London (1816: 10–11). Again in England, in 1834, Thomas Jevons wrote in his *Remarks on Criminal Law*, of the inadequacies of parents when it came to their delinquent children: 'If the neglect of a parent occasions his child to commit a crime, such parent is in fact the author of that crime, and ought to be made accountable to the state' (Sanders, 1970: 153). Jevons' suggestion was realised, to a degree, with the institution of parental prosecutions for neglect towards the end of century. Further, the removal of certain delinquent and neglected children to state-sponsored juvenile institutions across Europe was certainly intended to protect them from bad home environments but also to remind their parents and guardians of their duties both to the child and the nation.

With the expansion of more diffused and community-based child welfare programmes in the early twentieth century the potential for public regulation of private homes increased dramatically. To cite Donzelot, the policing of children and youths was very much part of a wider 'policing of families' (1980). A further important claim made by Donzelot is that some families colluded with external authorities in this process, that they 'invited' experts into their homes. Yet, in Ancien Régime Seville, as Tikoff (2002) has shown, both plebian and elite parents used the Toribios as a disciplinary device. English sources from the early modern period on-wards show how many 'ordinary' parents were prepared to place their wayward children in the Bridewell, house of correction or in similar institutions (Innes, 1987: 47; Shore, 1999: 10–11, 31–3). Assumptions about good and bad family life therefore did a great deal to shape reformatory strategies. Those children removed from their own families, for whatever reason, and placed in nineteenth-century juvenile institutions were being consciously placed in alternative 'families'. These institutions were com-monly designed to emulate, and improve upon, the supposed security, stability and order of an ideal family home. At Mettray in the 1840s, boys were divided into 'families': 'Each family resides in a distinct house ... The boy feels that his master is not a mere officer to watch him and enforce discipline, or a mere instructor to teach him, but is a relation – a friend – to sympathize with him and assist him' (Carpenter, 1851: 326–7). Again, however, 'family'-style institutions like Mettray and many others were subject to much debate in the nineteenth and twentieth centuries. And again, much of the debate dwelt on the nature of the children admitted and, by extension, the primary purpose of the institution. Were children sent to such places to be punished, or to be protected? If they were sent to be punished, was the family model 'too lenient'? If they were sent to be protected, was it still 'too harsh'? The search for the 'ideal' juvenile institution, like that for the 'ideal' family, continues in many parts of Europe today.

Conclusion

In summary, investigation of such issues over a wide timespan and broad demographic context shows how conventional criminological and his-torical chronologies can be usefully challenged and how the conventional boundaries of 'modernity' can be usefully questioned. Yet it seems clear that while we can acknowledge crucial early modern antecedents, the nineteenth century represents a watershed in the definition and management of social disorder, and particularly youthful disorder, across Europe. While it would be unwise to argue that there was a uniquely European construction or response to juvenile delinquency, it is clear that from the nineteenth century certain themes came to dominate European discourses of delinquency, which continue to inform our understandings, perceptions, fears and anxieties about the child criminal.

Notes

1. See the introductory and other papers in P. Cox and H. Shore (eds), *Becoming Delinquent: European Youth, 1650–1950*. Aldershot: Ashgate, 2002.

References

Alaimo, K. 'Shaping adolescence in the popular milieu: social policy, reformers, and French youth, 1870–1920', *Journal of Family History*, 17, 4, 1992, pp. 419–38.

Andresen, A. 'Gender, after-care and reform in inter-war Norway', in Cox, P. and Shore, H. (eds), *Becoming Delinquent: European Youth, 1650–1950*. Aldershot: Ashgate Press, 2002, pp. 23–40.

Bailey, V. *Delinquency and Citizenship: Reclaiming the Young Offender, 1914–1948*. Oxford: Clarendon Press, 1987, pp. 47–57.

Beggs, T. *An Inquiry into the Extent and Causes of Juvenile Depravity*. London: Charles Gilpin, 1849.

Berlanstein, L. 'Vagrants, beggars, and thieves: delinquent boys in mid-nineteenth century Paris', *Journal of Social History*, 12, 1979, pp. 531–52.

Cain, M. (ed.) *Growing Up Good: Policing the Behaviour of Girls in Europe*. London: Sage, 1989.

Cale, M. 'Girls and the perception of sexual danger in the Victorian reformatory system', *History*, 78, 1993, pp. 201–17.

Capul, M. *Abandon et Marginalité: Les Enfants Placés sous L'Ancien Régime*. Toulouse: Privat, 1989.

Carpenter, M. *Reformatory Schools for the Children of the Perishing and Dangerous Classes and for Juvenile Offenders*. London: Charles Gilpin, 1851/1968, p. 2.

Cavallo, S. *Charity and Power in Early Modern Italy: Benefactors and their Motives in Turin, 1541–1789*. Cambridge: Cambridge University Press, 1989.

Christiaens, J. 'A history of Belgium's Child Protection Act of 1912: the redefinition of the juvenile offender and his punishment', *European Journal of Crime, Criminal Law and Criminal Justice*, 7, 1, 1999, pp. 5–21.

Christiaens, J. 'Testing the limits: redefining resistance in a Belgian boys' prison, 1895–1905', in Cox, P. and Shore, H. (eds), *Becoming Delinquent: European Youth, 1650–1950*. Aldershot: Ashgate Press, 2002, pp. 89–104.

Cohen, S. *The Evolution of Women's Asylums Since 1500: From Refuges for Ex-Prostitutes to Shelters for Battered Women*. Oxford: Oxford University Press, 1992.

Cox, P. 'Rescue and Reform: Girls, Delinquency and Industrial Schools, 1908–33', unpublished PhD thesis, Cambridge University, 1997.

Cox, P. 'Race, delinquency and difference in twentieth century Britain', in Cox, P. and Shore, H. (eds), *Becoming Delinquent: European Youth, 1650–1950*. Aldershot: Ashgate Press, 2002, pp. 159–77.

Cox, P. *Gender, Justice and Welfare: Bad Girls in Britain, 1900–1950*. Basingstoke: Palgrave, 2003.

Cunningham, H. *Children and Childhood in Western Society since 1500*. London: Longman, 1995.

Davis, N. *Society and Culture in Early Modern France*. Cambridge: Polity, 1987.

Dekker, J. 'Punir, sauver et eduquer: la colonie agricole "Nederlandsch Mettray" et la reeducation residentielle aux Pays-Bas, en France, en Allegmagne et en Angleterre entre 1814 et 1914', *Mouvement Social*, 153, 1990, pp. 63–90.

Donzelot, J. *The Policing of Families*. London: Hutchinson, 1980.

Driver, F. 'Discipline without frontiers? Representations of the Mettray Reformatory Colony in Britain, 1840–80', *Journal of Historical Sociology*, 3, 1990, pp. 272–93.

Farge, A. *Fragile Lives: Violence, Power, and Solidarity in Eighteenth Century Paris*. Cambridge: Polity, 1993 translation.

Fielding, J. *A Plan of the Asylum; or, House of Refuge for Orphans and Other Deserted Girls of the Poor in this Metropolis*. London: R. Franklin, 1758.

Fishman, S. 'Juvenile delinquency as a "condition": social sciences construction of the criminal child, 1936–46', in *Proceedings of the Annual Meeting of the Western Society for French History*, 24, 1997, pp. 92–100.

Fishman, S. 'Absent fathers and family breakdown: delinquency in Vichy France', in Cox, P. and Shore, H. (eds), *Becoming Delinquent: European Youth, 1650–1950*. Aldershot: Ashgate Press, 2002, pp. 141–57.

Gelsthorpe, L. and Morris, A. 'Juvenile justice 1945–1992', in Maguire, M., Morgan, R. and Reiner, R. (eds), *The Oxford Handbook of Criminology*, Oxford: Oxford University Press, 1994, pp. 949–93.

Griffiths, P. *Youth and Authority: Formative Experiences in England, 1560–1640*. Oxford: Clarendon Press, 1996.

Griffiths, P. 'Juvenile delinquency in time', in Cox, P. and Shore, H. (eds), *Becoming Delinquent: British and European Youth, 1650–1950*. Aldershot: Ashgate Press, 2002, pp. 23–40.

Harrington, J. 'Bad parents, the state, and the early modern civilising process', *German History*, 16, 1, 1998, pp. 16–28.

Harvey, E. *Youth and the Welfare State in Weimar Germany*. Oxford: Clarendon Press, 1995 .

Hendrick, H. *Child Welfare: England, 1872–1989*. London: Routledge, 1994.

Innes, J. 'Prisons for the poor: English Bridewells, 1555–1800', in Snyder, F. and Hay, D. (eds), *Labour, Law and Crime; A Historical Perspective*. London: Tavistock, 1987, pp. 42–122.

Jablonka, I. 'Philanthropic discourse in nineteenth century France: the rehabilitation of juvenile delinquents in agricultural reformatories', *Revue D'Histoire Moderne et Contemporaine*, 47, 1, 2000, pp. 131–47.

Kersten, J. 'The institutional control of girls and boys: an attempt at a gender-specific approach', in Cain, M. (ed.), *Growing Up Good: Policing the Behaviour of Girls in Europe*. London: Sage, 1989, pp. 129–44.

King, P. 'The rise of juvenile delinquency in England, 1780–1840: changing patterns of perception and prosecution', *Past and Present*, 160, 1998, pp. 116–66.

King, P. and Noel, J. 'The origins of "the problem of juvenile delinquency": the growth of juvenile prosecutions in London in the late eighteenth and early nineteenth century', *Criminal Justice History*, 15, 1993, pp. 17–41.

Koeppel, B. *Marguerite B. Une Jeune Fille en Maison de Correction*. Paris: Hachette, 1987.

Kumlien, M. *Uppfostran och Straff: Studier Kring 1902 ors Lagstiftning om Reaktioner mot Ungdomsbrott* (Upbringing and Punishment: Studies on the 1902 Swedish Reformatory Acts). Lund: Rättshistoriskt bibliotek LVI, 1997.

Leonards, C. 'From a marginal institution to institutionalised marginalisation: developments in the treatment of "criminal" children in the Dutch prison system, 1833–84', *Paedagogia Historica*, 26, 2, 1990, pp. 147–59.

Leonards, C. 'Border crossings: care and the "criminal child" in nineteenth century European Penal Congresses', in Cox, P. and Shore, H. (eds), *Becoming Delinquent: European Youth, 1650–1950*. Aldershot: Ashgate Press, 2002, pp. 105–21.

Magarey, S. 'The invention of juvenile delinquency in early nineteenth-century England', *Labour History*, 34, 1978, pp. 11–27.

Mahood, L. and Littlewood, B. 'The "vicious" girl and the "street-corner" boy: sexuality and the gendered delinquent in the Scottish Child-Saving Movement, 1850–1940', *Journal of the History of Sexuality*, 4, 1994, pp. 549–78.

Mahood, L. *Policing Gender, Class and Family: Britain, 1850–1940*. London: UCL Press, 1995.

May, M. 'Innocence and experience: the evolution of the concept of juvenile delinquency in the mid-nineteenth century', *Victorian Studies*, 17, 1, 1973, pp. 7–29.

Mitterauer, M. *A History of Youth*, trans. Graeme Dunphy. Oxford: Blackwell, 1992.

Nilan, C. 'Hapless innocence and precocious perversity: constructions of the child criminal in late eighteenth and early nineteenth century France', *Proceedings of the Annual Meeting of the Western Society for French History*, 24, 1997, pp. 81–91.

Nilan, C. *Precocious Perversity: Childhood, Crime and the Prison in July Monarchy France*. (Forthcoming).

Pearson, G. *Hooligan: A History of Respectable Fears*. London: Macmillan, 1983.

Radzinowicz, L. and Hood, R. (eds) *A History of English Criminal Law and its Administration from 1750. V. The Emergence of Penal Policy*. Oxford: Clarendon Press, 1990.

Roberts, B. 'On not becoming delinquent: raising adolescent boys in the Dutch Republic, 1600–1750', in Cox, P. and Shore, H. (eds), *Becoming Delinquent: British and European Youth, 1650–1950*. Aldershot: Ashgate Press, 2002, pp. 41–57.

Rush, P. 'The government of a generation: the subject of juvenile delinquency', *Liverpool Law Review*, 15, 1992, pp. 3–43.

Sanders, W. *Juvenile Offenders for a Thousand Years: Selected Readings from Anglo-Saxon Times to 1900*. Chapel Hill, NC: University of North Carolina Press, 1970.

Shore, H. *Artful Dodgers: Youth and Crime in Early Nineteenth Century London*. Woodbridge: Boydell & Brewer, 1999.

Shulamith, S. *Childhood in the Middle Ages*. London: Routledge, 1990.

Smith, D. 'Juvenile delinquency in Britain in the First World War', *Criminal Justice History*, 11, 1990, pp. 126–7.

Spierenburg, P. *The Prison Experience: Disciplinary Institutions and their Inmates in Early Modern Europe*. New Brunswick, NJ: Rutgers University Press, 1991.

Springhall, J. *Coming of Age: Adolescence in Britain, 1860–1960*. Dublin: Gill & Macmillan, 1986.

Stack, J. 'Reformatory and industrial schools and the decline of child imprisonment in mid-Victorian England and Wales', *History of Education*, 23, 1, 1994, pp. 59–73.

Tikoff, V. 'Before the reformatory: a correctional orphanage in Old Regime Seville', in Cox, P. and Shore, H. (eds) *Becoming Delinquent: European Youth, 1650–1950*. Aldershot: Ashgate Press, 2002, pp. 59–75.

Chapter 7

'Scoundrels and scallywags, and some honest men ...' Memoirs and the self-image of French and English policemen, c.1870–1939

Paul Lawrence

The self-image which police officers hold of themselves, as well as their attitudes towards the profession and their opinions of those they deal with on a daily basis, are notoriously difficult to assess. It is often hard enough for the historian/criminologist even to ascertain the 'facts' surrounding policing practice (i.e. who did what, when) – without attempting to stray into the highly subjective field of thoughts and feelings. Yet, as Robert Reiner notes, 'an understanding of how police officers see the social world and their role in it – "cop culture" – is crucial to an analysis of what they do, and their broad political function' (Reiner, 2000: 85). To this end, for the contemporary period, a number of criminological studies are available which attempt to delve into these issues (notably, *inter alia*, Skolnick, 1966; Reiner, 1978; Waddington, 1999; Reiner, 2000). Reiner himself claims that despite the existence of variant 'subcultures', in fact 'police forces in modern liberal democracies do face similar basic pressures that shape a distinctive and characteristic culture' (Reiner, 2000: 86). The key elements of this culture, for him (and other commentators), are a sense of mission, a love of 'action', the prevalence of machismo, a sense of solidarity and a 'pragmatic, concrete, down-to-earth, anti-theoretical perspective' (Reiner, 2000: 101).

However, an understanding of 'cop culture' is just as important for the historian of crime as for the contemporary criminologist, but historical studies of these issues are far more sparse (although not non-existent – see, for example, Clapson and Emsley, 2002; Shpayer-Makov, 2002). Moreover, most analyses, both contemporary and historical, tend to focus on either Britain or the United States. Comparative approaches involving other European countries are rare. This study will attempt partially to remedy this lacuna via an analysis of the range of memoirs written by English and French police officers, primarily detectives, between the beginning of the Third Republic and the outbreak of the Second World War. This was a period in which an unprecedented number of officers published reminiscences of various kinds, and these certainly are intriguing sources for the historian. All represent themselves as inherently factual, with most claiming rather predictably (usually in the preface or foreword) to contain 'the truth, the whole truth, nothing but the truth' (see, for example, Macé, 1885: 2). Indeed, many authors specifically set up a distinction between their writings and detective fiction, which often portrayed 'real-life' detectives as bumbling fools (at least up until the creation of the Criminal Records Office in 1901: Hobbs, 1989: 42). Many also expressly disclaimed any literary pretensions which might perhaps have implied embellishment. G. H. Greenham, for example, claimed that he had 'abstained as much as possible from clothing his tales with phrases of flowery language, with a view to giving the actual facts, and neither more nor less' (Greenham, 1904: 7).

Clearly, however, despite their claims merely to narrate real events, there are problems in judging where fact and fiction collide in these works. A limited number of episodes are verifiable from archival sources, but such authentication is time-consuming and in any case not always possible.[1] Taken individually, therefore, the utility of each memoir for the historian is perhaps limited. Taken en masse, however, patterns of presentation and linguistic trends begin to emerge, as do similarities in outlook and opinion between officers. Yet, historical study of policing memoirs per se is markedly lacking. The work presented here thus falls into two sections. Initially, an attempt is made to consider the memoirs written during this period as a whole. Questions are posed as to whether they constitute a specific 'genre' and, if so, what literary conventions can be identified. Also, what does study at this general level reveal about the French and English police, and the differences between the two? Then, more specifically, the utility of policing memoirs in revealing the self-perceptions of officers – historical 'cop culture' – is considered. How did officers perceive themselves? Or rather, how did they wish to portray themselves? French and English historical examples are contrasted, and then both are compared to the findings of contemporary studies.

Police memoirs/autobiographies as a 'genre'

The first policing autobiographies/memoirs began to appear quite early in the nineteenth century (see Richmond, 1827; Vidocq, 1828). As would be expected, these emerged coincidentally with the development of new forms of policing in both England and France and the increasing spread of literacy. Initially, these writings were dogged by scandal and did not sell in significant numbers, but a number of bogus memoirs (written by journalists) later captured the public imagination (see, for example, Waters, 1849), and subsequently more authentic material began to appear. However, it was not until post-1870 that publication levels began to reach appreciable proportions, co-incident with the rising popularity of detective fiction (an issue which will be discussed in the conclusion below). As Figure 7.1 shows,[2] the 1880s saw an early peak of interest in both France and England, and there was another wave of publications in the interwar period (possibly related to the retirement of the first detectives perceived by the public as fully professional) (Hobbs, 1989). There was a marked bias towards memoirs written by officers from large urban forces, particularly detectives, although as a rule books written by most types of officer can be found.[3]

In general, police autobiographies appear to have been more popular in England (and the USA) than in France. Undoubtedly more were printed in England, although this may have been because English-language texts could tap into the American market with relative ease. It was certainly the

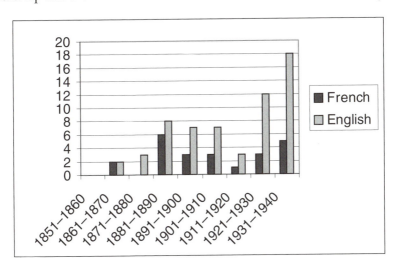

Figure 7.1   Policing memoirs published in England and France, 1850–1939.

case that some French texts were translated into English (often in an abridged form), but never vice versa (see, for example, Goron, 1907). Some texts by French authors even seem to have been published solely in English (for example, Belin, 1950). However, the general trends of publication (an initial peak of interest in the 1880s/1890s, further sustained interest and then a larger surge in the 1930s) seem to have occurred in both countries.

It is difficult to assess exactly how popular these works were, as publishers details rarely survive. However, what evidence does exist appears to suggest that many probably had quite robust sales figures. Greenham's memoirs, for example, were published in 1904 by George Routledge & Sons, whose archives are held on microfilm at the British Library. The company had initially operated in a 'raffish manner', producing cheap pirate copies of popular fiction in the mid-nineteenth century, but by the turn of the century this was a legitimate, respected publisher. While its publications still sold cheaply, this no longer implied deficient quality. Rather, low prices were achieved via large print runs and widespread advertising. A number of the more popular memoirs went through three or four editions (see, for example, Canler and Macé). Others were serialised in newspapers, which would again seem to indicate an avid readership. For example, Charles Arrow published some of his reminiscences in the *London Evening News*.

Of course, this public popularity brings with it another set of problems for the historian. While the sources thus exist in abundance, it becomes hard to ascertain how representative they are. Works issued by commercial London publishers may well have been selected for their perceived similarity to already existing (and commercially successful) memoirs. As David Vincent has noted in his study of working-class autobiography, 'concern for their profits and consequent sensitivity to the values of a largely middle-class readership might be expected to lead to a bias in the type of manuscript accepted and possibly to the censoring of accepted texts' (Vincent, 1981: 9). However, it can be argued that in the case of police officers, when the whole range of texts is considered, there is a very wide variety of style and content. Given this, then, to what extent can these books be considered as forming a 'genre'?

It is tempting initially to conceptualise them as autobiographies. Certainly these authors are writing about themselves, and appear to follow certain popular autobiographical conventions (for example, the frontispiece photograph of the distinguished author in later life, and the familiar protestation that, while not a literary man, family and friends have requested the publication, and so on). However, autobiography is both a problematic term to define and a complex source to utilise. Part of the problem is that, as Philippe Lejeune has noted, autobiography is necessarily 'a fiction produced under special circumstances' (Lejeune, 1988: xiii). No literary work can convey an accurate record of an entire life, and hence all such attempts are necessarily selective, adapting and filtering reality. However, unless we concede some basis in referential fact, the autobiography loses its status as a distinct genre, and merely collapses into fiction. As Lejeune again aptly summarises it, 'telling the truth about the self, constituting the self as complete subject – it is a fantasy', yet 'in spite of the fact that autobiography is impossible, this in no way prevents it from existing' (Lejeune, 1986: xiv). Lejeune's own definition of autobiography attempts to sidestep this fact/fiction paradox by claiming that autobiography is 'the retrospective prose narrative that someone writes concerning his own existence, where the focus is his individual life, in particular the story of his personality' (Lejeune, 1988: 14). In other words, it is the attempt to understand and define the self that characterises autobiographical writing, rather than any putative *verité*.

Such a definition clearly excludes the writings of police officers. The quest for personal understanding that Lejeune highlights is markedly absent from all the police writings examined. While initially some cursory personal details about the author are usually revealed, these writings are almost exclusively concerned with the period the author spent in work as a policeman. For example, René Faralicq only once mentions his family life (Faralicq, 1933: 68). He details how he was sitting up late at night with his wife who had cancer and was awaiting an operation in the morning. However, he only gives this detail as an incidental explanation of why he was awake when the telephone rang at 3 a.m. to inform him of a double homicide. No follow up information on the fate of his wife is ever proffered! This is not to say that these works are entirely narrative, merely that the details of thoughts and feelings given relate almost entirely to 'the job'.

However, other definitions of autobiography are possible. Linda Peterson argues that 'autobiography distinguishes itself as a genre by the act of interpretation rather than the act of presentation, in the fact that its emphasis lies in the understanding of events rather than in the art of narrating them' (Peterson, 1986: 4). This definition can perhaps be seen to apply partially to police writings. Certainly, the authors often sought to explain events – crime, criminality, the workings of society – and their relationship to them. Certainly, too, most authors aimed via this exposition to enlighten their readers as well as to entertain them. Despite this, these police writings are probably better termed memoirs or work histories rather than autobiographies. Despite the protestations of their authors, many were certainly far from factual, suffering from many of the problems of verifiability of autobiographies, and must to some extent be counted as fiction. But, as argued below, they do still have utility to the historian. While the 'facts' narrated cannot be relied upon, they do at least enable a consideration of the perceptions the police held of themselves and others.

It should be noted that there are no hard and fast 'rules' when considering policing memoirs. Literary analysis of this type inevitably involves a degree of generalisation, but it is possible tentatively to identify two specific 'types' of memoirs, which might be termed 'narratives of improvement' and 'career success stories'.[4] While exceptions exist, it is not a distortion to note that the majority of British memoirs might be termed 'narratives of improvement' and the majority of French memoirs 'career success stories'. In the English case, many individuals had worked their way up the rank structure from the level of constable. In establishing the Metropolitan Police in 1829 Sir Robert Peel had 'made a policy decision that his constables were to be recruited from the working class and that, by merit, the same men were to be promoted to fill the senior ranks' (Emsley and Clapson, 1994: 270). These men often desired, via their memoirs, to outline the route via which they had both improved their own personal situations and contributed to the bettering of society. In the French case, it was far more common for high-level policing appointments to be sideways transfers, often from the civil service or the judiciary. As such, the memoirs of these officials customarily display more of a 'bureaucratic' outlook.

While this was not specifically a class distinction, certainly it was common for French and English authors to have very different backgrounds (Shpayer-Makov, 2002; Berlière, 1991). To an extent none were 'typical', in that all were clearly successful in their profession, but it would appear that French writers were usually higher up the social ladder to begin with. For example, Robert Fuller, a London detective of the 1880s, came from a farming community background, and had little by way of formal education (Fuller, 1912). Louis Hamon, a Paris detective of the same period, had a father who was a lawyer and municipal councillor (Hamon, 1900). Hamon himself initially worked for a financial journal, then worked in the civil service and only subsequently transferred to the commissariats.

This tentative distinction can also be seen in the way the job is often described. English writers described policing as a practical, rough 'trade' to be worked at. Fuller, for example, noted that 'all detectives ... start from scratch and work their way forward ... Detectives have rough work to do and must learn betimes to endure harshness, which can only be learned early and in a rough school' (Fuller, 1912: 18). Likewise, Charles Arrow, when describing his first brush with a policeman, noted that he had 'never seen a police-man so unlike a policeman, and the business-like, "rough and ready" style of the man filled me with an admiration for his cloth which I have never lost' (Arrow, 1926: 15). In the French case it was much more likely for authors to lay emphasis on the way in which entry into the police formed part of the steady progression of an office-based career. At the highest level, for example, Claude, Chief of Police under the Second Empire, initially trained as a lawyer, found this tedious, and hence accepted a position at the Court of the Tribunal of the Seine and then worked his way upwards. Lower down, Louis Hamon (mentioned above) was similarly matter of fact about his entry into the police, noting that 'after the war came the Commune, and several weeks after that I left the offices of the Prefecture to enter into the Police Commissariats of Paris as the Secretary of the 12th Arrondissement' (Hamon, 1900: 37).

This putative distinction between those authors who had worked their way up from the streets and those with a more bureaucratic/fonctionnaire background is also perhaps reinforced by a glance at the contents pages of a number of volumes. In the English case, the texts tend to be episodic, with each chapter/vignette relating the details (discovery, apprehension, capture, sentencing) of a particular case or criminal. Charles Arrow, for example, has chapters headed 'A Destiny-Shaping Adventure', 'Tubby Smith's Gang', 'A Blotting Pad Clue', 'The Begging-Letter Impostor' and 'The Great Burglary at the Diamond Merchants Alliance' (Arrow, 1926). In France, authors were far more likely to tend towards a 'classificatory' structure. Hamon, for example, has chapters headed 'Types of Murderers', 'Infanticide', 'Prostitution', 'Executions' (Hamon, 1900). Counter examples can, of course, be found, but even those French authors who tend towards a more episodic structure usually also included a number of 'classificatory' chapters. Gustave Macé, for example, in his chapter on vagrants, initially divided them into three distinct categories – 'the needy, the lazy and recidivist, and thieves and fugitives from justice' (Macé, 1885: chapter 20). These categories are then further subdivided (those who beg from doorways, those who travel from town to town, those who run scams, etc.) in an effort to identify common characteristics. Both types of writing might be termed narratives of control, in that the authors are attempting to describe ways in which the boundaries of acceptable/unacceptable behaviour can be mediated. However, in the English case this control is portrayed as being administered by personal confrontation, with an emphasis on physicality. In the French case, control is achieved by an almost academic 'knowledge' or typology.

Thus it can be posited that two main types of memoirs exist. A more 'up from the streets' mentality is usually in evidence in the British case, supporting Reiner's conclusion for the contemporary period that, 'overall,

British chief officers do not have fundamentally different cultural styles from the rank and file, having come from similar backgrounds and worked their way up the force hierarchy' (Reiner, 2000: 103). Shpayer-Makov agrees that, historically too, 'a clear divide cannot be drawn between supervisory ranks and the rank and file' (Shpayer-Makov, 2002: 18). A more 'civil service' or managerial mentality, with a desire to classify, order and theorise, is far more evident in the case of memoirs written by high-ranking French officers. However, as noted above, this distinction is by no means impermeable. There are certainly French examples where the stress on physicality is firmly in evidence (for example, Cassellari, 1930; Belin, 1950) and there are equally English examples where a managerial style is readily apparent (see, for example, Macready, 1924; Howgrave-Graham, 1947; Scott, 1954).[5] These latter individuals, of course, had not worked their way up from walking the beat, but were high-level entrants, either as ex-military men (Macready) or bureaucrats (Scott and Howgrave-Graham). Thus rather than a firm national distinction, it might be better to note subdivisions within police culture. Many contemporary studies have made distinctions between the 'bobby' and 'new centurion' (peace-keepers and law-enforcers) and the 'managerial professional' (one equipped for the largely public relations functions of senior rank) (Reiner, 2000; Shearing, 1981; Brown, 1981). It may simply be that the latter were slightly more preponderant in France, while the former approach was more common in England, or that there was less of a public appetite for a certain type of memoir in France.

However, given these preliminary, general remarks, can anything more specific be asserted about the respective self-images of English and French officers. As noted earlier, Reiner (and others) have observed a number of common features of police cultures in modern, liberal democracies. Perhaps foremost among these features is a 'sense of mission' or 'the feeling that policing is not just a job but a way of life with a worthwhile purpose' (Reiner, 2000: 89). In addition, many officers have stressed the hedonistic, action-centred aspect of 'cop culture', often describing it as a 'game' of wits and skill (Crank, 1998). Commentators have also noted the marked internal solidarity of police officers, sometimes coupled with social isolation (Crank, 1998: chapter 15; Waddington, 1999: 99–101). Writing of East End detectives in particular, Dick Hobbs has noted the vital 'entrepreneurial' skills shared by East End detectives and villains alike, and the sense that policing and criminality could often be two sides of the same coin (Hobbs, 1989). Were these perceptions and attitudes shared by officers from a previous century, or was the job so different at that time that different cultural values applied? What similarities and differences in French/English policing culture are apparent from the memoirs?

Memoirs and self-image

Perhaps one of the more fruitful avenues via which to investigate officers' perceptions of policing are the reasons each author cites for his initial decision to join the force. Given that most of these officers were writing at the end of a long career which sometimes extended to thirty or more years, it can perhaps safely be assumed that we can never know with objective certainty why they joined the police. All that can be gleaned from their memoirs is why they later *said* they joined the police – another question entirely. An analysis of this question allows some insight into what officers at the end of their career (and projecting backwards, perhaps) felt were the most important/attractive aspects of their work.

It was extremely common for officers to recall a 'formative incident', which usually took place in childhood or early adolescence, that led them to realise their professional calling, their sense of 'mission'. Charles Arrow, for example, narrated 'A Destiny Shaping Adventure' (Arrow, 1926: chapter 1). When a bag was stolen from his school, he swiftly organised a hunt with some fellow pupils and the offender was soon tracked down at the edge of the village. Richard Jervis detailed 'A Wreck on the Coast', a chapter in which (as a small boy) he noticed some men thieving from a wreck, assisted in their capture and then vowed to be a policeman (Jervis, 1908). Similarly, Louis Canler related how (as a young man) he came across a crowd outside an apartment block and learned that a thief was trapped inside. The onlookers were too apathetic to act, but he alone managed to enter the building and hold the thief (who had tried to escape up the chimney) until the police arrived (Canler, 1882). Jean Belin noted that thefts had taken place from a shop near his mother's house. He and a friend had been blamed, and thus he had laid in wait for the real thief, arranged his capture and then vowed to join the police (Belin, 1950).

What is common to these formative incidents is that the thrill of the chase is cited as the major attraction of a career in the police, rather than (for example) the desire to change society or the lure of a steady job. As contemporary commentators have noted, officers often refer to the adrenaline-filled 'legitimate man hunt' as one of the prime attractions of the job (Crank, 1998), and certainly this is reflected in both English and French memoirs. Arrow, for example, used the exact phrase 'legitimate man hunt' (Arrow, 1926: 15). Claude described himself as 'a tenacious hunter of the most dangerous and crafty criminals', while Cassellari noted that 'the thrill of the man hunt eclipses all other sensations in the world' (Claude, 1881–82: 18; Cassellari, 1930: 81). Jervis, too, referred to himself as 'one who has for over thirty years made the hunting of men his business' (Jervis, 1907: 61), while René Faralicq admitted that he found himself 'attracted by the mysterious and adventurous elements in the policeman's trade' (Faralicq, 1933: 1).

Allied with this, another theme that is strongly represented in almost all memoirs is the way in which policemen liked to portray themselves as straddling (and yet maintaining) a dividing line between respectable and outcast society – Reiner's 'sense of mission'. In both French and English cases, much is made of an easy familiarity with the 'netherworld' of the criminal and the very poor. Clearly this is an image which officers enjoyed, rather than viewed as a necessary but distasteful part of the job. McLevy, for example, claimed with relish that

> many may not know of the 'Happy Land' I allude to – not other than
> that large tenement in Leith Wynd ... divided into numerous dens,
> inhabited by thieves, robbers, thimblers, pickpockets, abandoned
> women, drunken destitutes, and here and there chance-begotten
> brats, squalling with hunger, or lying dead for days after they should
> have been buried. Well do I know every hole and corner of
> it ... (McLevy, 1975: 1)

Similarly, Claude, too, was anxious to establish his underworld credentials. Writing of his early policing experiences he noted that:

> In those days the quarter called specially the Cité, was the
> rendezvous of all the evil-doers of Paris ... It was in these damp and
> noisome regions, where foetid alleys led to filthy stairways, that a
> mass of outlaws, human vermin, swarmed; here the most monstrous
> crimes were planned ... (Claude, 1881–82: 32)

Partly, of course, this posturing may have been useful in terms of boosting sales, but clearly also, many officers relished an image of themselves as 'hard men', mediating between respectable society and the residuum, protecting one from the other. This was almost certainly part of the attraction of the profession for many.

However, many officers went further than merely depicting themselves as *au fait* with the seamier side of society, protecting the weak and the respectable. Authors were often keen to demonstrate that they were also familiar with criminals themselves – indeed, that their acquaintance with the underworld went further than merely knowing villains and their methods, and often extended to friendly or even sympathetic exchanges. It was common for some officers to conceptualise crime and policing as two sides of the same coin, or two constitutive elements of the same nether-world, much as Hobbs has noted in relation to the East End in the 1970s

(Hobbs, 1989). Arrow, for example, offered the following vignette, clearly demonstrating this view:

> When he was placed in his cell I gave him a handful of tobacco from my pouch, and, as he took off his boots ... he said, 'Well, guv'nor, we've all got to live. If I hadn't been a fief I might have been a policeman!' He did not add, 'and vice versa', but I think it was in his mind. (Arrow, 1926: 36)

This easy familiarity – in this instance, the sharing of tobacco and casual conversation – is common in English memoirs, perhaps due to the class background and career path of officers, as discussed above.

It is still possible to find such passages in French memoirs, but officers are much more likely to be looking down socially on criminals, even when familiarity is in evidence. Cassellari related an episode (almost certainly bogus) in which he had foiled a butler who had been stealing from his wealthy employers. He eventually arranged for the butler to leave the country (to avoid scandal) and goes on to state:

> Occasionally, when I am in England, I visit the restaurant [the butler has opened an eatery] and have my lunch there. The butler ... greets me with great deference, though I am sure he has never forgiven me for depriving him of half a million francs. (Cassellari, 1930: 110)

Evidently, familiarity between detective and criminal exists in this instance, but clearly demarcated social space also exists between the two. Officers from both France and England seem often to have relished an image of themselves as familiar with the criminal netherworld and friendly with criminals, but in the French case this informality was usually tempered with respect (on the part of the villain) while English officers made much more of their 'streetwise' insider knowledge.

When assessing self-image, it can also be constructive to consider the abilities which officers presented as intrinsic or vital for successful police work. Again, this probably reveals relatively little about actual policing practice, but can perhaps offer rather more insight into the conception officers had of their own abilities and their public role. Two quite contradictory tendencies are apparent here. On the one hand many authors stressed the 'routine' aspects of the job – minute observation, keeping tabs on suspicious characters, the monotonous checking of alibis. On the other hand, there is an inconsistent stress (particularly in detective memoirs) on an almost supernatural ability to 'see through' subterfuge. This is described here as inconsistent because it often appears in the same memoirs where the routine aspects of the job are also stressed. Two examples will serve to illustrate these conflicting representations. Belin noted that 'the science of detection depends in the main on accurate and trained observation ... The detective ... must be possessed of unlimited patience and perseverance' (Belin, 1950: 3). By contrast, one of the most immoderate descriptions of the detective's 'eye' is related by Claude. When describing the moment he realised that he was destined to be a police officer, he relates his attendance at a high-society dinner party, where he was introduced to a popular up-and-coming young lawyer. Erudite conversation flowed, but, as the meal progressed, the man's appearance began to change in front of Claude's eyes:

> As the man became transformed, or rather, as the mask fell from him, ... I now saw him for what he was – a criminal ... These magnetic impressions, these luminous perceptions, have, since then, often come to me at the sight or the contact of an evildoer. (Claude, 1881–82: 5)

These two conflicting representations are hard to interpret. Certainly, the idea of the 'detective eye' is strong in early detective fiction. Martin Kayman notes that in Dickens' *On Duty with Inspector Field* (1851) the motif of 'the detective's eye' is 'probably the main characteristic of Dickens' mythology' (Kayman, 1992: 108). For the fictional detective the eye was 'the means by which he penetrates, like the philanthropic social researcher, into every part of the "secret world" ', and it became a staple literary device for many subsequent novelists (Kayman, 1992: 108). It may well have been the case that, despite their protestations to the contrary, many real-life authors drew more heavily on their fictional counterparts than they liked to imagine. It may also, of course, have been the case that after thirty years of detection, a form of intuition (or at least a highly acute sense of suspicion) did develop, which was then projected back by authors when reviewing their careers. What is certain, however, is that what the memoirs do reveal, particularly those from the nineteenth century, is a certain amount of confusion as to exactly what was required to be a good police officer/detective. With little by way of formal training in either country until the late-nineteenth century, it is certainly possible that officers sought to define and locate their own legitimacy in their memoirs. Some did this, as noted, by stressing the 'trade' nature of the job – routine, hard graft. Others did this by laying claim to an innate vision of the world accessible only to a few. It would appear that as police training increased throughout the twentieth century, memoirs depicting detective work as an innate gift gradually declined and the motifs of hard work and luck proliferated.

A final issue on which policing memoirs can be informative is in revealing the nature of the relationship between police authors (who were, after all, writing as individuals) and the organisations/departments for which they had worked. Almost all memoirs reveal that officers generally possessed a very strong sense of institutional loyalty. Most had nothing but admiration for the institution which provided them with such a fulfilling and exciting career. The caveat must, of course, be raised that these were possibly atypical individuals, defined by both the extremely successful nature of their career and by their literary ability. However, this sense of institutional loyalty is certainly something which features quite strongly in contemporary studies of the police (Waddington, 1999).

Lejeune argues that middle-class autobiographical type writings of the nineteenth century naturally fall into three main categories – exemplary, apologetic and critical (Lejeune, 1988: 172). Exemplary autobiographies are stories wherein success has been achieved by adherence to the dominant social discourse and are written primarily as examples. Apologetic reminiscences are written by those who have failed, or have been perceived to have failed, and wish to justify themselves. Critical writings are those which specifically set out to call into question existing social institutions. Lejeune claims that exemplary autobiographies are the most common and this is certainly true in the case of police memoirs. Although apologetic and critical exemplars can also be found, most police authors wished to demonstrate, via the sense of accomplishment they depict, the necessity and validity of the police. Clapson and Emsley note that the Smilesian notion of self-help had 'a double resonance for the hierarchical institution of the Victorian police, first in the promise it offered to recruits, and second in the way that it encouraged personal identification in contrast to others' (Clapson and Emsley, 2002), and certainly many of those who wrote their memoirs are explicit in their depiction of the institution of the police as a vehicle for both personal and societal advancement. In his introduction, Arrow revealed 'I have in mind the young man at the threshold of a career in search of a profession, and if anything I have written should influence him to follow my example and join the police … I shall have my reward' (Arrow, 1926: 12). Belin similarly noted, 'I am glad I chose the police as a career. It has entailed a life of hard work with small pay but it has had its reward of personal satisfaction and a sense of something accomplished' (Belin, 1950: 5).

With few exceptions, all criticism of the police (both general and specific) is reserved for the period before the author joined the force. Canler, for example, noted that he joined the police at a time of political upheaval (April, 1820). He highlighted how he deplored the political venality of the police service at that time, and the culture of denunciations that prevailed. Unsurprisingly, all this changed when he was put in charge! Claude, too, is eager to stress his rejection of this aspect of the French police, claiming that 'I have had the satisfaction in my long career never to have mingled in any unworthy machinations in spite of the times in which I have lived; to have never served either the cupidity or the base purposes of the courtiers of the Empire' (Claude, 1881–82: 184). Some authors do express open criticism of other elements of the criminal justice system – magistrates, the court system, lawyers and prisons all feature in a number of works – but invariably the image presented of the police service is of a male fraternity of brothers, each able to rely entirely on the others. This was, of course, not always the case, but the fact that so many authors were keen to present it as such surely indicates that institutional loyalty was a key feature of police culture for many officers, even during the nineteenth century.

It should be noted, however, that this institutional loyalty in memoirs was often combined with a desire on the part of the authors to display their independence, to provide evidence that they were not just 'yes men'. Many make a point of noting how they broke the rules when they had to. Fuller, for example, claimed that while generally an officer should not 'transgress the laws of the land', it was nonetheless true (albeit paradoxical) that 'if he waited for statutory authority for one half of his actions, he would not be worthy of his hire' (Fuller, 1912: 17). Faralicq, too, notes an occasion when he went to arrest a suspect, only to realise he had mistaken his identity. However, he proudly details how he pressed on regardless:

> I showed him my warrant, that was made out in the name of Fremyet and not of Guillet, but I held it sufficiently far away from him that he could not see the actual wording. Of course, I had gone beyond my powers, but it was too late to think about that now. (Faralicq, 1933: 104)

It would appear likely that this tension between loyalty to the institution of the police, and the attraction of the freedom of discretionary action which police work inevitably entails, was a common feature of police work.

Overall then, policing memoirs can be extremely useful in analysing how policemen/detectives thought about themselves and the job they did. There is certainly scope for more work in this area, but it would appear that there was a high degree of congruence in police culture across the Channel, with many representations of police work common to both French and English memoirs. Most authors were strongly attracted to the physical elements of the job, and liked to present themselves as 'hard men', crossing boundaries where the middle classes feared to tread in their mission to protect the innocent and reform society. While possessed of a strong institutional culture, many were not afraid to step outside the bounds of official authority when they deemed fit (although this aspect of police work becomes increasingly less common during the twentieth century). A more 'managerial' style of policing, predicated on the officer/ detective as a socially superior expert, is perhaps initially more apparent in the French case. However, analysis of the flurry of publications in the interwar period shows that the 'rough and ready' English memoir and the more bureaucratic French work history gradually converged as a new style of memoir, strongly reminiscent of the popular detective novel, came to the fore.

Conclusion: fact or fiction?

As has been demonstrated, policing memoirs are a rich and diverse source for comparative historians. They can be useful in an analysis of the past self-image of police officers, as discussed above. They could also potentially be utilised in relation to a range of other issues (for example, historical policing practice and public/police service relationships) for which there has not been space to explore here. This contention is, of course, not entirely new. Many historians studying the police have used memoirs and work histories. However, there has as yet been little consideration of these life-writings as a 'genre'. It has been argued that it is only when analysed en masse, with the application of some form of literary analysis (albeit rudimentary) that their full significance is revealed. Awareness of the links between this type of memoir writing and prevalent literary trends has often been missing from historical analysis.

Yet, it is essential for the historian to read the memoirs written by police officers during this period with one eye on the development of detective/ policing fiction. The major waves of publication of police memoirs coincided precisely with the establishment and increasing popularity of fictional representations of police work. As Figure 7.1 above shows, it was during the latter half of the nineteenth century that memoirs and work histories became popular. It was during the same period that fiction pertaining to crime and detection (called 'enigma' stories until the 1880s, when the term 'detective fiction' was coined) gained in popularity. For example, Poe's *Dupin* (1840s) provided perhaps the first template for fictional detective representation. Dickens' *Detective Anecdotes* (1850) and *On Duty with Inspector Field* (1851) swiftly followed. (As an aside, it is interesting to note in these early works the way in which Poe's Dupin, working in France, focused on issues of 'theory' rather than being a 'simple agent of action' (Kayman, 1992: 139). Dickens' work, by contrast, evinced a specific emphasis on the realism of the street.) Conan Doyle's first Sherlock Holmes story, *A Study in Scarlet* (customarily, but erroneously, regarded as founding the genre – Kayman, 1992) was initially published in 1887.

Clearly the two literary trends – police fiction and policing memoirs – overlap and intertwine. Certainly, for example, 'real-life' detectives were interested in detective fiction, even to the extent of comparing their methods with those of their fictional counterparts (see, for example, Massac, 1889 and Bercher, 1906). Equally certainly, memoirs published during the interwar period increasingly adopted the literary style prevalent in detective novels. It became common for authors, even in France, to present their work in a 'The Case of ...' style, leaving the denouement/explanation of the crime to the very end. This element of suspense was often not in evidence in earlier nineteenth-century memoirs, where a brief précis of the details of the case were often given prior to the officer's thoughts on the matter. This convergence of styles cannot have been coincidental.

In terms of contents, authors gradually evinced less desire to educate or enlighten their readers by providing examples which illustrated particular moral points. A far greater emphasis came to be placed on the 'entertainment' value of memoirs, via the claim that the multiplicity of real-life crime provided a treasure-trove of material which no fictional author could match. The covers which publishers produced for memoirs also became far more lurid and sensational as the century progressed. The cover of Greenham's memoirs, for example, depicts a furious struggle between a police officer and a villain taking place on top of a hansom cab, the wheels of which are spinning at great speed. Fuller's *Recollections of a Detective* has an eye-catching representation of the author on the cover, leaning over his desk to point menacingly at a middle-class woman.

It seems likely then that the prevalence and popularity of policing memoirs in the 1920s/1930s (see Figure 7.1) is fairly easily explained as a consequence of the public vogue for detective fiction at that time. However, what is harder to account for is the initial proliferation of both memoirs and fictional accounts of police work in the 1880s. Why did this type of literature – fictional and non-fictional accounts of crime and policing – assume such unprecedented (and lasting) prominence at during this particular period? It would appear that a number of conjoined factors were at work here. Firstly, of course, increasing public literacy in both England and France during the latter half of the nineteenth century contributed to the formation of a 'reading public'. The rise of the novel itself (primarily a nineteenth-century concept) must also be cited. After all, it was only in 1870 that Trollope testified that 'We have become a novel-reading people. Novels are in the hands of all us all: from the Prime Minister down to the last-appointed scullery-maid' (Kayman, 1992: 172). The period between c.1840 and c.1870 also saw a fierce literary debate between proponents of the 'sensation novel' and serious fiction. As the sensation novel gradually lost this battle, it was perhaps the detective novel which took its place as a public favourite. Equally, given that detective forces (and indeed the 'New' police itself) were only instituted during the early part of the century, it is possible that the wave of publications in the 1880s can partly be explained by the career ends of the first fully professional officers.

However, it perhaps appropriate to search briefly for deeper, under-lying causes for even these trends. Two possible factors can be cited here. Firstly, it could be argued that the enormous narrative production of the nineteenth century, and particularly crime fiction and policing memoirs, reflects a culmination of anxiety at the loss of what Peter Brooks has termed 'providential plots' (Brooks, 1984). As he notes:

> The emergence of narrative plot as a dominant mode of ordering and explanation may belong to the large process of secularisation … which marks a falling-away from those revealed plots … that appeared to subsume transitory human time to the timeless. (Brooks, 1984: 27)

In other words, with no 'divine plan' to order human affairs, the actions of individuals or institutions takes on a new importance in literature. It may well have been that, in a period of acute social upheaval (the 1880s were a turbulent period in both France and England), policing memoirs may have helped readers (and authors) to explore/reinforce the lines demarcating acceptable and anti-social behaviour. In this way, police memoirs con-tinued the prevalent tradition of the spiritual autobiography, in which right and wrong were defined for the reading public via personal testament.

A second factor which might be cited is the significance of the 1880s/ 1890s for the consolidation of the institutional identity of police forces in England and France. David Vincent, writing about working-class auto-biography at the start of the nineteenth century, notes that such works helped both to promote and reinforce the first stirrings of class con-sciousness (Vincent, 1981). The end of the century was a period during which police forces were becoming increasingly professionalised. Yet at the same time specific training and better working conditions were still only just being introduced. It could thus be argued that, as well as their relevance for the reading public, memoirs helped serving police officers to consolidate their group identity and define their role within society.

While undoubtedly complex sources to study, police memoirs can be thus be of use to the historian on a number of levels. They can be mined for factual detail, which can later be substantiated from archival material. They can be assessed en masse as a literary 'genre' indicative of emergent societal anxieties, or they can be investigated as an indirect source of insight concerning police officers' attitudes and opinions. Whichever level of analysis is considered, however, it should also not be forgotten that they are 'always of interest to those who love a good story!' (Smethurst, 1914/ 1995: 3).

Notes

1. For example, Superintendent James Bent portrayed himself as a humanitarian and friend to the poorer classes in several chapters of his memoirs (Bent, 1891). Evidence drawn from the *Manchester Courier* and other newspapers establishes that he did indeed set up a soup kitchen at Old Trafford Police station in the 1880s, and that he continued to help feed homeless children well into his retirement. For more information on the extent to which these memoirs reveal the social welfare functions undertaken by many officers, see (Lawrence, 2000).

2. This graph has been compiled from works noted in the British Library in London, the Bibliothèque Nationale in Paris, the Greater Manchester Police Museum and the Senate House Library of London University. While the most significant memoirs are utilised in this study, and are hence cited in the references following these notes, comprehensive bibliographies have been compiled by Martin Stallion (Stallion, 1998, 2000). Wherever possible, English translations of French memoirs have been cited; in all other cases the translations are by the present author.

3. Although, it should be noted that while quite a number of memoirs written by English officers who served (at least for a time) in rural areas exist, there are only two examples of autobiographies written by members of the French gendarmerie (La Roche, 1914; Forestier, 1983). I am grateful to Prof. Jean-Nöel Luc (Université de Paris IV) for his advice on this matter, and it would appear that this vacuum may have been due to the public's perception of the gendarmerie as not as glamorous as the army (a profession which produced a large amount of life-writing) and not as popular as the detective police.

4. The term 'narratives of improvement' was used by Dr Haia Shpayer-Makov in an unpublished conference paper delivered at the European Social Science History Conference (The Hague, The Netherlands, 27 February – 2 March 2002) – 'The Work Histories and Self-Image of British Detectives During the Late Nineteenth and Early Twentieth Centuries: A Study of Their Memoirs'.

5. I am grateful to Rob Mawby (Centre for Public Services Management and Research, Staffordshire University Business School) for his comments in this regard, following the presentation of a version of this paper to the seminar series of the European Centre for the Study of Policing (Open University).

References

Arrow, C. *Rogues and Others*. London: Duckworth, 1926.

Belin, J. *My Work at the Sûreté*. London: George G. Harrap, 1950.

Bent, J. *Criminal Life: Reminiscences of Forty-Two Years as a Police Officer*. Manchester: Heywood, 1891.

Bercher, J. *Etude médico-légale de l'oeuvre de Conan-Doyle et de la police scientifique au Xxe siècle*. Lyon, 1906.

Berlière, J.-M. *L'institution policière en France sous la Troisième République, 1875–1914*, Thèse pour le Doctorat, Université de Borgogne, 1991.

Brooks, P. *Reading for the Plot. Design and Intention in Narrative*. Oxford: Clarendon Press, 1984.

Brown, M. *Working the Street*. New York: Russell Sage, 1981.

Canler, L. *Memoires de Canler. Ancien Chef du service de Sûreté*, 2 vols. Paris, 1882.

Cassellari, R. *Dramas of French Crime. Being the Exploits of the Celebrated Detective René Cassellari*. London: Hutchinson, 1930.

Clapson, M. and Emsley, C. 'Street, beat and respectability: the culture and self-image of the late Victorian and Edwardian urban policeman', in Knafla, L. A. (ed.), *Policing and War in Europe*, in *Criminal Justice History*, Volume 16, 2002, pp. 107–32.

Claude, M. *Memoires de Monsieur Claude, Chef de la Police sous le Deuxième Empire*, Vol. 1. Paris: Rouff, 1881–82.

Crank, J. P. *Understanding Police Culture*. Cincinatti, OH: Anderson Publishing, 1998.

Divall, T. *Scoundrels and Scallywags (and Some Honest Men)*. London: Ernest Benn, 1929.

Emsley, C. and Clapson, M. 'Recruiting the English policeman c.1840–1940', *Policing and Society*, 3, 1994, pp. 269–86.

Faralicq, R. *The French Police from Within*. London: Cassell, 1933.

Forestier, I.-E. *Gendarmes à la Belle Epoque*. Paris: France Empire, 1983.

Fuller, R. A. *Recollections of a Detective*. London: John Long, 1912.

Goron, M.-F. *The World of Crime: True Detective Stories*. London: Hurst & Blackett, 1907.

Greenham, G. H. *Scotland Yard Experiences*. London: George Routledge & Sons, 1904.

Hamon, L. *Police et Criminalité – Impressions d'un Vieux Policier*. Paris: Flammarion, 1900.

Hobbs, D. *Doing the Business. Entrepreneurship, the Working Class, and Detectives in the East End of London*. Oxford: Oxford University Press, 1989.

Howgrave-Graham, H. M. *Light and Shade at Scotland Yard*. London: John Murray, 1947.

Jervis, R. *Lancashire's Crime and Criminals – with some Characteristics of the County*. Southport: J. J. Riley, 1908.

Kayman, M. A. *From Bow Street to Baker Street. Mystery, Detection and Narrative*. London: Macmillan, 1992.

La Roche, J.-F. *Souvenirs d'un Officier de Gendarmerie sous la Restauration. Publiés et Annotés par le Vth Aurélien de Courson*, 3rd edn. Paris: Librarie Plon, 1914.

Lawrence, P. 'Images of poverty and crime. police memoirs in England and France at the end of the nineteenth century', *Crime, Histoire et Sociétés*, 4, 1, 2000, pp. 63–82.

Lejeune, P. *Moi aussi*. Paris: Seuil, 1986.

Lejeune, P. 'On autobiography' (ed. and foreword P. J. Eakin), *Theory and History of Literature*, 52, 1988.

Macé, G. *La Police Parisienne. Le Service de la Sûreté*. Paris: G. Charpentier, 1885.

Macready, Sir N. *Annals of an Active Life*. London: Hutchinson, 1924.

McLevy, J. *The Casebook of a Victorian Detective* [Selections from his *Curiosities of Crime...* and *The Sliding Scale of Life*]. Edinburgh: Canongate, 1975.

Massac, R. *Le 'Detective Novel' et l'influence de la pensée scientifique*. Paris, 1889.

Peterson, L. *Victorian Autobiography. The Tradition of Self-Interpretation*. New Haven, CT and London: Yale University Press, 1986.

Reiner, R. *The Blue-Coated Worker*. Cambridge: Cambridge University Press, 1978.

Reiner, R. *The Politics of the Police*. Oxford: Oxford University Press, 2000.

Richmond, A. *Richmond: Scenes in the Life of a Bow Street Runner, drawn up from his private memoranda*. London, 1827.

Scott, Sir H. *Scotland Yard*. Harmondsworth: Penguin, 1954.

Shearing, C. 'Subterranean processes in the maintenance of power', *Canadian Review of Sociology and Anthropology*, 18, 3, 1981, pp. 283–98.

Skolnick, J. *Justice without Trial*. New York: Wiley, 1966.

Shpayer-Makov, H. *The Making of a Policeman. A Social History of a Labour Force in Metropolitan London, 1829–1914*. Aldershot: Ashgate, 2002.

Smethurst, T. *A Policeman's Notebook. The 1914 Notebook of Thomas Smethurst*. Bolton: Aurora, 1995.

Stallion, M. *A Life of Crime. A Bibliography of British Police Officers' Memoirs and Biographies*. Leigh-on-Sea: M. R. Stallion, 1998.

Stallion, M. *Cops, Flics and Mounties. A Bibliography of Overseas Police Officers' Memoirs and Biographies*. Leigh-on-Sea: M. R. Stallion, 2000.

Vidocq, E. *Mémoires de Vidocq. Forçat et Chef de la Police*. Paris, 1828.

Vincent, D. *Bread, Knowledge and Freedom. A Study of Nineteenth-Century Working Class Autobiography*. London: Europa, 1981.

Waddington, P. A. J. 'Police (canteen) sub-culture: an appreciation', *British Journal of Criminology*, 39, 2, 1999, pp. 286–308.

Waters, T. *The Recollections of a Policeman*. London: Winchester, 1849.

Wensley, F. P. *Forty Years of Scotland Yard*. London: Doubleday, Doran & Co., 1931.

Chapter 8

Policing the seaside holiday: Blackpool and San Sebastián, from the 1870s to the 1930s

John K. Walton

The origins of this chapter lie in an ESRC-funded research project on 'Crime, migration and social change in North-West England and the Basque Country' of northern Spain, which originally covered a longer time span, with a particular focus on the seaports of Bilbao and Liverpool and the seaside resorts of San Sebastián and Blackpool.[1] Any aspiration to a detailed comparative quantitative history of crime (as opposed to migration) foundered on the differences between social expectations, regional and class identities and ideologies, policing and legal systems, and ways of classifying actions and legal processes in the two regional settings. But these issues were important enough in themselves to take centre stage as the dominant subject matter of the project (Walton *et al.*, 1999).

This chapter narrows the original agenda to focus on the seaside resorts. Blackpool and San Sebastián were contrasting places in many ways. However, they shared an identity as (predominantly) leisure towns living mainly by a summer holiday season, with extensive seasonal comings and goings. This gave them an interest in negotiating the tensions between openness to pleasure and diversity, and made their rulers sensitive to the need to protect the lives and property of visitors in search of enjoyment and relaxation, and to the disruptive potential of conflict between classes, value systems and cultural expectations. These shared concerns make comparison not only viable but highly stimulating. These were distinctive places, but the heightened versions they offer of social tensions, conflicts and attempts at policing and resolution provide transferable insights into how societies were regulated, and regulated themselves, during a period of particular dynamism and transitional significance in both countries. The working definition of 'policing' goes beyond the deployment and policies of formally constituted police forces to embrace the control of behaviour through internalised consensus and senses of propriety and decorum, and the impact of cultural awareness of the limits of relaxed but acceptable standards in a liminal setting (Walton, 1997).

Seaside resorts are and have been distinctive kinds of urban environment, posing special problems of public order and policing. As 'places on the margin' and gateways between land and sea they have been associated with liminality and the contested freedoms that accompany that ambiguous intermediate status (Shields, 1991). As places identified with release from daily cares, responsibilities and conventions they seem obvious outlets for the carnivalesque, for the shedding of inhibitions, the turning of the world upside down, the celebration of excess and the temporary reversal of the 'civilising process', where they may be thought to have a stronger claim than the football stadium (Lewis, 1996). As places where transient seekers after enjoyment cross paths with equally transient seekers after opportunistic gain through casual labour, leading to un- familiar transactions with a high element of risk, both popular and elite seaside resorts might even be labelled 'crimogenic', in Gerald Mars's memorable formulation. This is a characteristic they share with (for example) the central entertainment areas of great cities, as documented historically by Judith Walkowitz in her work on Victorian London (Walkowitz, 1992). Moreover, as the self-described professional thief Paul Axel Lund explained to Rupert Croft-Cooke, talking rather vaingloriously about the immediate postwar years in Blackpool, the sheer pressure of visitor numbers could mean that at the height of the season:

> Villainy was too easy in Blackpool … The Law was kept busy finding lost kids, running round after sex cases, looking for bits of conviction wherever it came easiest and hadn't the time or the staff to look after us. It was a thieves' paradise … (Croft-Cooke, 1961: 82)

Crowded environments, pressure to maximise profits during a short season leading to problems of quality of provision (especially as regards food and accommodation), and the propensity of the resort setting to encourage relaxed attitudes to sexual behaviour and bodily exposure (especially in relation to bathing), with an associated capacity to shock, all contributed to these problems in popular resorts (Mars, 1994). As (in many cases) places where upper- and middle-class visitors share desirable space and amenities with people of lower status, different manners and contrasting leisure preferences, seaside resorts generated social conflicts focused on complaints of noise, nuisance and unruly or challenging behaviour, a situation that might be exacerbated when retired residents encounter assertively hedonistic groups of much younger pleasure-seekers. At an extreme, controversial resort entertainments, such as casino gambling and cabarets, might not only generate conflict between users and beneficiaries on the one hand and advocates of moral reform and even prohibition on the other: they might provide favourable environments for the emergence of racketeering and corruption (Denton and Morris, 2002; Sternleib and Hughes, 1983; Walton, 2001a).[2] Protection rackets might even flourish where small-scale informal entertainments lacked the muscle to protect themselves, as on Blackpool's Golden Mile in the mid-1950s when Scarface Jock and his 'razor mob' claimed to be making a comfortable living by intimidating the proprietors of booths and sideshows (Croft-Cooke, 1961: 94).

Seaside resorts thus have plenty of claims on our attention. In practice, of course, the fears of disorder and crime that were generated in these settings posed such potent potential threats to the economic well-being of resorts that particular care was taken to neutralise them, both by formal policing and by the development of informal visitor norms which reduced or channelled conflict. Significantly, we can follow up these themes in both of these apparently contrasting settings: the fashionable resort in the Basque Country of northern Spain, and the proletarian playground of Lancashire's (and later Britain's) densely-populated industrial districts on the unglamorous Irish Sea coast (Artola, 2000; Walton, 1998a).

Blackpool and San Sebastián were themselves experiencing transition, and expressed, reflected and helped to accelerate changes in the societies from which their visitors were drawn. As towns they grew at not dissimilar rates in population terms, although San Sebastián, as an old-established port, fortress town and commercial/administrative centre, grew from a larger base than Blackpool, which owed its urban standing entirely to the holiday trade. San Sebastián's turn-of-the-year population was 14,111 in 1860, from which it grew to 21,300 at the 1877 census, 35,583 at that of 1900 and 78,432 at that of 1930. Blackpool, at an early spring census, had just over 6,000 inhabitants in 1871, rising to nearly 24,000 in 1891 and doubling to over 48,000 in 1901 before reaching 100,000 in 1931 (Garate and Martin, 1995; Walton, 1974). So the English resort grew further and faster, and (briefly) explosively, while San Sebastián expanded at a more sedate pace. But they were never far out of line with each other.

Blackpool was always dominated by its holiday industry, with employment in retailing, construction and transport functioning mainly to service it, whereas San Sebastián kept and developed extensive commercial and administrative functions, never quite lost its old roles as port and garrison town though most international maritime activity shifted a few kilometres eastwards to Pasajes, and developed a ring of manufacturing industries on the periphery of the holiday and residential district (Larrinaga, 1999; Walton, 1974).

But the local press's emphasis on San Sebastián's dependence on tourism was increasingly apposite by the turn of the century, although much of the accommodation industry was hidden from the tax administrator's and other kinds of gaze in the spare rooms of modest flats, and what is visible in guidebooks and directories was the tip of the iceberg. Here, perhaps, we encounter one distinctive kind of white-collar 'crime', for board and lodging businesses were supposed to register with the appropriate trade organisation, which divided up the tax quota between its members according to the size of their businesses. A 'black economy' in accommodation, part of a characteristic pattern among small businesses in resort settings, may well help to explain the limited visibility of this sector. Moreover, lodging-house keepers in the late nineteenth century were still legally obliged, in theory, to furnish lists of their lodgers to the police, a requirement imposed in the 1860s, and occasionally invoked in the 1890s, by which time it was more honoured in the breach than the observance (*La Voz de Guipúzcoa*, 31 July 1891, 18 August 1891). There was, however, no direct tax on visitors themselves as in, for example, France and Germany (Chadefaud, 1987; Bennett-Ruete, 1987). Blackpool's local statistics were much more overt in representing the town's landladies, with over 5,000 appearing in the 1921 census, in the absence of any taxation regime directed at them as a group: general taxes on income and property values were harder to evade, although some occasional providers of short lets in summer were always beyond the statistician's reach (Walton, 1994). San Sebastián, on the other hand, appeared to provide much more precise visitor numbers. Blackpool's were guestimates, with favoured figures for visitors of all sorts (from day-tripper to the small minority who could afford a fortnight or longer) rising from around 600,000 in 1873 to 4 million in 1913 and 7 million in the 1930s (Walton, 1974: 263). San Sebastián's were superficially more convincing, based on counts of arrivals and departures at railway stations (though road transport began to make an impact by the 1910s and especially by the 1920s). This exercise produced an August average of around 10,000 staying visitors in the 1890s, doubling or trebling around the end of the First World War and then tailing off a little. But these figures do not match trends in entertainment tax receipts (the evasion of which must in practice have been another major aspect of little-recorded crime), and seem to be less reliable with the passage of time, producing inflated September totals (*El Urumea*, 12 July 1884; Walton and Smith, 1996). Blackpool's visitors were far more numerous, but they were also far less affluent and stayed for shorter periods.

Here, of course, was a major contrast, although its extent and significance ebbed and flowed over the period. Blackpool's key transition years came in the late nineteenth century, when it became the world's first working-class seaside resort. New York's Coney Island ran it close, but its visitors were overwhelmingly day and evening trippers (Kasson, 1978; Immerso, 2002). This was when Blackpool had to make room for, and change its culture to accommodate and attract, a huge and swelling volume of working-class Lancastrians from the 'cotton towns', with a growing admixture from the rest of Northern and Midland England. Conceptions of propriety, order, taste and good behaviour were all challenged in these years, the Edwardian outcome being an unwritten negotiated settlement in which the new visitors moderated their behaviour and policed each other, while their 'betters' beat a retreat to the margins of the resort and came to accept the 'trippers' with good humour as a spectacle in themselves, adopting a sort of anthropological gaze. Although Blackpool tried to reinvent itself in more upmarket guise in the interwar years with parks and formal promenades at its extremities, its unplanned and plebeian Victorian origins continued to set the tone, providing a tolerant central environment for what had become acceptable working-class exuberance (Walton, 1998a).

San Sebastián, meanwhile, consolidated its position as a planned resort for the Madrid aristocracy and its associates during the late nineteenth century, gaining an annual royal presence and the status of summer capital from 1887, which was also the year in which an international syndicate opened the Gran Casino, whose roulette wheels gave the local authority a stake in high society gambling and whose largesse soon seemed indispensable to local charities and programmes of attractions. The Casino brought international high society to San Sebastián during the First World War, benefiting from Spain's neutrality, and in their wake came international bookmakers, promoters and prostitutes. A second establishment opened in 1922 (Walton and Smith, 1996: 44–8). This would have been literally unthinkable in Blackpool.[3] It was, in fact, officially a serious crime (a *delito* as opposed to a *falta*) to operate a roulette wheel in Spain, and from time to time moral reformers on San Sebastián's local council reminded their colleagues of this. Periodic campaigns sometimes shut down the tables temporarily in the 1890s, and threatened to do so again in 1918. But generally a blind eye was turned to what might be seen as a further example of white-collar crime: a bending of the law and adjustment of administrative processes to accommodate an enterprise whose core activity was technically illegal but whose presence soon came to be regarded as essential to the resort's economic well-being (*La Época*, 23 July 1871, 22 August 1887; *La Voz de Guipúzcoa*, 31 July 1891 and subsequently; 8 August 1918). As in Blackpool, however, the 1920s marked a period of adjustment, as postwar social conflicts were followed by the Primo de Rivera dictatorship, which enforced the gaming laws, closed the casinos and left the local authority to prop up the entertainment regime as best it could. In 1929 the town's royal patron, Queen María Cristina, died, and the coming of the Second Republic two years later reinforced a sense of transition and threat. But the entertainment tax receipts remained buoyant, suggesting that the middle-class clientele from right across Spain, which had always provided most of the visitors, was the real foundation of the town's prosperity (Walton and Smith, 1996: 49–51).

Apart from roulette and the related de facto tolerance of high-class (and indeed lower-class) prostitution in the Casino and in the brothels, cabarets and dancing-saloons of the old town and the eastern suburb of Gros, the other outstanding contrast between the resorts was the enduring royal presence in San Sebastián, which raised significant policing issues of its own (Graves, 1936; Starkie, 1934). The royal family summered in the resort every year except one between 1887 and 1928, although Queen María Cristina, who had originated the custom as Queen Regent, was the mainstay by the 1920s. The royal palace, completed in 1894, occupied a strategic point on the shoreline at the end of La Concha bathing beach, and the season was regularly inaugurated by the royal procession from the railway station, featuring the household cavalry. Access to a section of the town's main asset was restricted, although in exchange the royal presence converted San Sebastián into Spain's summer capital, with an impressive attendance of ministers, scheming politicians and ambassadors. The royal family also attracted visitors as a spectacle and cynosure of fashion in its own right, although the gilt faded when the young king, Alfonso XIII, began to take most of his pleasures elsewhere shortly before the First World War. María Cristina herself was never a glamorous figure. Importantly, however, she enjoyed going for local excursions and shopping trips with the minimum of fuss, and the regular appearances of her donkey and carriage in the town centre, with no visible escort beyond an apparently unarmed policeman, reinforced the town's reputation as a relaxed and secure space for elite enjoyment (Calvert, 1909: 65–71).

Royalty was, of course, even more alien to Blackpool than roulette, apart from rare ceremonial occasions. Even so, the contrasts between the resists should not be exaggerated. By the 1930s San Sebastián had a planned core and an unplanned periphery, while Blackpool reversed this pattern (Walton, 2002a; Meller, 2001). Since the 1870s San Sebastián had played host to impecunious short-stay visitors on cheap trains from Madrid and points in between, while Blackpool retained and developed its middle-class clientele (although much more downmarket and provincial than San Sebastián's summer residents). There was no Basque echo of the Lancashire wakes holidays, but by the early twentieth century day-trippers were coming in from the surrounding industrial towns every Sunday and on special occasions like the big bullfights and the regattas for sea-going rowing-boats, and the leisure menu had its proletarian offerings (*El Diario de San Sebastián*, 11 August 1879; *La Época*, 19 August 1880; and see Iván, 1928). Some of the profiles overlapped, and so did some of the problems.

How were the holiday crowds policed? In Blackpool's case an important change took place in 1887 when the town was allowed to run its own police force and the first local Chief Constable was appointed. In earlier years the Lancashire county force had not always been willing to allocate extra resources to the Blackpool holiday season, nor had it taken the enforcement of local by-laws as seriously as the town's rulers preferred. By-laws governing land use, public behaviour and the use of the beach and streets were central to Blackpool's holiday regime, which needed to be able to discourage activities that went too far in challenging consensual attitudes to what constituted indecency, vulgarity, intrusive noise, obstruction and untidiness, or which imported raucous working-class mores into self-consciously 'better-class' areas. Moving frontiers posed recurrent problems here in the late nineteenth century. The Corporation, established in 1876, soon expanded the by-law regime it had inherited from the Local Board of Health, which had begun to regulate bathing, hawking and touting for custom in the streets in the early 1850s, and by the early 1880s, after expanded powers had been obtained by the Improvement Act of 1879, it was introducing its own inspectors for by-law enforcement, enforcing its regulations through the local magistrates' court. Discretion was important, for often the by-law powers were held in reserve for use against contentious developments, and (for example) prosecutions of obstructive street stalls in the popular central districts were seldom completed until the end of the season. A local police force, responsible directly to a municipal Watch Committee dominated in the late nineteenth century by representatives of the popular entertainment and drink industries, was much more reliable in imposing suitable definitions of and allowing appropriate relaxations of order than a body run by the county magistrates had been. From 1899 there was also a borough bench of magistrates, again dominated by local business interests. Even when the Watch Committee was opened out to less obviously interested parties in the new century, the concern to limit nuisance to a mainstream visiting public was always tempered by the need to allow visitors to enjoy themselves in their own way with a minimum of external interference (Walton, 1974; Walton, 1983). This was made easier by the ways in which the visitors policed themselves, working within a consensual vision of what was acceptable and always aware of the potentially censorious gaze of foremen, Sunday School teachers, workmates and neighbours who policed respectability in the towns from which they came. Cautionary tales by dialect writers illustrated the perils of stepping out of line. In the 1870s and 1880s Ben Brierley depicted Blackpool as reputedly full of predatory widows eager to enjoy themselves with unattached men, but the plots of his stories showed that wives, and indeed the fear that they would catch errant husbands out, were perceived to be potentially ever-present and ultimately impossible to evade (Brierley, 1872, 1881). It was under these circumstances that Blackpool in the early twentieth century could pride itself on low levels of prosecuted drunkenness and violence, although definitions of drunkenness certainly allowed for a lot more cheerful and obstreperous merriment at closing time than would have been the case 'at home'. But by the turn of the century it could be argued that the seaside was 'civilising' its working-class visitors, who were themselves losing their rougher edges as schooling and work became more disciplined and new commercial entertainments imposed new skills of attentive spectatorship. The development of recognisable social areas, with their own conventions about the limits to proper behaviour, was already becoming visible in the 1860s and helped to reduce tensions and conflicts: even the Pleasure Beach, which was growing up at the relatively upmarket southern end of the promenade from the mid-1890s, was tamed and made respectable by an increasingly potent alliance between proprietors and local government (Bennett, 1996). An indicative result was the banishing of gipsy fortune-tellers, whose challenge to values of individual self-determination, religiosity and personal responsibility was sufficiently dangerous to lead to much heavier fines than those that were imposed on Blackpool's handful of visible prostitutes. Blackpool remained a haven for palmists and occult practitioners, however, as befitted its enduring association with freak-shows and the display of ambiguous sexualities, and by the 1890s it already had more than its fair share of phrenologists, astrologers, psychometrists, graphologists and similar fauna, who were able to escape the attentions of the Corporation by occupying their own premises (Davies, 1999: 254–5). If anything, the concentration had increased by the

1930s, with large numbers of landladies offering tea-leaf readings while the petty impresario Luke Gannon had spiced up the Golden Mile still further with exhibitions of starving honeymoon couples, the unfrocked Rector of Stiffkey and the sexually ambiguous Colonel Barker. In San Sebastián there were occasional panics about the activities of *curanderas*, or female alternative healers, who were associated both with fortune-telling and abortion, but the local female population, rather than the visitors, were seen as the victims here. In Blackpool, in contrast with San Sebastián, the focus on the speculative and the grotesque indicated that sex was more in the repressed imagination than the actual doing, despite a reputation for lubricity that the amateur anthropologists of Mass-Observation failed to confirm in the late 1930s, despite endless rumour, innuendo and retrospective boasting. A firm association between Blackpool and sexual laxity was to be reserved for the late twentieth century (Cross, 1990: 117–19, 185–91; Collis, 2001; Walton, 1998a). Despite all this activity on dry land, which the Corporation and its police force tried unavailingly to discourage, the beach itself had been brought firmly under corporate control by the turn of the century, its liminality brought to heel through by-laws and the renting of stalls, and (from 1923) many of its votaries had been persuaded to transfer themselves to the municipal bathing pool at South Shore, where crowds of spectators reinforced the Corporation's rules about proper dress and behaviour. Sea-bathing, as opposed to sitting on the sands and paddling, had become such a minority activity that it no longer posed a threat to norms governing exposure of the person (Walton, 2001b: 272–98).

The beach attracted much more attention from the authorities in San Sebastián, where there was no municipal pool and the rise of the fashion for sun-bathing and skimpy costumes in the late 1910s ushered in a generation of conflict between followers of international fashion and fierce Catholic moralists. A special subsection of San Sebastián's local force, the *celadores de la playa*, looked after order, decency and the protection of property on the bathing beaches, which remained central to the resort's identity and appeal, and their close allies were the *bañeros* who ran the bathing-machines and (after 1925) cabins. They had a vested interest in requiring bathers to use their facilities, and a result of this was that the local working class were pushed to the margins, leaving the best beaches to the affluent visitors and bathing as best they could on the dangerous terrain of the river estuary and the generally plebeian suburb of Gros (Walton, 2002b). This sense of knowing one's place was replicated within the town, as the fashionable promenade of the Alameda was divided into minute social subdivisions whose boundaries were barely visible but intimately known (Walton, 2001c). It did not prevent sustained conflict from developing within the middle and upper classes over sunbathing and the ostentatious display of scantily clad bodies on the beach, which became a staple of debate in the local press between the second decade of the twentieth century and the outbreak of the Civil War, reaching a shrill crescendo with the campaigns of 1934–5 for the imposition of regulations which would have widened the existing gap in tolerated practices between San Sebastián and its French rivals, thereby (it was argued) threatening its status as an international resort (Walton, 2001b).

It might be argued that whereas Blackpool seems to have found policing the holiday crowds easier with the passage of time over this period (this was to change in the late twentieth century), in important ways San Sebastián found it more difficult, despite the shared propensity for people of different classes to 'know their place', literally, and internalise and observe social boundaries, except on specific occasions when they deliberately transgressed them to make a point. The policing system was more complex here. The municipal force, whose summer uniform included a replica of the classic British helmet but in white, dealt with day-to-day issues like traffic control (a big issue from the early twentieth century in San Sebastián, with reinforcements brought in from Madrid during some summer seasons), public order in the streets, and the capture of malefactors such as pickpockets and confidence tricksters (*El Diario de San Sebastián*, 25 July 1876; *La Voz de Guipúzcoa*, 19 July 1886; Walton, 1999). The conventional rhetoric of the local press was that these came in from less virtuous environments to enjoy the rich pickings of the summer season, especially from alien haunts of iniquity like Madrid, Barcelona and Paris; and representations of the force's success in this latter field oscillated between praise for the perspicacity of the officers in charge, and denunciations of sloth and negligence (*El Diario de San Sebastián*, 26 July 1879; *La Voz de Guipúzcoa*, 15 July 1886). But these varied in tone as much according to the complexities of local politics and the state of relations between the governing coalition on the local council and the newspaper in question, as to the genuine effectiveness of the force. The conventional rhetoric of Basque virtue deployed by almost all local commentators assumed that serious malefactors would come from without, although strict measures were taken against indecent words and actions in public places wherever the offenders came from, and the police were regularly praised for picking up suspicious persons on arrival and deporting them by train to other parts of Spain, a policy that would have left few traces in the official statistics (*El Diario de San Sebastián*, 2 August 1879; Artola, 2000: 357–8). No such extravagant expectations regarding local virtue existed in Blackpool, although the holiday crowds were represented throughout the early decades of the twentieth century as friendly, open, easily controlled and practically self-regulating, and the popular media figure of the 'gradely' Lancastrian, represented as unpretentious, witty and quick to deflate pretensions, but ultimately decent and disciplined even when on the spree, provided a self-fulfilling stereotype with a different pedigree (Joyce, 1991). Where outside help was brought in on set-piece occasions like the Carnivals of 1923 and 1924, it was to help identify opportunists with criminal 'form' who had been drawn in from Manchester or Liverpool by the publicity: to police those who battened onto the crowd, rather than the crowd itself, which came to be romanticised as essentially innocent except when groups within the town sought to highlight alleged rowdyism for purposes of their own (Blackpool Carnival, 1923; Walton, 1998b).

When the local working class transgressed boundaries in San Sebastián, it was as rioters, whether over prices, politics (sometimes with a nationalistic tinge) or trade union issues; and here the provincial police, the national Civil Guard and the garrison were more likely to come into the equation, backed up by the civil and even the military governor. The politics of this could be complex, and the important thing to stress is that San Sebastián, unlike Blackpool, regularly experienced confrontations between consumers and producers, capital and labour, on its central streets during the holiday season, especially during the disturbed years around and beyond the end of the First World War. From time to time there were deaths, and tramway strikers, in particular, were prone to placing small bombs on the tracks. This, like the issues surrounding casino gambling, would have been unthinkable in Blackpool, although strikes were not absent from the English resort (Walton and Smith, 1994; Luengo, 1990). It is therefore not surprising that one aspect of San Sebastián's pre-emptive policing system was an unusually well-endowed system of charities for the relief of poverty, boosted from the revenues of the Gran Casino until 1924, which helped to justify the prevailing hard line against beggars and street vendors which made the town unique in Spain. It was assumed, of course, that these too would be outsiders. Blackpool had the Chief Constable's clothing club for poor children, and voluntary bodies like the Ladies' Sick Poor Association, which vetted recipients very carefully, but it had nothing to match San Sebastián's infrastructure here (Artola, 2000: 355, 357; Walton, 1998).

Despite the perceived propensity for disorder among the local working-class population, the rapid throughput of short-term migrants among holiday industry workers as well as visitors, and environments conducive in obvious ways to excess, what stands out about these resort experiences up to and including the 1930s is the success of local authorities in policing holiday crowds who were generally willing to go with the conventional flow.[4] Rates of recorded crime in both places were low by comparison (in San Sebastián's case) with the rest of Spain, and (in that of Blackpool) with most of the industrial towns of the resort's hinterland, especially if we allow (as the statistics do not) for the huge seasonal population increases in the Lancashire resort. In Blackpool the main conflicts arose between sections of the changing visiting public, peaking during transitional years towards the turn of the century; in San Sebastián the main flashpoints involved changing conventions of beach behaviour in the 1920s and 1930s, and, more enduringly, the perceived propensity to disorder of the local working-class population. But what won out almost all the time, in both places, was a shared perception that the holiday industry was economically vital and that a reputation for order and stability was a necessary prerequisite for the relaxed enjoyment of the visitors. The interpretation of what constituted an appropriate version of order, and still more of suitable behaviour in public places, varied between and within the resorts and changed over time, but the preoccupation remained inescapable.

Notes

1. ESRC award reference number L210252026. Collaborators on the original project were Colin Pooley, David Tidswell, Martin Blinkhorn and Mike Winstanley.
2. The most obvious example is, of course, an inland resort in the United States: see most recently Denton and Morris (2002). But see also, for example, Sternlieb and Hughes (1983) and Walton (2001a: 19–25).
3. Blackpool's willingness to embrace large-scale casino development, including roulette, at the beginning of the new millennium marked a remarkable transformation in attitudes in response to the urgent need for a new remaking of the resort's image, although Atlantic City in the 1970s was a more convincing comparator than was Las Vegas at any time.
4. For less optimistic postwar perceptions of Blackpool see Croft-Cooke (1961), and for a more recent novelist's treatment see Nick Oldham's, *Nightmare City* which contrasts the happy-go-lucky public face with 'the massive and continually expanding drug culture ... burglary, theft, violent robberies and overdoses ... serious assaults (outside night-clubs) by itinerant, untraceable offenders ... the growing problem of child sex and pornography ...' (Oldham, 1997: 25). For a picaresque view of San Sebastián's underworld in the mid-1970s see Aguirre Alcalde (1976).

References

Alcalde, Aguirre. *Guía secreta de Guipúzcoa*. Madrid: Taurus, 1976.

Artola, M. (ed.) *Historia de Donostia/San Sebastián*. Hondarribia: Nerea, 2000.

Bennett, P. *A Century of Fun*. Blackpool: Blackpool Pleasure Beach, 1996.

Bennett-Ruete, J. 'The Social History of Bad Ems', unpublished PhD thesis, University of Warwick, 1987.

Blackpool Carnival: Official Souvenir Programme, June 9th to 16th (inclusive) 1923, British Library catalogue no. 103609 47.

Brierley, B. *Ab-o'-th'-Yate: adventures at Blackpool*. Manchester: Heywood, 1872.

Brierley, B. *Ab-o'-th'-Yate: drop't on at Blackpool*. Manchester: Heywood, 1881.

Calvert, A. *Royal Palaces of Spain*. London, 1909.

Chadefaud, M. *Aux origines du tourisme dans les pays de l'Adour*. Pau: Université de Pau, 1987.

Collis, R. *Colonel Barker's Monstrous Regiment: A Tale of Female Husbandry*. London: Virago, 2001.

Croft-Cooke, R. *Smiling Damned Villain*, 2nd edn. London: Four Square Books, 1961.

Cross, G. (ed.) *Worktowners at Blackpool: Mass-Observation and Popular Leisure in the 1930s*. London: Routledge, 1990.

Davies, O. *Witchcraft, Magic and Culture 1736–1951*. Manchester: Manchester University Press, 1999.

Denton, S. and Morris, R. *The Money and the Power: The Making of Las Vegas and Its Hold on America, 1947–2000*. London: Knopf, 2002.

Garate Ojanguren, M. and Martín Rudi, J. *Cien anos de la vida económica de San Sebastián*. San Sebastián: Dr Camino, 1995.

Graves, C. *Trip-tyque*. London: Nicholson & Watson, 1936 .

Immerso, M. *Coney Island: The People's Playground*. New York: Rutgers University Press, 2002.

Iván, V. *Costa de Plata*. San Sebastián, 1928.

Joyce, P. *Visions of the People. Industrial England and the Question of Class, 1848–1914*. Cambridge: Cambridge University Press, 1991.

Kasson, J. *Amusing the Millions: Coney Island at the Turn of the Century*. New York: Hill & Wang, 1978.

Larrinaga Rodríguez, C. *Actividad económico y cambio estructural en San Sebastián durante la Restauración, 1875–1914*. San Sebastián: Fundación Kutxa, 1999.

Lewis, R. 'Football hooliganism in England before 1914: a critique of the Dunning Thesis', *International Journal of the History of Sport*, 13, 1996, pp. 310–39.

Luengo Teixidor, F. *Crecimiento económico y cambio social: Guipúzcoa, 1917–1923*. Leoia: Universidad del Pais Vasco, 1990.

Mars, G. *Cheats at Work: An Anthropology of Workplace Crime*, London: Allen and Unwin, 1982.

Meller, H. *European Cities, 1890s–1930s: History, Culture and the Built Environment*. Chichester: John Wiley & Sons, 2001.

Oldham, N. *Nightmare City*. London: Headline Feature, 1997.

Shields, R. *Places on the Margin*. London: Routledge, 1991.

Starkie, W. *Spanish Raggle-Taggle*. London: Murray, 1934.

Sternlieb, G. and Hughes, J. *The Atlantic City Gamble*. New York: Harvard University Press, 1983.

Walkowitz, J. *City of Dreadful Delight; Narratives of Sexual Danger in Late-Victorian London*. London: Virago Press, 1992.

Walton, J. K. *The Social Development of Blackpool, 1788–1914*, PhD thesis, Lancaster University, 1974.

Walton, J. K. 'Municipal government and the holiday industry in Blackpool, 1876–1914', in Walton, J. K. and Walvin, J. (eds), *Leisure in Britain, 1780–1939*. Manchester: Manchester University Press, 1983.

Walton, J. K. 'The Blackpool landlady revisited', *Manchester Region History Review*, 1994, pp. 23–31.

Walton, J. K. 'Seaside resorts and maritime history', *International Journal of Maritime History*, 9, 1997, pp. 125–47.

Walton, J. K. *Blackpool*. Edinburgh: Edinburgh University Press, 1998a.

Walton, J. K. 'Popular entertainment and public order: the Blackpool carnivals of 1923–4', *Northern History*, 34, 1998b, pp. 170–88.

Walton, J. K. '"The Queen of the Beaches": Ostend and the British from the 1890s to the 1930s', *History Today*, 51, 8, 2001a, pp. 19–25.

Walton, J. K. 'Consuming the beach: seaside resorts and cultures of tourism in England and Spain from the 1840s to the 1930s', in Furlough, E. and Baranowski, S. (eds), *Being Elsewhere: Tourism, Consumer Culture and Identity in Modern Europe and North America*. Ann Arbor, MI: University of Michigan Press, 2001b.

Walton, J. K. 'Policing the Alameda', in Gunn, S. and Morris, R. J. (eds), *Identities in Space: Contested Terrains in the Western City since 1850*, Historical Urban Studies. Aldershot: Ashgate, 2001c.

Walton, J. K. 'Planning and seaside tourism: San Sebastián, 1863–1936', *Planning Perspectives*, 2002a, pp. 1–20.

Walton, J. K. 'The waters of San Sebastián: therapy, health, pleasure and identity', in Anderson, S. and Tabb, B. S. (eds), *Water, Leisure and Culture: European Historical Perspectives*. Oxford: Berg, 2002b.

Walton, J. K. and Smith, J. 'The rhetoric of community and the business of pleasure: the San Sebastián waiters' strike of 1920', *International Review of Social History*, 39, 1994, pp. 1–31.

Walton J. K. and Smith, J. 'The first century of beach tourism in Spain', in Barke, J. Barke, M., Newton, M. T. and Newton, N. (eds), *Tourism in Spain: Critical Issues*. Wallingford: CABI Publishing, 1996.

Walton, J. K., Blinkhorn, M., Pooley, C., Tidswell, D. and Winstanley, M. 'Crime, migration and social change in north-west England and the Basque Country, c.1870–1930', *British Journal of Criminology*, 39, 1999, pp. 90–112.

Chapter 9

'The greatest efficiency': British and American military law, 1866–1918

Gerry Oram

Military law remains foreign territory to many criminologists and historians. Yet it has affected millions of people – most significantly during wartime. Arguably, however, it is the periods of relative peace that are of greatest interest to the historian: only then did opportunities exist for reform of a code regarded as sacrosanct during wartime. Broadly speaking, these opportunities were missed and a military code drawn up in late seventeenth-century England, dominated by ideas of deterrence, survived well into the twentieth century on both sides of the Atlantic. It was not so much that military law proved resilient to reform but that what debate existed was too easily marginalised in societies that isolated their armies.

This essay will examine developments during the late nineteenth century before considering how the unprecedented enlargement of military manpower and authority in the First World War impacted on prewar structures. Paradoxically, given the constitutional differences between the two countries, the key issue for both hinged on the question of autonomy. In many ways this was not new and I will show how this debate was merely a continuation of pre-existing concerns that also persisted beyond our period. Furthermore, I will challenge the commonly held view that excesses of military discipline during the Great War resulted in widespread and meaningful reform.[1] Instead, I will show how limited appeasement of critics during this era ensured that military discipline remained largely beyond the reach of the legislature in both the United States and Britain.

There are a number of reasons why pre-1914 American and British military codes warrant comparison. They share common origins and traditions (military and legal). Both armies remained relatively small and relied on the voluntary principle of recruitment, a principle later compromised by the exigencies of modern warfare. The codes retained a 'separateness' from other legal forms that was less evident in the mass armies of continental Europe, and the military occupied a peculiar, often precarious, position in the two countries that, outwardly at least, espoused individual liberty and eschewed despotism. Military activity during the late nineteenth century was characterised for both armies by gendarmerie-style operations against indigenous people and in the early twentieth century by larger conflicts – Britain in South Africa, America in Mexico and Cuba. There was, however, a deeper historical context to our period.

Background

British military law, in a modern form, originated with the Mutiny Act 1689. This partly reflected the shift from royal prerogative to parliamentary control, but the relationship between sovereign and army was a complex one that was not easily disentangled. The sovereign retained a special executive responsibility for army discipline while Parliament approved military law. This contradiction defined later developments and provides the key to understanding the American problem: it was this system that the fledgling United States inherited from its former colonial master.

Prior to 1689 the British army was subject to civil law during peacetime with Articles of War issued by the Crown during conflict. Soldiers were tried by tribunals presided over by Earl Marshals who, as early as the sixteenth century, were assisted by lawyers to advise them on civil law. In 1666 this role was formalised with the appointment of the first Judge Advocate General (JAG), Dr Samuel Barrow. The office of JAG was retained after the Mutiny Act and in it was personified the relationship between the military and civil codes – a relationship that would become increasingly remote (Stuart-Smith, 1963: 223–46; Manual of Military Law, 1914: 6–14; for the origins of courts martial and earlier developments see Squibb, 1959). The circumstances surrounding the Mutiny Act were not entirely the outcome of the transition of power from sovereign to Parliament. In March 1689 soldiers of the Royal Scots Regiment mutinied. The pre-existing Articles of War did not allow courts martial to sentence soldiers to loss of life or limb and so the Mutiny Act was rushed through Parliament. Given the circumstances of its inception it is not surprising that the Act never successfully resolved the underlying question of who really controlled the army. Originally intended as a temporary expedient and with limited scope, the Mutiny Act, with all its inherent contradictions, formed the basis for the control of British and, by extension, American armies until the twentieth century.

Early American military law was also founded on a temporary expedient and reflected the emergency situation facing the revolutionaries. British military law appeared to be a sound basis from which to proceed and the Massachusetts Articles of War, which closely resembled the British, were drawn up as early as April 1775 and adopted by the Continental Congress only two months later. Military expediency and fear of the consequences should the rebellion fail justified the severity of the new code. For example, officers and men who 'shamefully abandon any post committed to his charge, or shall speak words inducing others to do the like, in time of an engagement, *shall suffer death immediately* (Winthrop, 1920: 955 [my italics]).

Execution without trial, however, did not survive John Adams's revision the following year, which also required a general court martial to complete a full report to Congress or the commander-in-chief (C-in-C) before a sentence could be confirmed (Lurie, 1992: 5). But the urgency surrounding the issue of effective control of the militia cannot be overstated. As one historian has observed 'they [courts martial] predate our federal district courts by more than a decade, and can thus accurately be said to have been among the first (if not *the* first), federal courts authorized by the United States' (Lurie, 1992: 5). Thus the first truly 'New World' army adopted 'Old World' practices. This was not initially problematic, but the failure to adapt what was effectively an old code to a new constitution merely deferred resolution of its inherent contradictions to later generations. Claims that 'the British system served as a firm stepping stone for the American system which thereby got a running start in 1775' (Schleuter, 1980: 144) might be considered overenthusiastic. Although benefiting from long established practices within English law (many of which such as the concept of due process went back as far as 1215 with *Magna Carta*), the relationship between courts martial and the Bill of Rights continues to provoke debate (for example, the debate on the sixth amendment (right to counsel) – see Henderson, 1957: 293–324, and Wiener, 1958: 1–49).

In Britain the Mutiny Act received its annual renewal with only perfunctory debate and in America the military code survived intact despite the occasional 'bad press' such as the 'Somers' affair of 1842. The execution at sea of three junior officers serving aboard the US Navy Brig *Somers* attracted considerable public attention. This was hardly surprising given that one of the condemned conspirators to mutiny was Philip Spencer, the 18-year-old son of John Spencer, US Secretary of War. Critics, including literary figures (Henry Wadsworth Longfellow and James Fenimore Cooper), attacked a system that allowed the captain to convene the trial, selected the members of the court, then order the conviction and condemnation of the defendants. Finally, as the confirming authority, he was also responsible for overseeing its 'legality'. Militarists, on the other hand, saw in the captain's actions a decisiveness that prevented a potential mutiny at sea. The US Navy effectively condoned the captain's actions, but public attention focused on a military authority seemingly beyond control. Critics were accused of posing a threat to national security merely by suggesting that discipline might be subjected to due process rather than unalloyed military authority (Lurie, 1992: 22): a recurrent theme in Britain, America and France (Dreyfus). Despite the issues raised by the affair, any challenge to military autonomy was destined to fail because of two supposedly infallible tenets of military justice both later acknowledged by Abraham Lincoln: 'Armies [or navies perhaps] cannot be maintained unless desertion shall be punished by the severe penalty of death ... [Also that] The commander in the field is the better judge of the necessity in any particular case' (see Lincoln, 1953: 237). Similar arguments dominated the debate concerning military justice in Britain where attention focused on the role of the JAG whose duties involved 'perusing the proceedings of courts-martial of soldiers and officers, to ensure that such hearings had been conducted lawfully' (Rubin, 1997: 45). This advisory post did not limit the disciplinary power of the C-in-C whose twin roles – the preservation of discipline *and* justice – came under parliamentary scrutiny as his relationship with the JAG was increasingly strained towards the end of the nineteenth century. The latter, we should recall, symbolised the connection between military and civil codes and the debate *must* be viewed in this context (for a European comparison, see Oram, 2001). Military justice, though, was multi-layered and it was impossible for the JAG to peruse the many thousands of cases each year. Most of these cases were conducted in relatively informal courts – regimental courts martial – and bore little resemblance to civilian trials. Broadly speaking these courts only heard relatively minor cases and powers of sentencing were restricted. It was also possible for minor punishments to be imposed extra-judicially. In 1879, for example, there were 252,296 recorded minor punishments and only 15,512 trials by courts martial (Army Courts Martial Returns for 1879, War Office, 1881). These minor punishments were beyond the control of politicians and JAG alike.

Balancing the needs of discipline and justice

According to the *Manual of Military Law*, the standard reference book for practitioners in the British army:

> The object of military law is to maintain discipline among the troops and other persons forming part of or following an army. To effect this object, acts and omissions which are mere breaches of contract in civil life – e.g. desertion and disobedience to orders – must, if committed by soldiers, even in time of peace, be made offences, with penalties attached to them; while on active service, any act or omission which impairs the efficiency of a man in his character of a soldier must be punished with severity. (*Manual of Military Law*, 1914: 6)

This established a number of principles. Firstly, the code was underpinned by the needs of discipline and not jurisprudence. Furthermore, military law was regarded as distinct from civil law – effectively criminalising breaches of contract. It also reflected the emphasis attached to deterrence. Finally, and perhaps most intriguing of all, was the need for an efficient character of a soldier. The meaning of this ambiguous term might not be as elusive as it appears provided we consider its context. In *The Soldier's Small Book* – a handbook containing personal details, advice on how to prevent sore feet, warnings about the 'common women' of India and even recipes – British troops were informed that 'OBEDIENCE IS THE FIRST DUTY OF A SOLDIER [*sic*]' (cited in Baynes, 1967: 265). This included courage because soldiers were expected to obey orders to stand and fight regardless of other factors. A soldier's resolve – his morale – was, therefore, intrinsically linked to his discipline – his obedience. To most militarists of the nineteenth century cowardice in an individual simply reflected a lack of discipline (see Oram, 2000: 73–133; 134–87). Efficiency was synonymous with obedience and military law was constructed with this in mind.

Crucially, the Mutiny Act had not placed the army under the control of Parliament, but had retained the royal prerogative personified through the office of C-in-C (for much of our period this was George, Duke of Cambridge – grandson of George III – who commanded the army from 1865 to 1904). But the lines remained blurred and in 1872 this triggered a dispute over the role of the JAG who remained responsible to Parliament for army discipline.[2]

The Army Discipline and Regulation Act 1879 rationalised existing law and formalised existing practices, but did little to resolve the question. The power to confirm or commute sentences remained with the sovereign or, if overseas, the C-in-C, or other officers in certain (usually minor) cases.[3] The role of the JAG did not feature in the act, which *appeared*, therefore, to confirm the primacy of the C-in-C and, by implication, of army discipline over jurisprudence.

Concurrent with the debate concerning control of military discipline was a separate – though not unconnected – concern over the severity of military punishments. This became more pressing after the death from flogging of Private Slim in 1867. A partial abolition of flogging followed although it was retained for mutiny or insubordination with violence at any time and for desertion and drunkenness during wartime (Oram, 2001: 96). The less common and therefore less visible capital punishment attracted no such attention from reformers. Flogging might also have escaped total abolition had there not been a sharp increase in its use in Zululand in 1879, which attracted the attention of reformers, including Gladstone, resulting in complete abolition in 1881.

The range of punishments meted out by courts martial was vast. Capital punishment was rare, but corporal punishments were surprisingly common. The returns for the army during the years 1865–67 show that corporal punishments (flogging and marking) were applied to between 5 and almost 8 per cent of all cases. However, this was steadily decreasing even though the total number of trials was increasing year on year, as illustrated in Table 9.1.

Table 9.1   Returns for court martial sentencing 1865–67[*]

Sentence	1865	1866	1867
Solitary confinement	6	18	8
Imprisonment/solitary confinement with hard labour	571	600	627
Imprisonment	16,227	18,639	19,219
Marked with 'D'	1,562	1,464	1,615
Marked with 'BC'	74	120	190
Discharged	106	122	184
Stoppages	10,572	13,134	14,074
Flogged	601	510	150
Total	29,719	34,607	36,067
% flogged/marked	7.5	6	5.4

*Figures taken from The Second Report, pp. 255–78.

But the debate over military punishments was merely a distraction from the real issue – the control of military discipline, which remained firmly in the grasp of the C-in-C. Furthermore, this distraction had occurred at a crucial time. In capitulating to pressure for reform of military punishments the army command had unwittingly removed from public attention the key issue of who controlled military law. The symptom of severe punishments might have been relieved but the cause – unfettered military authority, or 'efficiency' – remained. The *advisory* role of the JAG might have been expanded to balance this 'efficiency'. But it was not. The army had for centuries constructed its ideas about discipline around the central tenet that the army knew best and any suggestion of outside interference in its affairs was deeply resented. A change of commander near the end of the century did nothing to alter the situation. Viscount Wolseley, C-in-C from 1895 to 1900, 'repudiated the idea of civil rights for soldiers as essentially mischievous and misconceived' (Rubin, 1997: 75).

This was reflected in the recommendations of the Royal Commission appointed to inquire into courts martial and punishments, which reported in 1869 and saw no reason to adopt practices in other European armies. Some armies, such as the Russian army, provided legal training and 'each tribunal has a *procureur militaire* (Judge Advocate) to conduct the prosecution. He has several assistants, civil or military, all of whom must have studied law, and for this purpose a military law academy has been established'.[4] Even the reputedly draconian Prussian army had an 'auditor's department [which] is a *civil* [my emphasis] branch of the War Office, the members of which have been educated and have taken their degrees as lawyers. The auditor-general has the relative rank of major-general, and his bureau consists of five superior and seven inferior officials' (*The Second Report*, 1868: 220). Civilian officials also prosecuted in Italian courts martial. But the report regarded these as alien, pointing out how practices in Prussia 'so materially differ from those of the English army' (*The Second Report*, 1868: 220) or how the more egalitarian approach of the French 'appears strange to us … and I am not sure that it works' (*The Second Report*, 1868: 223).

The British army was not unique in jealously guarding its privilege and excluding the unwanted attention of lawyers. In America military courts had proved an expedient method for trying cases arising from the Civil War and a relatively large number of trials involved civilians. Extending the jurisdiction to civilians naturally resulted in increased public attention on the courts themselves, but also on the nature of the military code. Although not strictly courts martial, challenges to these military tribunals had at least brought a ruling from the Supreme Court that military judicial authority was 'not reviewable by civilian courts'.[5] This did nothing to enhance public confidence in the military commission charged with trying the conspirators in the case of the assassination of Lincoln. One historian has suggested military commissions were regarded with deep mistrust because they were comprised of 'officers too worthless for field service, ordered to try, and organised to convict' (Turner, 1982: 139). However, we should beware of drawing too much inference from the Lincoln case because circumstances were really quite different and in the highly charged atmosphere surrounding the case standards of evidence were allowed to slip.[6] The trial, involving civilian defendants, did have implications for courts martial: in finding against the original conviction the Supreme Court conceded that 'when dealing with military personnel [military courts] were beyond the reach of civil federal courts' (Lurie, 1992: 41).

The flogging debate in Britain had raised concerns within the army over possible outside interference in matters of discipline. This caused the War Office to look again at practices in other armies. The resulting memorandum written by General Sir Charles Ellice, Adjutant-General of the British Army, was intended to pre-empt accusations of excessively severe punishments. The Russian Army, it was noted, had increased the use of corporal punishments, from little more than 3,000 cases in 1860 to almost 7,000 in 1868. In Austria corporal punishment had been abolished in 1868, but the power to pass sentences of 'tying-up' or to 'put in irons' had been retained. In Germany, however, the new code of 1872 did not meet with Ellice's approval. The parliamentary committee responsible for the new code had included General von Moltke, but Ellice was more concerned that it was 'chiefly composed of civilians'. The new laws, he suggested, were so lenient that 'the Allied [German] governments hesitated to approve them, but gave way for the sake of a settlement'.[7] These comments reflected concerns of militarists in Britain where the practice of flogging was moribund. But the most telling remarks were reserved for the American Army. It was noted that despite the abolition of flogging in 1861, 'it is well known, that during the American Civil War corporal punishments of varied, but sometimes extreme, severity were often inflicted upon soldiers in the United States [Union] Army' (Ellice Report, 1879). Moreover, it was emphasised that the Judge Advocate-General in 1879 had advised courts martial on methods that avoided the label of corporal punishment:

In view of the abolition of the corporal punishments by the 98th (new 54th) Article of War [which prohibited flogging, branding, marking or tattooing], courts-martial must needs often draw upon the customs of the service for a penalty which shall insure the description of a corporal punishment. Thus, the accused may be adjudged to carry a loaded knapsack for a certain time, stand on a barrel, or suffer any other ignominy which would naturally result in a degree of bodily pain or fatigue, provided the same were not excessive and physically injurious. (Ives, 1879: 172, cited in Ellice Report, 1879)

Similar developments can be detected in the British code around this time. Branding, or marking, had been abolished in 1871 and an 1881 draft of proposed summary punishments to replace flogging suggested:[8]

(a.)   Putting the offender in irons.
(b.)   Attaching the offender, while on the line of march, to a cart, wagon, or horse, so as to compel him to move onward at a walking pace. Whilst so attached, he may be handcuffed or otherwise secured so as to prevent his escaping, but he must not be in fetters.
(c.)   Requiring the offender to carry extra burdens or weights not calculated to injure his health.

The approved measures were couched in broader terms when eventually formalised so that 'such punishment shall be of the character of personal restraint or of hard labour, but shall not be of a nature to cause injury to life or limb'.[9] These developments, however welcomed by campaigners against the excesses of military punishments, did nothing to address the fundamental issue of soldiers' rights. Even Article 47 of the American code, which required the assent of the President before the execution of any death penalty, could be bypassed in times of war for deserters and mutineers. Such was the strength of the 'disciplinary necessity' argument.

Not all challenges to military judicial authority came from outside liberal reformers: some came from within. In 1889 James Fry, a retired US army colonel, argued that 'the ascertainment of truth' cannot 'be at variance with the objects of the military code, and they ought to be applied to it'. More significantly, he pointed out that 'all available means of ascertaining truth are not invariably resorted to by Courts-martial' (Fry, 1889: 183, cited in Lurie, 1992: 43). The emphasis on prompt punishment was, he suggested, the cause of this iniquity, but Fry's solution – establishing a military court of appeals under the control of the C-in-C – was not adopted.

Lord Roberts, C-in-C of the British army (1900–4), faced accusations of exercising 'despotic power' by removing Lieutenant-Colonel Kinloch from his command of the 1st Battalion, Grenadier Guards, in a way that had circumvented normal procedures. Briefly, Lord Roberts, following a secret War Office Court of Inquiry, had dismissed Kinloch for allowing the unlawful trial and corporal punishment of two subalterns (one the son of Lord Belhaven, the other related to Lord de Saumarez). Kinloch's request to be tried by court martial was denied. Roberts's action to address what he viewed as a situation prejudicial to military discipline might have been carried out with the decisiveness expected by other militarists, but it was not universally appreciated. The problem was that some viewed the C-in-C's actions as unconstitutional. On 28 April 1903 the Duke of Bedford asked the Upper Chamber:

> From whence is derived this authority which overrides an Act of Parliament and confers on the office of C-in-C a despotic power which is beyond all law, and which has never been allowed under our constitution to any single individual in any department of Government? ... I do not understand how the discretionary powers of a C-in-C can be used to infringe the provisions of an Act of Parliament. It was not, continued the Duke, merely 'a matter of military law or military procedure. It is a question of the infringement of the provisions of an Act of Parliament'. (Parliamentary Debates (Hansard), vol. CXXI, col. 618)

The debate hinged not so much on the merits of the case than on the accountability of the army's high command and the rights of those subject to that command – a point neatly made by the Duke of Northumberland:

> In this case the real issue is whether His Majesty's Government, the Secretary of State for War and the C-in-C have utterly disregarded Acts of Parliament and the regulations of the Service and substituted a procedure of their own which gives the accused no chance of fair play. (Parliamentary Debates (Hansard), vol. CXXI, col. 633)

Winston Churchill put a similar point to the Commons: 'May I ask why an officer of the army has not the same privileges [the right to trial by court martial] as an officer of the Navy?'[10] In fact, according to Lord Bedford, Kinloch's privileges had been breached

> because the C-in-C and the Secretary of State for War have disregarded the explicit terms of the Parliamentary contract [contained in the Army Act], and violated the rules established by Parliament for the vindication of the character and military reputation of officers in His Majesty's Army. (Parliamentary Debates (Hansard), vol. CXXI, col. 626)

Nor was this the first occasion that Lord Roberts had clashed with politicians over the matter of autonomy. In a private note to Lord Kitchener on 9 March 1901, in which he rejected a parliamentary motion to try officers who surrendered their posts to the Boers, Roberts stated:

I have pointed out to [William] Broderick [Conservative MP for Surrey South West and Guildford and Secretary of State for War 1900–3] the *danger* to the Army of allowing the House of Commons to deal with questions regarding the conduct of officers [my emphasis]. (Lord Roberts to Lord Kitchener, in Wessels, 2000: 164–5)

Political interference, from whatever quarter, was invariably resisted to preserve the army's putative independence – a view expressed by Lord Harris when commenting on the Kinloch case on 4 May 1903:

The whole object of the authority which is given to the C-in-C, and to commanders of units, will, it seems to me, be imperilled if noble Lords are encouraged to take the opportunity of membership of this House to call in question the decisions of the C-in-C on military matters. (Parliamentary Debates (Hansard), vol. CXXI, col. 1177)

The Kinloch matter eventually blew over without resolution other than a gentle reminder to the War Office, the Secretary of State and the C-in-C that the autonomy of military law *could* be compromised by suggestions of malpractice. It was no coincidence that the Kinloch affair had involved only well connected officers and this no doubt had brought it to the attention of Parliament just as the 'Somers' affair in America had also involved the son of a high-profile politician. The next major scandal concerning British military law – this time during the First World War – also involved an officer with influential relatives and friends.

Total war, and two systems found wanting

Sub-Lieutenant Edwin Dyett of the Royal Naval Division, an infantry formation deployed under army command, was executed for desertion during the 1916 Battle of the Somme. Again, we need only concern ourselves with the impact of the case.[11] The son of a naval commander, Dyett's case was taken up by Horatio Bottomley in his journal *John Bull* on 23 February 1918. Later, the case would also inspire the writer A. P. Herbert,[12] but the publicity whipped up by Bottomley in 1918 ensured an immediate political response. Backbenchers pressed for an assurance that procedures of courts martial and standards of justice were of the highest order. One member even suggested that members of the House should take it upon themselves to review the evidence in the case.[13] Unfortunately, this could not be done without the consent of Dyett who by this time, of course, was dead. That effectively postponed the debate.

In America, too, the war helped to focus attention onto military law. The JAG, Enoch Crowder, had been concerned with revising the American code since 1912. The new Articles of War were finally approved in 1916, but did little to alter existing law or procedure. America's entry to the war in 1917 took Crowder away from his JAG role to oversee new draft laws. His role was, therefore, delegated to his deputy, Samuel Ansell. There then followed a dispute between them over the precise nature of this role. In short, Ansell interpreted his function as a reviewer of sentences to safeguard against possible excesses or injustices carried out by the military – a one-man appeal court. Central to this view was Ansell's understanding of section 1199 of the code. Originally enacted during the Civil War, the clause required the JAG to 'receive, revise, and cause to be recorded the proceedings of all courts-martial, courts of inquiry and military commissions' (cited in Lurie, 1992: 52). Ansell's interpretation of the word 'revise' was that this placed a judicial appellate responsibility on the JAG and not merely an advisory one as had been understood previously. A memorandum to this effect distributed to US forces angered General Pershing, commander of the American Expeditionary Force in France, who appealed to the Secretary of State for War, Newton Baker, who in turn alerted Crowder to this threat to military efficiency. The threat became an open challenge to military authority when, in October 1917, Ansell unilaterally reversed the verdict of a court martial arising from an alleged mutiny at Fort Sam Houston in Texas. The unwarranted charges against three non-commissioned officers, he suggested, had arisen from the 'capricious conduct of a very youthful and inexperienced officer' (Lurie, 1992: 54). Crowder's response was to warn Ansell of the need for prompt and expedient discipline during wartime which, he reminded his deputy, was an emergency situation (Lurie, 1992: 68).

The debate became more than theoretical when, in December 1917, the War Department became aware of a serious incident that threw American military law into the public glare once again. In August 1917 a mass execution of black soldiers had been carried out following a mutiny in Texas. A court martial convened to hear 63 cases following the mutiny, which had resulted in a number of white civilian deaths, found 58 of the men guilty and 13 were sentenced to death. The men were all hanged the following day. This 'Second Texas Mutiny' only came to the attention of the War Department and the JAG when featured in the Washington papers some four months later. Ansell's fears, it seemed, had been realised and the War Department acted immediately – issuing General Order No. 7 forbidding the execution of any death sentence until 'reviewed' by the JAG who could refer cases back to the commanding officer for retrial or amendment. Additionally, a JAG office was established in France. However, this amounted only to a minor dilution of military authority and, according to Crowder, 'courts martial remained instrumentalities [sic] of the executive [military commander's] power' (cited in Lurie, 1992: 73). It is worth noting here that the only American soldiers executed in France during the war were ten black troops convicted of rape or murder (Oram, 1998: 29).

Postwar recriminations

After the war the Ansell–Crowder dispute became increasingly personal as it attracted public and political attention. This was partly because of the Senate Committee on Military Affairs chaired by Senator George Chamberlain, an Oregan Democrat and outspoken critic of President Wilson. By the end of 1918 the Committee focused its attention on the nature of military justice, effectively grafting itself onto the Ansell–Crowder dispute. In February 1919 Chamberlain presented to the Senate an unsuccessful Bill 'to promote the administration of military justice', which envisaged a greater judicial role for the JAG, tighter political control of military law and supervision of the C-in-C in matters of discipline.

Concerns raised by the Dyett case persisted in postwar Britain and on 10 April 1919 the Army Council set up a committee, chaired by Privy Councillor, member of the King's Bench Division and former Conservative MP, Sir Charles Darling. The broad remit 'to enquire into the law and rules of procedure regulating Military Courts-Martial, both in peace and war, and to make recommendations',[14] might have obscured the influence of the Dyett case but for the inclusion of Bottomley on a committee otherwise packed with militarists.

There was no such gesture in America where the three-man board established by Baker to 'consider all recommendations looking to the improvement of the present system of military justice' was staffed entirely by regular army officers and chaired by Major-General Francis Kernan, a reputed disciplinarian. Predictably, the Kernan Report, published on 17 July 1919, reflected concerns of the military authorities, but rather less predictable was its alarmist tone. Ansell's proposals, the report argued, were 'open to be questioned as an attempt by law to emasculate the legitimate and heretofore undisputed authority of the President'.

Suggestions that the accused be judged by men of equal rank were 'out of harmony with the American conception of democracy' and 'more in harmony with that form of discipline which in Europe recently resulted in the establishment of soldiers' and workers' councils' (Kernan Report 1919).

By the time the Chamberlain Committee reported at the end of 1919 the war was fast receding in the minds of people, press and politicians. The new Articles of War, issued in June 1920, formalised the review role of the JAG, but placed responsibility for this on a board of army officers within the JAG's office. The limits of military authority had been defined but at the same time power had been consolidated rather than diluted.

The Darling Report had the same impact on British military law. Here, also, any appellate procedure was regarded as injurious to the needs of discipline and unnecessary because '[a] soldier is in a better position [than a civilian]' thanks to the confirming role of the C-in-C and the review role of the JAG. The emphasis, though, remained on disciplinary efficiency:

> In regard to sentences, we consider that, subject to the right to petition for clemency, the decision ought to be left, as at present, to the military authorities, who alone are in a position to form a correct judgment [sic] as to what sentences the state of discipline in the Army, or of a particular force, requires. (Darling Report, 1919: 11)

The rationale that underpinned this argument was a lingering mistrust of lawyers and the resentment of outside interference in matters that civilians could not understand. It was the same argument and the very same concerns and mistrust that had polarised the debate in America. Major-General David Shanks, in evidence to the Kernan inquiry, had put it more explicitly than the Darling Committee could possibly have dared:

> Courts-martial should be free from wrangling of lawyers and hair-splitting technicalities ... Nothing can be more discouraging to the seasoned officer who knows the difficulties connected with the control and management of soldiers than to find that all of his experience which has taken him a lifetime to acquire is set aside to the whim of some lawyer who has a hobby to ride ... When the sentence is reached it should be imposed by men who know the soldier and not by a bookworm who knows a little law. (Kernan Report 1919, cited in Lurie, 1992: 116)

Conclusion

Military law was defined by its origins – expedient reactions to emergencies (mutiny in Britain, revolution in America). Its continuation was not anticipated beyond the immediate necessity, a point recognised by Judge Blackstone in 1765:

> For martial law, which is built upon no settled principles, but is entirely arbitrary in its decisions, is, as Sir Matthew Hale observes, in truth and reality no law, but something indulged, rather than allowed to law. The necessity of order and discipline is the only thing which can give it countenance; and therefore it ought not to be permitted in time of peace, when the King's courts are open for all persons to receive justice according to the laws of the land. (Blackstone, 1809: 413)

Despite this, both codes existed until the mid-twentieth century with only the more visible excesses curbed by Parliament. The fundamental issue of military authority and accountability remained unresolved. Why were both governments reluctant to wrest control from the army?

In America and in Britain the army's relationship to the rest of society was not a close one. Both countries relied on the voluntary principle of recruitment, at least until the First World War. Armies were invisible during times of peace and only came to public, and therefore political, attention at moments of scandal such as the 'Somers' or Kinloch affairs and even then it was ephemeral. During wartime the military expediency argument was unassailable. In America this had been recognised by none other than John Adams and Abraham Lincoln. In Britain the army was compared to the crown – beyond the reach of politicians. Nothing could be more sacred.

In countries where a large conscript army was maintained the relationship was different and this was reflected in the military codes: courts of appeal and political supervision were commonplace in the mass armies of continental Europe. Only in Prussia was the military held to be above such control, but this merely reflected the feudal nature of that society and was extinguished upon the unification of Germany which established a constitutional state, or *Rechsstaat*. By compelling men to serve these states accepted a responsibility towards its troops and recognised them as citizens rather than mere soldiers.

Britain and America, on the other hand, only confronted the responsibilities associated with mass armies in 1916 and 1917 respectively. Until that moment soldiers were viewed less as citizens but rather 'a mob –

dangerous to all but the enemies of their country' (Darling Report 1919: 11). The greatest challenge to military authority came at the end of the First World War when the relationship between soldier and state had been redefined by the introduction of compulsory service. This took the form of political pressure – largely the result of increased public concern about what were perceived as excessively severe military punishments. This potent mix of genuine humanitarianism and political opportunism, which had been brewing since the earliest days of the war, meant that military executions were frequently debated by the British Parliament and in 1918 caused the Under-Secretary for War, James Macpherson, to acknowledge the 'widespread anxiety in the country' (cited in McHugh, 1999: 236). For the opportunists a weakness had been exposed by which they might attack the army itself. Despite this, the prevailing official view remained that 'a Commander-in-Chief, who is entrusted with the safety of his Army, must not be fettered in his decision as to a point which so vitally affects the discipline of that Army' (Darling Report 1919: 12). Nevertheless, the campaign in Britain did gain momentum and by 1930 the death penalty was abolished for most military offences,[15] but was (and is) retained in the American army. Political interference in punishments was one thing, but the very idea of any political influence over courts martial remained anathema to militarists who resisted any threat to 'efficiency' because as the US Secretary of War had explained to Congress in 1878, 'A small army, such as ours, manifestly needs all that strict discipline can do to supply, by the greatest efficiency, whatever may be lacking in numerical strength' (cited in Ellice Report 1879: 2).

Postscript

In 1950 the American government set up a court of military appeals – a civilian rather than a military court. In Britain courts martial procedures were modernised by the Army Act 1955, but many fundamental features remained. In 2002, following a ruling by the European Court of Human Rights, all British courts martial were suspended.

Notes

1. Campaigners often targeted the excesses of military punishments and neglected the underlying causes – inadequate safeguards and lack of independent appellate procedures. More recently, historians have fallen into the same trap and what little has been written on the subject all too often

focuses on military punishments and fails to analyse adequately the structures that legitimised those practices. See, for example, Moore (1974), Babington (1993), Putkowski and Sykes (1992), Spiers (1992). However, some legal historians have redressed the balance: see Rubin (1997: 45–84), Lurie (1992).

2. A full discussion of the dispute over the role of the JAG is beyond the scope of this essay. In any case it would be impossible to improve upon the excellent study by Rubin (1997).

3. Section 57 of the Army Discipline and Regulation Act 1879 was effectively a rationalisation of sections 16, 23, 24 and 25 of the Mutiny Act.

4. *The Second Report of the Royal Commissioners appointed to inquire into the Constitution and Practice of Courts-Martial in the Army, and the Present System of Punishment for Military Offences.* London: HMSO, 1868: 216; hereafter referred to as *The Second Report.*

5. Judgment in the case of *Vallandigham* (1864), cited in Lurie (1992: 34).

6. Evidence was accepted from a witness who had previously perjured himself. Moreover, the defendants were not allowed to testify. Although acceptable in criminal trials at this time, this was not normal practice in American courts martial. See Lurie (1992: 36).

7. Memorandum on the Various Methods of Punishment adopted by Foreign Armies for Soldiers in the Field, 1879, PRO WO32/604; hereafter referred to as the Ellice Report.

8. Copy of Draft Rules as to Summary Punishments Proposed to be made by the Secretary of State Under Section 4 of the Army Discipline and Regulation (Annual) Bill (1881–2), (London: HMSO, 1881: 1), return to an order of the House of Commons dated 25 March 1881.

9. Army Discipline and Regulation (Annual) Act 1881, section 4 (1).

10. Parliamentary Debates (Hansard), vol. CXXI, col. 276.

11. The Dyett case continues to dominate the attention of historians of military discipline during the First World War and accounts of it can be found in Babington (1993), Putkowski and Sykes (1992) or, more specifically, in Sellers (1995).

12. Herbert's novel is generally accepted to have been based on the Dyett case.

13. Mr J. H. Thomas, House of Commons debate on army estimates, 20 February 1918.

14. *Report of the Committee Constituted by the Army Council to Enquire into the Law and Rules of Procedure Regulating Military Court-Martial.* London: HMSO, 1919: 2; hereafter referred to as the Darling Report.

15. This was achieved in two stages, firstly in 1928, and then in 1930 when desertion and cowardice ceased to be capital crimes. Mutiny remained a capital offence in the British Army until 1998 when, to conform to European convention, it was finally abolished. In the USA, however, desertion remains a capital offence during wartime (Article 85, Uniform Code of Military Justice).

References

Babington, A. *For the Sake of Example: Capital Courts-Martial 1914–18 The Truth*. London: Leo Cooper, 1993.

Baynes, J. *Morale: A Study of Men and Courage*. London: Cassell, 1967.

Blackstone, Sir W. *Commentaries on the Laws of England*, Volume 1, 15th edn. London: Cadell & Davies, 1809.

Bottomley, H. 'Shot at dawn', *John Bull* (London), 23 February 1918.

Henderson, G. 'Courts-martial and the Constitution', *Harvard Law Review*, 72, 1957, pp. 293–324.

Herbert, A. *The Secret Battle*. London: Methuen, 1919.

Lincoln, A. *Collected Works*, vol. 6, ed. Roy Basler. New Brunswick, NJ: Rutgers University Press, 1953.

Lurie, J. *Arming Military Justice*, Volume 1, *The Origins of the United States Court of Military Appeals, 1775–1950*. Princeton, NJ: Princeton University Press, 1992.

McHugh, J. 'The Labour Party and the parliamentary campaign to abolish the military death penalty, 1919–1930', *Historical Journal*, 42, 1, 1999, pp. 233–49.

Manual of Military Law, London: HMSO, 1914 edn.

Moore, W. *The Thin Yellow Line*. Barnsley: Pen & Sword, 1974.

Oram, G. *Worthless Men: Race, Eugenics and the Death Penalty in the British Army during the First World War*. London: Francis Boutle, 1998.

Oram, G. ' "What alternative punishment is there?": military executions during World War One', unpublished PhD thesis, Open University, 2000.

Oram, G. ' "The administration of discipline by the English is very rigid": British military law and the death penalty (1868–1918)', *Crime, histoire et sociétés / Crime, History and Societies*, 5, 1, 2001, pp. 93–110.

Putkowski, J and Sykes, J. *Shot at Dawn: Executions in World War One by Authority of the British Army Act*. London: Leo Cooper, 1992.

Rubin, G. 'Parliament, prerogative and military law: who had legal authority over the army in the later nineteenth century?', *Legal History*, 18, 1, 1997, pp. 45–84.

Schleuter, Captain D. 'The court-martial: an historical survey', *Military Law Review*, 87, 1980, pp. 129–66.

Sellers, L. *For God's Sake Shoot Straight!* London: Leo Cooper, 1995.

Spiers, E. *The Late Victorian Army 1868–1902*. Manchester: Manchester University Press, Manchester, 1992.

Squibb, G. *The High Court of Chivalry: A Study of the Civil Law in England*. Oxford: Clarendon Press, 1959.

Stuart-Smith, J. 'Without partiality, favour or affection: an account of the history and present functions of the Judge Advocate General at a British court martial', *Revue de Droit Pénal Militaire et de la Guerre/The Military Law and the Law of War Review*, 2, 1963, pp. 223–46.

Turner, T. *Beware the People Weeping: Public Opinion and the Assassination of Abraham Lincoln*. Baton Rouge, LA: Louisiana State University Press, 1982.

Wessels. A. (ed.) *Lord Roberts and the War in South Africa 1899–1902*. Stroud: Army Records Society, Sutton Publishing, 2000.

Wiener, F. 'Courts-martial and the Bill of Rights: the original practice I', *Harvard Law Review*, 72, 1, 1958, pp. 1–49.

Winthrop, W. *Military Law and Precedents*. Washington, DC: US Government Printing Office, 1920 edn.

Chapter 10

The decline and renaissance of shame in modern penal systems

John Pratt

One of the most significant features in the realignment that has taken place in the penal systems of anglophone societies in the last twenty years or so has been the re-emergence of shaming punishments. These take two distinct forms. First, there are the reintegrative shaming practices advocated by John Braithwaite (1989), now more usually known as restorative justice and to be found in varying degrees and capacities across all such countries. Second, there is stigmatic shaming. In the United States and parts of Australia this takes the form of judicially imposed penalties, specifically designed to humiliate their recipients (see Pratt, 2000). There are also a range of extra-penal, extra-legal activities running through these societies usually designed to humiliate adjudicated offenders, sometimes local troublemakers, sometimes those just thought to be different in unacceptable ways. This ranges from the naming and shaming posters in shops, community centres and so on warning off, or warning of, local unsavoury characters which can be found in New Zealand[1] to the concerted acts of local vigilante groups in Britain which came to a head in a spontaneous conflagration of anti-paedophile activity in the summer of 2000.

Obviously, there are political, ethical and strategic differences between these respective outlets for shaming. Indeed, those involved in the restorative justice movement have been keen to emphasise the difference that exists between the shaming they espouse and the other forms it can take, to the point where these differences have effectively been essentialised: they have fundamentally different and contradictory conditions of existence in modern society. As such, restorative justice/ reintegrative shaming has had a historical, normative, legitimate existence in modern society. On this basis, the 'other' – stigmatic shaming – is seen as some kind of aberrational, illegitimate distortion: 'during the 19th century and well into the twentieth, the system became less punitive and the shaming more reintegrative ... but by the late twentieth century we had seen both a general weakening of shaming and some shift with neo-classicism back to stigmatic and away from reintegrative shaming' (Braithwaite, 1993: 10).

As a consequence of being able to construct such firm dividing lines between the two (cf. Morris, 2002), their contestation then takes the form of a latterday, evangelistic struggle between good (reintegrative shaming) and evil (stigmatic shaming). What I want to suggest in this chapter, however, is that both these types of shaming have more in common than is usually recognised. Indeed, I want to suggest that they both emerge out of the same historical conditions of existence. The shaming of individual criminals – of one kind or the other – takes place in modern society when the central state is weak, ill-functioning or contracting. The corollary of this, and which I shall attempt to show here by reference to English penal developments, is that for much of the modern period penal shame came to be *expelled* from these societies as the authority of the state grew and punishment came to be administered through its bureaucratic organisations. It thus became a scientific, administrative task performed by penal experts, with the emotive force of shame stripped away from it. Indeed, over the course of the nineteenth and much of the twentieth centuries, shaming itself, of whatever kind, became an aberrational rather than normative feature of modern penal systems.

What now determines the *particular* form that shaming will take is then likely to be dependent on the availability of local cultural values, memories and folk lore of what punishment 'used to be like'. In other words, the local space for it is likely to be entirely contingent: there is no essentialised quality to it, no inevitability, no necessary path to good or bad shaming, no firm boundary between good and bad. In these respects, while the productive, reintegrative shaming that takes place in Japanese society[2] is the model (in Braithwaite, 1989) for the desired form that shaming *should* take, it is also entirely possible that it can take on a very different form. And thus, in sharp contradiction to Japanese-type shaming, specific to the conditions of Japanese society, I want to examine the longevity of the utterly stigmatic, brutalising practices to be found in the Deep South[3] of the United States over much the same period: another contingent form that shaming *may* take under particular circumstances, as opposed to the form that it *should* take. The chapter will then conclude with a discussion of how this historical understanding of the relationship between shaming, penality and modern society relates to the presence and possibilities of the renaissance of shame today.

Modernity and the decline of shaming punishments

From the late eighteenth century up to the mid nineteenth, punishment in modern society underwent a profound series of changes. At the start of this period, it was still possible to see and participate in the full range of 'the spectacle of suffering' (Spierenburg, 1984), including shaming punishments, usually directed at the body of the offender and performed in public: ducking stools, stocks and pillories, whipping and, of course, highly ritualised and dramatised public executions. At the same time, there was also an array of informal local community sanctions in existence. One such took the form of a carnivalesque parade, known variously as the charivari, skimmington or skimmity ride,[4] where citizens would mock, shame and embarrass local troublemakers, adulterers and so on, often with a view to driving away such people altogether. Among upper-class men, duelling was a way of resolving disputes, particularly if aspersions had been cast upon one's honour. This would then be played out according to an elaborate and highly codified etiquette (see Andrew, 1980). Essentially, however, the challenge to a duel *had to be taken up*, otherwise one risked being 'posted' – labelled a coward in the press or some other form of community notice, with one's reputation forever shamed and ruined.

Nonetheless, by the 1860s, this framework for the imposition of shaming punishments had disappeared. Public whippings had rapidly fallen into disuse in the early nineteenth century, as had the charivari tradition. The pillory was hardly used after 1815 and was finally abolished in 1837. Duelling fell into rapid decline after 1843, with the last recorded duel taking place in 1852. The ducking stool was last used in 1817 and the stocks in 1860. Public executions were abolished in 1868. In place of a penality that was able to accommodate shaming of various kinds, we find instead the emergence of a recognisably modern penal system, revolving around the idea of imprisonment as the main penal sanction. What had brought about these changes? One significant influence was the role played by changing sensitivities among middle-class elites to such spectacles. Public shaming punishments and other public displays of violence, cruelty, excessive celebration and so on became increasingly distasteful to this class. Opinion formers such as Dickens, other novelists, essayists, social reformers and so on began to influence the political process and eventually helped to variously shut down, codify, sanitise or fence off these various sights and scenes that might range from 'hunting, wrestling, football and hurling, single sticks, boxing and sword fighting, bull and bear baiting, to hanging and whipping. Cock fighting was the most popular sport of all' (Trevelyan, 1961: 281). As John Stuart Mill wrote:

> ... one of the effects of civilization ... is that the spectacle, and even the very idea of pain, is kept more and more out of the sight of those classes who enjoy in their fullness the benefits of civilization ... it is in avoiding the presence not only of actual pain, but of whatever suggests offensive or disagreeable ideas, that a great part of refinement exists. (Mill, 1836: 130–31)

Thus, in relation to penal developments, legislation abolishing the degrading, insensitive public executions were described by *The Times* (14 August 1868: 12) as being 'in keeping with the spirit of the age'. In addition, social structural changes made the informal sanctioning of duelling and the charivari impractical and impotent. As regards the former, growing importance was attached to men of industry and wealth rather than men of honour in Victorian England: this had become the way to achieve respectability, rather than braggadocio concerns about character slights. As regards the latter, local community traditions and interdependencies were being broken down by urbanisation and industrialisation. Such declines in the informal modes of conflict resolution then strengthened the central state's monopolistic control of the power to punish.

These developments thus spelt the end for shaming sanctions in modern society. What followed thereafter, again prompted largely by the sensibilities of penal reformers and the ameliorative tendencies that were pursued by modern penal bureaucracies are a series of attempts to remove the shaming effects of various other features of the modern penal system by now in existence, particularly those associated with imprisonment. Unwarranted prison visits from a curious and insensitive public quickly provoked outrage: 'We think the introduction of the visitors who now attend on Fridays the readings to the women [prisoners], highly improper. On one occasion, when we were present, there were 23 visitors' (Report of the Inspectors of Prisons of the Home District, 1836: 19). Similarly, the days of social commentators and journalists able to wander around prisons at their leisure were quickly brought to an end (see Dixon, 1850; Chesterton, 1856).

Having excluded the public from gratuitous prison visiting which had contributed to the shame of the prisoners, so too the prisoners' sojourns beyond its walls (transfer to court or another prison or employment on public works) came to be more restricted and camouflaged. Again, one of the reasons for this was a desire to prevent the unnecessary shame and humiliation of the prisoners. Many commented on this in their prison writings. Oscar Wilde, for example, described such an experience while waiting for a train to take him to Reading prison:

> I had to stand on the centre of the platform of Clapham Junction in convict dress and handcuffed, for the world to look at ... of all possible objects I was the most grotesque. When people saw me they laughed. Each train as it came up swelled the audience. Nothing could exceed their amusement. (Hart-Davis, 1962: 490–1)

Eventually, travel to, from and between prisons came to be more discreet, usually in shuttered railway carriages or buses exclusively reserved for prisoners. In 1948 the rule was that '[prisoners] shall be exposed to public view as little as possible, and proper safeguards shall be adopted to protect them from insult and curiosity' (Fox, 1952: 164–5). From the late nineteenth century, the authorities had also recognised (see Report of the Committee on Prison Rules and Prison Dress, 1889: 44) and then steadily tried to remove the shaming consequences of some of the prison rules relating to personal hygiene, appearance and clothing. Again, their mortifying effects had become a regular theme in prisoner biographies throughout this period:

> There appeared a person dressed in the most extravagant garb I had ever seen outside a pantomime. It was my first close view of a convict ... the clothes were of a peculiar kind of brown ... profusely embellished with broad arrows. His hair was cropped so short that he was almost as closely shawn as a Chinaman. A short jacket, ill-fitting knickerbockers, black stockings striped with red leather shoes ... (Balfour, 1901: 36)

In these respects, the sight of prisoners – shamed, cowed and humiliated as a result of everyday prison conditions – came to be deeply troubling to prison officials and reformers in the early twentieth century. Prison Commissioner Alexander Paterson regretfully commented on a prison visit he made to Dartmoor in 1909:

As [the prisoners] saw us coming, each man thereafter ran to the nearest wall and put his face against it, remaining in this servile position, till we had passed behind him ... the men looked hard in body and in spirit, healthy enough in physique and colour, but cowed and listless in demeanour and response. (Ruck, 1951: 26)

Thereafter, a series of reforms were introduced, aimed at sanitising these features of prison life. For example, in relation to clothing, 'the Commissioners have done their best to get a better standard of neatness and cleanliness in the appearance of the prisoners' (Report of the Prison Commissioners, 1942: 35), and in relation to dining arrangements, there was to be a replacement of 'old wooden dining tables with tables having inlaid linoleum tops and many of the forms for seating were replaced by wooden chairs' (Report of the Prison Commissioners, 1949: 65).

Care must be taken, of course, not to characterise these trends as being unidirectional. From time to time, there were attempts to reverse this ameliorative route of penal development, and by so doing restore some shaming features to the penal system. The postwar introduction of short, sharp shock detention centres was one example. But these were later abandoned because prison officers now found these regimes unpalatable, based around deliberate attempts to humiliate those who were sent there (Dunlop and McCabe, 1965). The cultural values necessary to support such kinds of shaming had by then all but disappeared. As it was, the drives to further expel shaming continued, spreading beyond the prison itself. One of the issues relating to the introduction of community service orders in the early 1970s in Britain was the concern to ensure that the offender's identity would not become known to their non-offending colleagues as they undertook community work in reparation for their crimes (Young, 1981). Similarly, the Rehabilitation of Offenders Act 1974 introduced provisions to 'wipe' the criminal convictions of many offenders, so they would no longer have to live with the consequences of their stigmatic, shameful past. By legislative fiat, as it were, that part of their lives had been rendered invisible.

Such developments, specific to England but part of a similar pattern taking place elsewhere (Pratt, 2002), point the way in which modern penal systems over this period effectively became shameless. Shaming had become incompatible with the growing authority of the central state, which exercised its now monopolistic power to punish through its bureaucratic organs of government, and as a result of the dominance of the cultural sensitivities of penal reform and other elite groups. As Hermann Mannheim (1949: 228) noted as he reflected on postwar trends toward reform through rehabilitation, 'it is no use denying that in its practical consequences, individualization of treatment, that dominating principle of modern penology, is bound to clash with the traditional requirements of justice as understood by the man in the street.' By now, there was a fundamental cleavage between the scientific knowledge that bureaucratic experts brought to bear on the issue of punishment, as opposed to commonsensical, emotive, unrestrained public opinion. One of the consequences of the dominance of the former was that, formally, the re-integration of offenders did indeed become central to penal development over this period. This was to be achieved, however, by expelling all residual shaming components from the penal system, and then, through rehabilitation or other administrative measures, eliminating an indi-vidual's criminal past. Reintegration, as a bureaucratic accomplishment, would take place on the basis that the criminal's past has been eliminated in such ways, not forgiven (the kernel of the reintegrative shaming/ restorative justice movement), nor, for the most part, even publicly known about.

Indeed, and notwithstanding the formal commitments to rehabilitation and reform that had by now come into existence, it was the anonymity of the penal system, and the growing power of the bureaucratic forces that regulated it that had become the identifying characteristics of punishment in modern society. It had become the domain of expertise and scientific knowledge, incomprehensible to 'ordinary people' as Mannheim had intimated. At the same time, it was this expertise and those who possessed it that now attempted to regulate penal development according to calibrated, objective scientific principles. In contrast, then, to the historical account of restorative justice, the history of penal development in much of modern society precluded any of the emotive shaming capabilities associated with it.

The Southern United States: a shaming and shameful region

Nonetheless, against this general pattern of development, as late as 1930 it was possible to witness the following scene in the Deep South of the United States:

> James Irwin was chased all night by hundreds of man-hunters. When captured next morning, the sheriff along with the accused negro was seized by the mob ... [t]here quickly assembled a thousand or more men, women, and children. The accused negro was hung up in a sweet-gum tree by his arms, just high enough to keep his feet off the ground. Members of the mob tortured him for

more than an hour. A pole was jabbed in his mouth. His toes were cut off joint by joint. His fingers were similarly removed, and members of the mob extracted his teeth with wire pliers. After further unmentionable violations, the Negro's still living body was saturated with gasoline and a lighted match applied. As the flames leaped up, hundreds of shots were fired into the dying victim. (Southern Commission on the Study of Lynchings, 1931: 40)

How do we explain the presence of such monstrous barbarities, such utterly shameful degradation in this region, which by this time would surely be inconceivable across the rest of these societies? It was possible, I maintain, because of the historical background to penal development in the South in the modern period. The colonisation of this region had begun in the late seventeenth century, usually by poorer sections of English society. Georgia, for example, was eventually established in the early eighteenth century as a penal colony for English debtors. Due to the shortage of white labour and the remoteness of the new colony, they petitioned for the importation of slaves, to the effect that, by around 1750, there were four slaves for every white male in that state (Flanders, 1933: 22). From thereon, Georgia enjoyed a period of prosperity, attracting immigrants whose wealth and power came to be founded on the plantation and its produce, primarily cotton, rice and indigo. Plantation owners were likely to delegate disciplinary control of their estates to a white overseer (also known as 'the whipping boss') – with labour being performed by black slaves. In these respects, an economic base was developed in the South that was organised around small, paternalistic, highly authoritarian communities, at a time when modern penal development was moving in the opposite direction. In effect, it was as if a new aristocracy had been created here (Wyatt-Brown, 1982), where 'honour' and personal character were still valued at a time when such qualities were being overridden by respectability through industry and hard work elsewhere. Although the Southern gentry had no long or noble lineage, it nonetheless looked to the social structure and values of the pre-industrial English aristocracy as a way of defining and modelling its own existence. By the same token, we find an emphasis on pageantry and military display to a far greater extent in the ante-bellum South than to be found elsewhere. To become an officer, or have some corresponding rank of which there was a profusion in the extravagantly costumed and frequently parading local militia, was another way to establish one's prestige and acceptability among one's fellow whites (Franklin, 1956).

What it was thus possible to see in the South before the Civil War, and how it was possible to behave, had become very different from elsewhere.

In terms of what it was possible to see, 'Southern stores were very much like the Northern ones, visitors noted – except that they stocked negro whips and mantraps on their shelves' (Larkin, 1988: 292). In terms of what it was possible to do, slights to one's honour had to be avenged, all the way down the white social structure, whether in the highly codified duels that the Southern aristocracy participated in all the way up to the outbreak of the Civil War (Ayers, 1984), or, for the rest, other forms of highly ritualised physical combat: 'to gouge out an eye or otherwise mutilate the face of an enemy was the most common object of men involved in fist fights. With the possible exception of battle wounds, the mutilation itself was dishonouring, no matter how it was actually acquired. In a sense, all mutilations were equal, because men read the character of other men through the external features of the body' (Greenberg, 1990: 67).

Against this social structural and cultural background, Southern penal development in the ante-bellum period was of an almost entirely different order from what became the pattern for the rest of modern society. Penitentiary development was very limited and was extremely unpopular. There was instinctive opposition among the white plantation class to any enlargement of state power that it necessitated and the levying of taxes needed to sustain it. Instead, crime problems could be dealt with *in situ* on the plantation while, by the same token, most inter-white conflict (especially over 'honour' offences) could be settled by duels or fist-fighting. Indeed, as a Tennessee lawyer later noted, 'questions affecting personal character were rarely referred to courts of law ... to carry a personal grievance into a court of law degraded the plaintiff in the estimation of his peers and put the whole case beneath the notice of society' (Williams, 1980: 25). At the same time, institutional confinement was seen as unnecessarily dishonouring for whites, for whom stoic endurance of physical punishment might become a way to reclaim one's honour.

These circumstances ensured that a particular kind of penal shaming flourished here while it was in decline elsewhere. The individual sovereignty of the plantation owners rather than state sovereignty was paramount, thereby leading to the discouragement of strong, central state law enforcement. Instead, 'the whipping boss' could usually deal with trouble on the plantation. Beyond the plantation, the charivari continued to have strong local roots: 'the tarring and feathering of a thief near Charleston, the wrecking of a house of ill repute by a mob in Edgefield, and the hanging of a presumed horse stealer in Ninety Six by spectators who disagreed with a jury's "not guilty" verdict, were episodes of wrath in the history of South Carolina crime and punishment' (Williams, 1959: 121). At the same time, an almost obligatory community involvement among whites on law enforcement issues was then used to defend the existing social structure as it seemed increasingly endangered in the build up to the civil war. 'Vigilance committees' and 'vigilance clubs' emerged in the 1830s and 1840s, which hunted proselytisers from the northern anti-slavery movement, while enforcing curfews on their increasingly suspect black population. Indeed, such was the presence of these vigilance societies in some localities that the British consul in Charleston in 1859 wrote of the situation as being but little short of a 'reign of terror … persons are torn away from their residences and pursuits, sometimes tarred and feathered; ridden upon rails, or cruelly whipped' (Williams, 1959: 124). In the absence of any functioning state authority, these local groups could come together and impose sanctions which seemed appropriate to their cultural values and traditions, rather than those which fitted modern bureaucratic expectations.

Post-bellum penality in the south

However, after defeat in the Civil War and its consequences – the breakdown of its plantation-based economy and the imposition of new ruling elites from the North – the social structure in which shaming penalties had been able to flourish had been destroyed. Even so, local cultural values continued to have a strong penal presence as a result of the still largely undeveloped bureaucratic infrastructure of government, alongside a hesitant, fledgling and more or less bankrupt local state. Penal development, formal and informal, still bore the imprint of these penal values specific to the South, while the values themselves became distended and exaggerated in the aftermath of defeat.

Formally, in relation to the power to punish now vested in the state rather than the plantation owners, one of the immediate problems was how this should be exercised over the black population, who were to be punished for crime as free men rather than slaves. In the absence of both the financial and administrative resources necessary to follow modern penal developments elsewhere, the convict lease system was introduced in the late 1860s. Under these arrangements (almost exclusively black) prisoners could be hired out to the private sector and put to work on a variety of reconstruction tasks that involved labouring in public – effectively recreating plantation servitude (McKelvey, 1935). Nonetheless, the lease system was disbanded in the early twentieth century after persistent reports of brutalities and corruption had come to the attention of the central state authorities. A federal law of 1906, backed by the US Supreme Court, now prohibited forced labour of this kind (Mohler, 1924–5: 566).

Although the local Southern states now had to assume bureaucratic and financial responsibility for their convicts as opposed to simply contracting them out to the private sector, they were still used on public works tasks long after such practices had been discontinued elsewhere: 'partly because climatic conditions in the North are not so favourable to work ... and partly no doubt due to an earlier development of sensitiveness on the part of the public to the degrading spectacle of men working in public in chains [however] in the South ... the chain gang system has persisted ... the presence of [the black] race has been a factor in the continuance of the system' (Steiner and Brown, 1927: 17–18). Again, one could still see sights in the Deep South that would now be thought intolerable elsewhere. However, alongside the way in which cultural values would be able to put such a firm imprint on the shape of formal penal policy, the same combination of social structural and cultural forces also allowed informal punishment practices to continue, in new forms, and to flourish. After the Civil War, the changed realities of Southern life – the sense of dispossession, shame, dishonour, resentment – allowed the prewar vigilance committees to take on new life as a more institutionalised, organised force. Its foremost representative, the Ku Klux Klan, emerged in the late 1860s, borrowing the robes and trappings of former charivari practices and some of its nomenclature (e.g. 'Grand Cyclops') and commenced a reign of terror. How it was possible to behave in the South still seemed entirely different from elsewhere. Between 1889 and 1930 there were 3,714 lynchings in the United States, 90 per cent occurring in the twelve Southern states (the most in Georgia). Ninety per cent of those lynched in the South were black (only 71 per cent across the United States as a whole, Couch, 1934). Who were those involved in such activities? The mobs ranged from five to 15,000 in number: 'The majority of persons who took an active part in the lynchings were unattached and irresponsible youth of 25 or less, many of them not yet out of their teens ... older men looked on sympathetically and took part once activities got under way ... Southern community leaders were in the mob, as were women and children' (Southern Commission on Lynchings, 1931: 37).

Why did they happen? The immediate precipitating causes were likely to be allegations of murder, followed by similar allegations of assaults on white women and attendant fears of miscegenation (Hall, 1979). But what then prompted such responses to these suspicions? Again, the absence of or respect for any strong state authority (as in the Irwin lynching above, sheriffs would often hand over victims to the mob for fear of their own lives) seemingly gave free rein to such manifestations and outpourings of local community sentiments. They were most likely to occur in towns of less than 2,500 and knowledge of them would spread by word of mouth from one nearby community to the next. As such, it was as if they re-affirmed white solidarity and were a demonstration of its residual power and the possibility of continued resistance to those forces responsible for the defeat of the South; hence, as well, their extraordinary brutality. By contrast, lynchings along the west coast frontier (the second most prolific area for them), in addition to being more likely to be inflicted on whites, tended to be speedy affairs, conducted with little ceremony and designed only to bring about a swift and certain death (Kelly, 1985). In the South, however, these very acts of community disavowal, drawing on the available culture of violence as a way of resolving disputes, not only locked the participants together in their anger but at the same time, the more brutal the occasion became, the stronger the symbol of defiance it seemed against the despised central state authority. In these respects, there was no need for any attempt to disguise the identity of participants in lynching: they were not only asserting what they thought to be the natural law of white supremacy, but were, in effect, being authorised to do so by the complicity and forbearance of local community leaders (Southern Commission on Lynchings, 1931; Hall, 1979).

However, both these formal and informal penal arrangements were set in decline towards the end of the first half of the twentieth century. This became inevitable as state authority began to gather strength, coincident with a dilution of the previously hegemonic force of Southern cultural values. The breakdown of the plantation system as the basic unit of economic production, allied to the subsequent growth of industrialisation and urbanisation, inevitably led to a blurring of what had previously been the South's homogenous population structure. As Ayers (1984: 22) has written, subsequent diversity strengthened the authority of the law. Conflict between rival ethnic and economic groups created a widely perceived need for a system of law that stood above this. Again, the growth of a recognised state authority, now needed to regulate the more diverse system of trade and industry, began to extend itself to the resolution of crime and punishment in the early part of the twentieth century. There were growing reports in the 1920s of sheriffs resisting the demands of lynch mobs to hand over suspects (Southern Commission on Lynching, 1931). Local elites, particularly women's groups, newspaper editors and mayors, began to speak out more regularly against Southern penal brutalities and injustices. Modern communication processes (newspapers, radio and film) expressing condemnation of the lynching and chain gangs began to override word-of-mouth communication that glorified and romanticised them.

In these ways, some of the more notorious lynching cases, for example, assumed a significance that went well beyond the boundaries of the South and galvanised the opposition of national bodies to such practices, as happened after the lynching of Leo Frank in 1915 which brought protests from national Jewish organisations (Hall, 1979). Equally, in relation to the chain gangs, the famous biography of John Burns (1932) and the 1934 film based on this brought national attention to these Southern practices and 'idiosyncracies' of the South which were increasingly seen as shameful for the whole nation.

In effect, the growing power of the central state and the more diverse influences beginning to shape Southern cultural values were able to reorientate the fusion of punishment that had been created after the end of the Civil War. In the early 1930s, state executions exceeded the number of lynchings for the first time since the Civil War in Georgia (Clarke, 1998). In these respects, it was as if the formal punishment powers of the state could now act as a funnel for the previously unrestrained dominant cultural values of the white population. Prisons, too, came to be reorganised in that state in 1946: 'For many years, Georgia had had a grim record of prison cruelty. The nation had been shocked by stories of beatings and mis-treatment of convicts ... often stories of almost medieval brutality have been proved true, not by crusaders from "up North", but by Georgians, sickened by what they found. At the official inquiries in the past years, Georgia convicts have told of being beaten with rubber hose and ax handles, of being crowded into steaming "sweatboxes" as punishment for misbehaviour' (*Time Magazine*, 13 April 1946: 93).

The response to these scandals was the establishment of a State Board of Corrections in 1946.[5] Here, then, was the beginning of the bureaucratic control of penal development in that state. Although this would still have to bear the legacy of its past for some years to come, the shameful penal legacy it had inherited was eventually disowned. The Report of the State Board of Corrections (1961: 4) referred to 'the changes of the last few years; from notorious chain gangs of international disrepute to modern penitentiaries'. Finally, and for all formal purposes at least, exactly in line with penal developments in the rest of modern society, the Report of the State Board of Corrections (1965: 5) advertised the slogan 'Rehabilitation Pays' and referred to 'programs aimed at returning inmates to a society as useful and productive citizens – [and] correctional officer training is being provided, so they are not just prison guards'.

The renaissance of shame

Overall, the shaming of individual offenders had effectively been expelled from modern penal systems. In what amounted to a transformation of its moral economy, shaming had increasingly come to be directed instead at those areas of modern society, like the Deep South, where shaming punishments and its effects could still be found. Nonetheless, as we know, shaming has since returned to modern penal systems: most obviously in the United States (but also in parts of Australia), where in recent years offenders have been compelled to wear t-shirts that indicate their crimes, forced to post a 'scarlet M' sign in their window to warn others that they are a convicted sex offender, or made to perform humiliating public works (see Pratt, 2000). This is in addition to the reintroduction of chain gangs in some American states and (across most of these societies) the publication of names, addresses and photographs of known criminals or returning ex-prisoners in local police/community news bulletins and television commercials. Even so, we still find attempts to reduce the shame of conviction and imprisonment with 'clean slate' reforms as currently called for in New Zealand in some political circles and the mainstream media (*The Dominion*, 16 January 2003: 16). Notwithstanding such examples, there has thus been another reversal of the moral economy of shame: shaming punishments are used again on individuals, while the shaming of societies (in relation to high, previously unthinkable prison populations) has been relaxed. If my argument is correct in relation to the historical preconditions necessary for the presence/absence of penal shame in modern society, then the reasons for its current renaissance are self-evident. These relate to the declining authority of the central state and the collapse of faith in the authority of its penal experts (Garland, 1996), and are allied to the growth of public anxieties and insecurities, and insistent demands that punishment should follow their beliefs rather than the rational expertise of the bureaucrats (Pratt, 2002).

Clearly, then, the significance of the renaissance of shaming (of whatever kind) is indicative of a breakdown in the pattern of development that had steadily squeezed it out of existence in modern penal systems. This is the price that we have to pay for the renaissance of penal shame, whether this be in its 'good' or its 'bad' format. Whether the price seems high or low depends on our respective commitment to these reactivated practices and possibilities. Nor does the renaissance come with any guarantees, some kind of strict division between good (Japanese style) and bad (Southern USA style) shaming, although, of course, it may well be possible for individuals to influence the form that it takes in any location.

But what is also going to influence the form that shame takes is the availability of all those local penal heritages, memories and folklore that can now be repackaged in the space the neoliberal central state with its much narrower orbit of intervention has left for its reactivation. It is thus not surprising that in those societies with histories of colonisation, and where indigenous populations and values have recently been rekindled (as in Canada and New Zealand), the shaming punishments that have been developed draw on some aspects of these cultures. Even so, there are no guarantees that this will be the only form that shaming may take. Within the same jurisdiction, alongside 'good shaming' of this order and its identification with restorative justice, it is just as possible for bad shaming in the form of mob rule to exist. Alongside family group conferences in New Zealand, we find naming and shaming posters and growing vigilantism (West, 1998). In the United States, we find the reactivation of shaming as a form of humiliation imposed by court order – drawing no doubt on the still available memories of Southern shaming practices, no longer shameful in themselves – hence the reappearance of chain gangs in the Deep South (see Crist, 1996). In England, another pattern emerges. It would seem that its penal system is still more or less exclusively regulated by an entrenched state bureaucracy – more so than these other societies. It may then be the case that, denied any outlet within the formal penal system, the emotive public sentiments that drive shame manifest themselves there in the kind of extra-penal vigilante activities so evident in the summer of 2000.[6]

None of this is to say that the good shaming of restorative justice may not be worth pursuing. It may well be. What I would like to see more awareness of, however, is the price – the full price – that we have to pay for this. When we welcome the renaissance of shaming there is no certainty at all that it will take this benign form. Indeed, in the existing political and social climate, amid the prevalence of anxiety and insecurity, there is the potential that when opening the door to this welcome guest, we also usher in its malignant relative, which then becomes a more prominent and powerful presence.

Notes

1. For example, a child of seven has been 'named and shamed' in this way: 'a poster campaign which labels a 7 year old a serial shoplifter has outraged his family and the Children's Commissioner' (*Sunday Star Times*, 18 August 2002: 1).
2. See Leonardsen (2002) for a helpful review of Japanese culture and its link to crime control.
3. This term incorporates the twelve states of the Confederacy: Alabama, Arkansas, Georgia, Florida, Kentucky, Louisiana, Missouri, Oklahoma, North Carolina, South Carolina, Tennessee, Texas and Virginia.
4. See Thomas Hardy's *The Mayor of Casterbridge* (1886: 201), for a description of one such fictional incident in the early nineteenth century.

5. Initially, road work was allowed to continue but was justified differently: 'Georgia leads the rest of the nation in gainful employment of its prison labour ... prison officials from outside Georgia are amazed at the good work we are doing' (Report of the State Board of Corrections, 1950: 2).
6. For example, in the anti-paedophile activities provoked by the rape and murder of a young child (see Pratt, 2001, 2002).

References

Andrew, D. 'The code of honour and its critics: the opposition to duelling in England 1700–1850', *Social History*, 5, 1980, pp. 409–34.

Ayers, E. *Vengeance and Justice*. Oxford: Oxford University Press, 1984.

Balfour, J. *My Prison Life*. London: Chapman & Hall, 1901.

Braithwaite, J. *Crime, Shame and Reintegration*. Cambridge University Press, 1989.

Braithwaite, J. 'Shame and modernity', *British Journal of Criminology*, 33, 1993, pp. 1–18.

Burns, J. *I Am a Fugitive from a Georgia Chain Gang*. New York: Vanguard Press, 1932.

Chesterton, G. *Revelations of Prison Life*. London: Hurst & Blackett, 1856.

Clarke, J. 'Without fear or shame: lynching, capital punishment and the subculture of violence in the American South', *British Journal of Political Science*, 28, 1998, pp. 269–89.

Couch, N. *Culture in the South*. Westport, CT: Negro Universities Press.

Crist, C. 'Chain gangs are right for Florida', *Corrections Today*, 58, 1996, pp. 178.

Dixon, W. H. *The London Prisons*. London: Jackson & Walford, 1850.

Dunlop, A. and McCabe, S. *Young Men in Detention Centres*. London: Routledge & Kegan Paul, 1965.

Flanders, R. *Plantation Slavery in Georgia*. Cos Cob, CT, 1933.

Fox, L. *The English Prison and Borstal System*. London: Routledge & Kegan Paul, 1952.

Franklin, J. H. *The Militant South*. Cambridge, MA: Harvard University Press, 1956.

Garland, D. 'The limits of the sovereign state: strategies of crime control in contemporary society', *British Journal of Criminology*, 36, 1996, pp. 445–71.

Garland, D. *The Culture of Control*. Oxford: Oxford University Press, 2001.

Greenberg, K. 'The nose, the lie and the duel in the antebellum south', *American Historical Review*, 95, 1990, pp. 57–74.

Hall, J. *Revolt against Chivalry*. New York: Columbia University Press, 1979.

Hardy, T. *The Mayor of Casterbridge*. London: Wordsworth Classics, 1886/1994.

Hart-Davis, R. *The Letters of Oscar Wilde*. London: Rupert Hart-Davis, 1962.

Kelly, J. 'Shifting interpretation of the San Fransisco vigilantes', *Journal of the West*, 24, 1985, pp. 39–46.

Larkin, J. *The Reshaping of Everyday Life*. New York: Harper & Row, 1988.

Leonardsen, D. 'The impossible case of Japan', *Australian and New Zealand Journal of Criminology*, 35, 2002, pp. 203–29.

McKelvey, B. 'Penal slavery and Southern reconstruction', *Journal of Negro History*, 22, 1935, pp. 152–79.

Mannheim, H. *Criminal Justice and Social Reconstruction*. London: Routledge & Kegan Paul, 1949.

Mill, J. S. 'Civilization', in Robson, J. (ed.), *Collected Works*, XVIII. Oxford: Oxford University Press, 1836/1977.

Mohler, H. 'Convict labour policies', *Journal of the American Institute of Criminal Law and Criminology*, 15, 1924–5, pp. 555–82.

Morris, A. 'Critiquing the critics: a brief response to critics of restorative justice', *British Journal of Criminology*, 42, 2002, pp. 596–615.

Pratt, J. 'The return of the wheelbarrow men; or, the arrival of postmodern penality?', *British Journal of Criminology*, 40, 2000, pp. 127–45.

Pratt, J. 'Beyond "gulags Western style"? A reconsideration of Nils Christie's "Crime Control as Industry" ', *Theoretical Criminology*, 5, 2001, pp. 283–314.

Pratt, J. *Punishment and Civilization*. London: Sage, 2002.

Report of the Committee on Prison Rules and Prison Dress (1889). London: PP XLIX.

Report of the Inspectors of Prisons of the Home District (1836). London: PP XXXV.

Report of the Prison Commissioners (1942). London: PP (1946–7) Cmd. 7010.

Report of the Prison Commissioners (1946). London: PP (1947–8) XV Cmd.7271.

Report of the State Board of Corrections (1950). Atlanta: Department of Corrections.

Report of the State Board of Corrections (1961). Atlanta: Department of Corrections.

Report of the State Board of Corrections (1965). Atlanta: Department of Corrections.

Ruck, S. *Paterson on Prisons*. London: F. Muller, 1951.

Southern Commission on the Study of Lynching (1931) *Lynchings and What They Mean*. Atlanta: The Commission.

Spierenburg, P. *The Spectacle of Suffering*. Cambridge: Cambridge University Press, 1984.

Steiner, J. and Brown, R. *The North Carolina Chain Gang*. Montclair, NJ: Patterson Smith, 1927/1969.

Trevelyan, G. *English Social History*. London: Longmans, 1961.

West, A. 'Contemporary vigilantism: do-it-yourself justice in the 1990s', Victoria University of Wellington, unpublished Honours essay, 1998.

Williams, J. *Vogues in Villainy*. Columbia, SC: Columbia University Press, 1959.

Williams, J. *Dueling in the Old South*. College Station, TX: Texas A. & M. University Press, 1980.

Wyatt-Brown, B. *Southern Honour*. New York: Oxford University Press, 1982.

Young, W. *Community Service Orders*. Cambridge: Cambridge University Press, 1981.

Chapter 11

Practical and philosophical dilemmas in cross-cultural research: the future of comparative crime history?

Bronwyn Morrison[1]

Recently we have witnessed the growing use of cross-cultural comparative research techniques across many social science disciplines, criminology (and crime history) being no exception. However, while comparative methodologies have become increasingly popular with criminologists and crime historians, this growth in popularity has sometimes occurred in the absence of a broader appreciation of the problems and issues confronting cross-cultural comparative research. As crime historians enter into the international domain of comparative research in greater numbers, it is now both timely and necessary to explore the wider practical and philosophical implications inherent in cross-cultural historical research, especially if we hope to avoid some of the methodological dilemmas congenital in previous inter-cultural analyses.

This chapter will explore why we have seen the recent expansion of cross-cultural analyses within the social sciences, and will preliminarily examine some of the problems inherent in comparative methodologies with particular reference to crime history. Questions will be raised about how we should go about doing comparative crime history, who should carry out comparative research, and what we can realistically hope to achieve through cross-cultural histories of crime.

Globalisation and the internationalisation of knowledge

> The modern conference resembles the pilgrimage of medieval Christendom in that it allows the participants to indulge themselves in all the pleasures and diversions of travel while appearing to be austerely bent on self-improvement. To be sure, there are certain penitential exercises to be performed – the presentation of a paper, perhaps, and certainly the listening to the papers of others. But with this excuse you journey to new and interesting places, meet new and interesting people, and form new and interesting relationships with them; exchange gossip and confidences ... yet, at the end of it all, return home with an enhanced reputation for seriousness of mind. (Lodge, 1985: 1)

One might legitimately argue that David Lodge's fictional depiction of the 'modern conference' is somewhat divorced from the actual realties of international conference attendance. Certainly the concomitant stresses that accompany the international conference – jet lag, prolonged bouts of turbulence and the formidable threat of deep vein thrombosis, for instance – can often overshadow the 'pleasures' in the mind of the attendee. However, what Lodge touches on, and what I wish to develop more fully, is the notion of intellectual travel and the apparent system of knowledge exchange engendered by the international conference.

Almost two decades on from the publication of *Small World* the modern academic environment seems to have shrunk even further than Lodge anticipated. Indeed, the increased use of Internet facilities, coupled together with the proliferation of international journals, societies and conferences, has generated a growing awareness of academic work across the globe, and has enhanced opportunities for both cross-cultural collaboration and comparative research (see Johnson and Barak-Glantz, 1983; Sztompka, 1990; Gareau, 1985 quoted in Sztompka, 1990; Nelken, 1994, 1997; Heiland *et al.*, 1990; Karstedt, 2001, 2002).[2] In this sense, the contemporary academic community can indeed be described as occupying a 'small world'.

This academic shrinkage has not occurred in isolation, and can be viewed as part of a broader process of social contraction, as Sztompka notes, 'the social world has literally shrunk' (Sztompka, 1990: 51). Commentators have generally attributed this intellectual 'shrinkage' to the rising processes of internationalisation said to be engulfing the globe, whereby national ideologies are collapsing, giving way to a new globalised appreciation of the social world (Albrow, 1990; Findlay, 1999; Teune, 1990). Implicit in this purported rise in 'globalised appreciation' is the belief that people across the world are actually becoming more uniform and alike. As Sztompka asserts, 'Cultural experiences, ways of life and social conditions become more alike – and even if they remain different – the knowledge of foreign experiences, ways of life, social conditions – become more accessible – through travel, tourism, mass media, personal contacts' (Sztompka, 1990: 52).

Teune explains this process of cultural uniformisation through the use of 'The Convergence Theory', arguing that cultural convergence was the predictable outcome of new global technologies and methods of production (Teune, 1990: 52). Similarly Giddens holds that globalisation inevitably – albeit superficially – leads to a high degree of 'cultural standardisation' (Giddens, 2002: xxiv). An often exploited, but nonetheless useful, example of this 'convergence' in cultural experiences can be observed within the fast-food industry. Take, for instance, McDonald's, whose website once claimed, 'If you visit McDonald's anywhere in the world, the great taste of our world famous French Fries and Big Mac is the same – One Taste World Wide' (quoted in Schlosser, 2002: 279). Wherever in the world one consumes a Big Mac, then the taste and cultural experience ought (in theory at least) to be the same. As Scholsser asserts, the fast-food industry, along with other culturally transforming enter-prises such as the fashion industry, are helping to create 'a homogenised international culture' (Schlosser, 2002: 229).

Undoubtedly, as more people participate in global culture through the consumption of global tastes and fashions, and as more people travel outside their home country or alternatively vicariously participate in other cultures via the mass media coverage of world events from their own armchair, it appears the cultural gap between countries is diminishing. Certainly, it is fair to conclude that countries are no longer 'closed systems' (Teune, 1990: 52), as culture has become a commodity to be purchased, imported, exported and exchanged.

Today we often find that culture itself can no longer be solely conceived as a geographically bound entity, for a new unfixed chimerical global culture has emerged to occupy the vague and illusive new territories of the global context. A plethora of expressions has arisen to accommodate these new global arrangements, as today's societies are increasingly described as subsystems, being merely components in a bigger all-encompassing global community. We are said to be living in a 'single-network era' (Tilly, 1984), within a 'global information society' (Giddens, 2002: 78), being participants in a 'closely inter-linked world system' (Sztompka, 1990: 53; Wallerstein, 1974, 1980) and members of a vast 'global village' (McLuhon, 1964).

Many of today's social problems are increasingly being perceived in global terms. As Oyen notes, 'a national crisis is seldom merely national anymore' (Oyen, 1990: 2). Indeed, as the 'World Summit in Sustainable Development' recently held in Johannesburg demonstrated, hitherto local ecological and socio-economic problems have been reconstituted as global concerns, with the issues of 'global warming' and 'global poverty' becoming firmly affixed to the international agenda (see *The Times*, 28 August 2002: 13, 16). The crime problem, too, has become globalised. As Findlay asserts, crime is now seen as a 'global issue' and a 'world-wide problem', which necessarily requires 'global responsibility' (Findlay, 1999: 3, 10). Certainly, there seems to be a growing awareness that crime can no longer be confined within national boundaries, but instead transcends geographical borders and cultural barriers.

We have also seen the birth of new forms of crime made possible by the process of globalisation itself. Nelken, for example, draws attention to 'transnational' and 'cross-border' crimes now attracting academic attention, offering drug trafficking, money laundering and toxic waste disposal as evidence of these new global dimensions of crime (Nelken, 1994: 220–1). (In light of recent events, we could perhaps also add human trafficking and international terrorism to the list.) For Giddens these crimes represent the 'dark side' of globalisation (Giddens, 2002: xvi), as he acknowledges that the economic progress achieved through globalisation has come at the price of new global vulnerabilities and risks, whereby national boundaries now provide little protection from the threat of terrorism and other organised forms of crime (Giddens, 2002).

The rise of 'global' problems apparently necessitates global action, as the capacity to solve world problems is increasingly perceived to lie beyond the scope of any one nation state: as Giddens succinctly puts it, 'a globalising era demands global responses' (Giddens, 2002: 78). It is of little surprise, then, that in the last few decades we have seen the proliferation of aid societies and charities such as World Vision, Oxfam and Greenpeace, which are global in scope (Giddens, 2002: xxv). In terms of crime, we have also witnessed the development of transnational policing (Sheptycki, 1997; Karstedt, 2002) and seen the recent evolution of the International Criminal Court. In addition to these new international or transnational forums to combat crime, as Kartsedt has observed, modern crime policies are often transmitted on a global scale and travel from nation to nation, and although sometimes altering shape en route, often exhibit remarkable durability during their travels. For example, CCTV, Neighbourhood Watch and private prisons have been introduced around the world in notably similar forms (Karstedt, 2002: 114). This ability to transport crime policies, however, is somewhat dependent on the belief that around the world we are all becoming more alike, allowing 'transtheoretical meanings' (Sztompka, 1990: 52) to become available, which in turn enable the interchange and transportation of concepts, policies and solutions to crime problems.[3]

Accepting this perspective, the upsurge in cross-cultural comparative research in recent decades can be understood as a product of cultural convergence, whereby academics share ideas and increasingly occupy what Karstedt terms 'epistemic communities' (Karstedt, 2002: 113) based on common understandings. As Martin Albrow deduces, 'sociologists are adopting a global perspective ... precisely because globalism means they can no longer seek to explain processes within their own countries by reference to internal conditions' (Albrow, 1990: 11). In this sense, its seems researchers no longer hold the freedom to choose cross-cultural methodologies, but are compelled to do so owing to the inescapable interconnectedness imposed by new global arrangements.

Globalisation and the localisation of knowledge

In contrast to this line of argument, however, is the notion that while globalisation may encourage the adoption of a 'homogenised' global culture, this is merely a superficial veneer, as most cultures today are far from monolithic (Giddens, 2002; Godfrey, 2002). For Giddens, the more 'profound' effect of globalisation is not the removal of cultural boundaries, but rather the capacity of globalisation to produce greater local diversity. This 'push-down effect' of globalisation, as Giddens terms it, tends to promote a renewal of cultural identities in stark opposition to any homogenised 'global' culture. 'Globalisation' he asserts 'not only pulls upwards, but also pushes downwards, creating new pressures for local autonomy ... the nation becomes not only too small to solve big problems, but also too large to solve the small ones' (Giddens, 2002: 13). Globalisation therefore encourages local nationalism, which evolves to occupy the local context abandoned by the nation state.

Along a similar vein, Lowenthal argues that the modern cultural climate, with its concomitant anxieties and vulnerabilities, causes people to nostalgically latch onto their culturally diverse pasts as a means to resolve or buffer feelings of concern; 'nostalgia', he argues, 'reaffirms identities bruised by recent turmoil' (Lowenthal, 1985: 13). The preservation of the past, he further asserts, has now become a 'national crusade' whereby nations are increasingly taking ownership of their cultural heritage in order to conserve national identity (Lowenthal, 1985: 44). Indeed, many governments today have nationalised their nation's past by criminalising pillage and excavation by foreign archaeologists and collectors, demanding the return of heritage items previously plundered (Lowenthal, 1985: 46). Far from surrendering to the apparent onslaught of a homogenous global culture, then, we increasingly see pockets of resistance appearing which seek to privilege cultural identities and distinctions.

Godfrey, furthermore, argues that we are entering an era of 'global postmodern fracture' (Godfrey, 2002), whereby globalisation has caused the shatter of collective identities and explanations. This, Godfrey concludes, ought to be heralded as good news by those of us who wish to engage in cross-cultural comparative research, as the fragmented life of postmodernity surely multiplies opportunities to compare the resulting pieces: whether these be countries, communities, or other sub-groupings. However, as Godfrey rightly acknowledges, the postmodern context also tends to affect not only whom we study, but also how we study, by undermining the possibility of achieving any universal theories or explanations. In short, while postmodernity increases the potential units for comparison, it simultaneously reduces the possibility of explaining what connects them, and could potentially lead social science into the trap of radical relativism (a point we will return to below).

Postmodern uncertainties aside, however, we can see that globalisation encourages comparative work in two different ways. Firstly, it emphasises cultural convergence thereby compelling researchers to look beyond national boundaries for cultural similarities. Secondly – and somewhat paradoxically – the 'push-down' effect of globalisation leads to the renewal of cultural variation and national identities, creating new niches of cultural uniqueness ripe for comparison on the basis of difference. As Findlay notes, this represents the 'janus-faced nature' of globalisation, which 'unites, delineates, internationalises and localises' (Findlay, 1990: 3). At any rate, social science, or any academic discipline (including history), does not exist in a social vacuum, and has undeniably been affected by these social developments. An entirely new rhetoric has arisen to accommodate these changes with terms such as cross-national, cross-societal, cross-cultural and transnational all becoming a ubiquitous feature of modern academic discourse (Oyen, 1990). In addition to this rising rhetoric, certain methodologies have become increasingly fashionable, particularly cross-cultural comparative research.

As more academics travel to foreign conferences, it has now become almost a matter of intellectual etiquette to integrate some comparative aspect into conference presentations. Indeed it seems conferences are increasingly geared towards this end, adopting themes that place explicit emphasis on cross-cultural work and discussion.[4] This trend is by no means confined to British academia, as I found when I travelled to a New

Zealand Historical Association Conference in 2001, titled 'Connections from Local to Global'.[5] Preparing my paper for this conference, I found my research on nineteenth-century English media representations of female inebriation inadequate for this cross-cultural fixture, and felt obliged to integrate a comparative component into my research via the introduction of Australian and New Zealand media sources.

A cross-cultural comparative anecdote

Having little experience of comparative research, I adopted a formula akin to making a cake with no recipe, haphazardly combining my international ingredients together, hoping something coherent would result. As I quickly discovered, however, comparative research was more difficult than I had anticipated. Owing to time constraints, I was forced to sample the Australian and New Zealand newspaper sources, predicting appropriate time periods for analysis on the basis of my English data. However, after sampling several years of newspapers, I found little material on female drunkenness, with literally no level of description in the reports: overall a situation very different to my English data. What was I to conclude from this disparity? Was drunkenness simply not a problem in the late nineteenth-century South Pacific? Did women in Australia and New Zealand not drink, or get drunk? Alternatively, was female drunkenness so common that it was not considered particularly novel or newsworthy? Or perhaps there was an error in my methodological recipe: maybe I had selected the wrong years or the wrong papers for analysis? The possibilities seemed endless.

In the end, I ignored these problems and attempted to ice over the cracks in my research cake, fudging the distinctions between the different countries as I went. In reality my paper was intrinsically English-based, with some Australian and New Zealand research added in. I did not attempt to comment on cultural differences, but rather ignored the fact that these differences existed. On delivering the paper, I discovered that my predominantly English research findings were not directly transferable to the New Zealand context, learning that historical developments in New Zealand did not automatically replicate those of England. I had effectively – albeit unconsciously – made assumptions and predictions about New Zealand based on my experience of the English context. The result was that, rather than making my research more accessible and palatable to my audience, I had made it seemingly irrelevant.

This experience of comparative research raised a host of doubts and questions for me about the entire nature of comparative enquiry, in particular: ie why conduct comparative research? What are we really hoping to achieve through comparative analysis? Are we merely trying to secure invites to international conferences, pander to foreign audiences and enjoy research trips to pleasant locations, or is there a more theoretically sound rationale for undertaking comparative work? Are we looking to locate commonalities or differences? Are we trying to generate universal theories or theories of diversity? Furthermore, how should we effectively go about doing comparative research? How should we select the countries for analysis, and what kinds of rationale should inform this choice? Finally, who qualifies for comparative research? Must a researcher be sufficiently grounded in all the cultures to be studied – indeed, what counts as 'sufficient grounding'? Or, alternatively, should such research ideally be a collaborate effort between native researchers in each of the countries to be studied?

It is to these issues which we now turn, although it should be noted from the outset that simple answers to such questions are rarely attainable. Indeed, rather than offering straightforward solutions, the field of cross-cultural comparative research is inundated with a litany of debates about the practice, nature and philosophical implications of comparative work. It is the exploration of these debates which will form the crux of the following discussion.

The nature of comparative research

It is first necessary to establish what is meant by the term 'comparative research.' While this might appear to be a relatively straightforward question, commentators seldom agree on the nature of comparative enquiry, meaning that there are a number of competing definitions available. Jupp, for example, defines comparative research as 'the selection and analysis of cases which are similar in known ways and which differ in other ways, with a view to formulating or testing hypotheses' (Jupp, 2001: 45). Jupp's broad notion of comparative methodology thus seemingly applies to all forms of social research where any attempt at comparison is made; be it between different time periods, different individual cases, different sources or different cultures. If we accept this broad definition, then, we would also have to accept that we probably already use comparative methodologies throughout our research. This being the case, it would logically follow that comparative methods – whether we are comparing different individuals or societies – are basically the same, meaning that cross-cultural analyses do not merit the creation of new methodologies, nor require any special methodological consideration (Oyen, 1990).

This definition, however, is not without rivals. Contrary to Jupp, Johnson and Barak-Glantz define comparative work as something quite different to standard social science research, arguing that comparative research is restricted to cross-cultural forms, where countries act as the unit of analysis (Johnson and Barak-Glantz, 1983). Furthermore they argue that cross-cultural research signals a new 'scientific approach and an exercise in macro analysis ... where the purposes and meaning of a given activity are seen to be derived from the broad setting in which they are located' (Johnson and Barak-Glantz, 1983: 7). This definition is notably narrower than Jupp's, and suggests that comparative research does not merely involve the extension of normal social science methodologies to new forums, but instead signals a departure from old research practices. As Beirne argues, cross-cultural work is not simply a matter of transporting the tenets of any national discipline to other cultures; it must necessarily involve the reconfiguring and restructuring of disciplines and theories to fit the bigger picture (Beirne, 1983a). This is reiterated by Teune, who asserts that comparative work is 'a thing apart' from national disciplines, 'residing in disciplinary sub-fields' (Teune, 1990: 39). If we choose to favour this narrower definition, then, it seems we should direct some thought to the methodologies and problems to which this research gives rise.

Methodological implications

So, moving on from these definitional issues, how should we actually conduct comparative research? Cross-cultural comparative research continues to take several different forms, ranging from large statistical macro-analyses of international crime rates (favoured by criminologists), to the 'single-culture' studies (typically favoured by historians) where two countries are independently studied then compared, leading to conclusions of 'we do it this way, they do it that way' (Beirne, 1983a: 21). Both approaches have been criticised. With regard to the latter, Beirne argues that these studies miss the true spirit of comparative work, and provide only a shallow cross-cultural analysis which restricts the scope for theorising (Beirne, 1983a). Conversely, Nelken critiques the former large macro-level analyses, which he argues are 'over-ambitious' because they fail to adequately accommodate cultural variation, and while allowing for grand theorising, do so only on a very superficial level (Nelken, 1994: 227). To overcome this problem, Nelken advocates less ambitious analyses which look to include only two or three countries at a time (Nelken, 1994).

If we can overcome these initial obstacles, how are we then to select the countries for analysis, and what should inform this choice? Both Teune and Oyen agree that whatever we do by way of cross-cultural research, our comparisons must be 'theoretically justified' (Oyen, 1990: 3; Teune, 1990: 45). What this actually means in practice, however, remains ambiguous, although it is clear that both authors ideally believe that some greater force must lie behind comparative research than mere convenience. Nevertheless, Oyen freely admits that practical pressures, more often than not, govern most cross-cultural work (Oyen, 1990). Certainly it would be naive to ignore that in reality research decisions are frequently guided by issues of funding, time constraints, proximity and personal contacts, rather than being principally guided by any higher intellectual rationale. Cross-cultural investigations are, after all, an undeniably expensive undertaking, and for this reason alone, practical considerations will more than likely continue to outweigh theoretical ones.

Having selected the countries for analysis, who should subsequently undertake comparative research? Nelken recommends that comparative researchers should ideally have a 'genuine first-hand familiarity' with the countries they wish to study (Nelken, 1994: 228). This is supported by English philosopher Peter Winch, who argues that a comparative understanding can only be achieved by fully participating in the life of another culture, through immersing ourselves in the behaviour, language and systems of meaning of a society (Winch, 1966). Admittedly, for the historian, such criteria impose an obvious problem, as active participation in historical societies is barred from the outset. As Lowenthal observes, '... we can no more slip back to the past than leap forward to the future, save in imaginative reconstruction, yesterday is forever barred to us; we have only attenuated memories and fragmentary chronicles of prior experience and can only dream of escaping the confines of the present' (Lowenthal, 1985: 4). Taking this argument to its logical conclusion, however, would surely mean that we could never legitimately undertake historical – or indeed any – research at all. Therefore in order to avoid this academic nihilism we must accept that while some foreknowledge of the history and culture of countries is a prerequisite for comparative research, this need not always amount to active participation.

On the other hand, as Nelken points out, a native researcher may in fact be too over-familiar with a culture, being thus unable to identify what is particularly singular about their own society (Nelken, 1994). So it appears, therefore, that a researcher should be neither unrehearsed nor over-rehearsed in the cultures they wish to compare, although for the time being any real distinctions between under-familiarity and over-familiarity remain indiscrete. This sense of confusion and inability to draw distinctions seems to be part and parcel of the comparative research process.

Certainly there appears to be considerable disjunction amongst social scientists on defining and conducting comparative research. There seem to be no hard and fast rules of good practice, with comparative researchers rarely offering much insight into the rationales and guiding principles of their work. Indeed, there is seldom any explanation as to why we undertake comparative research at all.

Ontological considerations: the 'unity' vs. 'diversity' dichotomy

So why conduct comparative research? And what are we really hoping to achieve through cross-cultural comparative analyses? There appear prima facie to be two opposing aims of comparative research, namely the search for uniformity and the search for diversity. Whether comparative authors are looking to locate commonalities or differences, hoping to generate universal social theories or theories of diversity, is not always obvious. For theorists like Galtung, the sole purpose of cross-cultural comparisons is the generation of a 'universal social science' (Galtung, 1990: 108), whereby international variation becomes condensed and reconciled under a master umbrella theory. Similarly Karstedt, among others, envisions the evolution of a 'global criminology' (Karstedt, 2001: 303) based on universal understandings of crime and culture (Gottfredson and Hirschi, 1990). Beirne also accepts that the quest for universals drives comparative research, noting that the primary goal of comparativists is 'the construction of cross-cultural generalisation apart from cultural variation in meanings and values' (Beirne, 1983b: 386). In this sense, comparative research seeks to close the culture gap between different countries in the pursuit of all-encompassing social theories – a pursuit apparently furthered by processes of social contraction and the global convergence of culture.

On the contrary, however, Sztompka argues that we have moved away from this more 'traditional' style of comparative work, suggesting that in today's globalised world system, where people and cultures are becoming more alike, aims of uniformity have now given way to new aims of diversity. As Sztompka muses, 'What really becomes baffling and problematic is the preservation of enclaves of uniqueness amid growing homogeneity and uniformity' (Sztompka, 1990: 55). Although other commentators such as Giddens, Findlay and Godfrey might be less baffled by these pockets of diversity, they would perhaps also allow, as Sztompka does, that in this environment the point of comparative research is now 'to unravel the peculiarities of a given country … by contrasting it with others' (Sztompka, 1990: 55). In this scenario comparative research is transformed from a macro-level statistical-based enterprise into an exercise of hermeneutics, where the desire for qualitative description and interpretation of difference overtakes the desire for scientific universal truths.

In reality, however, it appears that much comparative research continues to waver between these two extremes, seemingly unsure of whether the point of comparison is to generate theories of divergence or theories of uniformity. The result is a muddling situation where it is not always apparent what the true object and predicted outcome of the research will be. Indeed, as Nelken alleges of international crime comparisons, it is often unclear whether we are examining culture as a means for explaining disparate crime rates, or whether we are, in fact, looking at crime in different countries as clues for making sense of culture (Nelken, 1994).

Whether comparative work seeks to identify universals or divergences is important nonetheless because the goal of comparisons will determine the types of methodology used: if the aim to is locate similarities, then we must examine a similar thing within different contexts, in other words we must search for functional equivalents in foreign settings (Karstedt, 2001). On the other hand, if we are looking to understand divergence, then we must accept that meanings are locally derived and look to interpret disparate practices in different contexts (Nelken, 1994). Each position carries serious philosophical implications both about the way we construct knowledge of humankind and the core nature of humankind itself.

If the aim is to devise universal theories based on similarities we must look to identify what Newman terms 'equivalent meanings' in different cultures (Newman, 1977). In doing so we assume that conceptual differences between countries can be resolved. We assume based on our knowledge of our country that similar things must exist elsewhere. We assume that definitions of social things are not culture-bound and may be shaken loose of their cultural roots and studied internationally. We effectively make assumptions about other cultures using our culture as the norm or baseline of comparison. As Nelken notes, 'an account of another culture is never an account from nowhere' (Nelken, 1994: 226). In this sense any attempt to identify cross-cultural similarities becomes tantamount to cultural imperialism (Beirne, 1983a), for we effectively judge sameness and divergence from a position of cultural superiority, assuming that our own country represents the norm. But what if functional equivalents cannot be found? In terms of historical research how do we accommodate changing definitions of the phenomenon we wish to study? What if definitions change at different rates and in different directions across different countries? What if, as is often the case, there is simply no common definition of the problem or thing we wish to study? And what bearing has this on comparative research?

Surely if we were to attempt to pursue our cross-cultural comparisons in the face of these obstacles we would be merely comparing the 'uncomparable' and trying to make sense where in fact no sense exists. Dubbed by Sztompka 'the problem of incommensurability' (Sztompka, 1990: 48), this lack of definitional 'fit' raises some broader questions about the entire nature of social enquiry. Cross-cultural work aimed at identifying similarity *ipso facto* assumes that all human meaning systems must have something in common (Berger and Kellner, 1981). This may, however, not be the case. As Beirne ponders, perhaps 'social behaviour is not of the same epistemic order as the behaviour of forces, such as celestial bodies in a physical system?' (Beirne, 1983a: 34). Perhaps human beings do not obey universal laws and are not necessarily the same the world over. Possibly, as Teune proposes, there exists 'infinite human diversity' (Teune, 1990: 47), which defies explanatory forces. As Beirne surmises, 'only with considerable discomfort can social behaviour be compressed into the artificial straitjacket of a generalisation in the case of cross-cultural analysis …' (Beirne, 1983a: 34).

The possibility of comparison aimed at difference, however, seems equally untenable. If we assume, as commentators like Beirne would appear to have us do, that concepts and things are completely culture-bound, then, as Archer notes, 'alien beliefs can never really be decoded, as they make sense only in that specific culture and are neither translatable nor transferable to other cultures' (Archer, 1990: 20). In the case of history this problem becomes confounded by the additional analytical layer imposed by time, as historians intent on undertaking cross-cultural analysis must jump across time periods as well as geographical borders (Teune, 1990; Newman, 1977). As Lowenthal notes, 'However faithfully we preserve, however authentically we restore, however deeply we immerse ourselves in bygone times, life back then was based on ways of being and believing incommensurable with our own … we cannot help but view and celebrate the past through present day lenses' (Lowenthal, 1985: xvi).

This position, typically defined as 'cultural relativism', therefore denies the possibility of comparative research from the outset (Beirne, 1983b). As Melossi states, 'the problem of comparison is first and foremost a problem of translation' (Melossi, 2001:403). He concedes that any translation is itself impossible as 'any term, even the simplest is embedded within a cultural context … that gives it its meaning' (Melossi, 2001: 404). More problematic still (even if we were able to appreciate a particular concept in its native context) is how we then set about translating this in order to report back to the culture from which we have come. We almost certainly enter into the endless problem of trying to understand the translations (Beirne, 1983b). As Archer contends, if meaning is entirely a matter of local cultural construction, social scientists (and of course crime historians) would become 'eternal tourists but ones who could hazard no generalisations about their trips' (Archer, 1990: 19). More critically, she contends that if we deny the possibility of human universals it logically follows that we 'abolish the human subject altogether' causing us to enter into a phase of 'theoretical anarchism' whereby the whole discipline of social science (and indeed history) is doomed, as the answer to every question would simply be 'it depends'. As Leavitt argues, the pursuit of knowledge in this event would thus fall victim to 'the problem of solipsism', where meanings are viewed entirely as the product of individual creation, thus leading us back to an epistemological era of 'provincial mysticism' where rain is produced by dances and economical progress by 'rugged individual efforts' (Leavitt, 1990: 24).

The future of comparative crime history?

So where does this leave comparative crime history? Is the future of cross-cultural historiography doomed from the outset, or can a case for comparative history be made? What potential relevance do these late modern (and at times postmodern) discussions of globalisation hold for the study of the past? And what possible bearing do these polarised arguments of 'unity' vs. 'diversity' have on the future of comparative historiography? For authors such as Karstedt, these debates are not only viewed as insignificant but also dismissed as a hindrance to the development of social knowledge per se. As Karstedt states, 'the dichotomy "unity" vs. "diversity" does not further the tasks of cross-cultural criminology' (Karstedt, 2001: 302). Further still, she asserts that 'any tendencies towards such dichotomies are inimical to the development of the discipline' (Karstedt, 2001: 302). But are these dichotomies really as hostile to the advancement of comparative crime history as Karstedt implies? I would argue not, for in two quite separate ways the universal/ divergence debate – and its relation to emerging global arrangements and cultural trends – can be seen as both intrinsic and advantageous to cross-cultural historical enquiry.

Firstly, as Lowenthal suggests, in the vulnerable climate of today's globalised society, we utilise the past in different ways, both trying to forge common roots between nations to alleviate feelings of international insecurity and vulnerability, while conversely attempting to preserve cultural identity through the nationalisation of cultural pasts (Lowenthal, 1985). Whether a historian wishes to emphasise common historical heritage or alternatively carve out distinct cultural pasts will necessarily impact on their analysis and subsequent findings. As Mandelbaum notes, 'whatever "truth" a historical work contains is relative to the conditioning processes under which it arose and can only be understood with references to those processes' (Mandelbaum, 1967: 19). In this sense, processes of globalisation and internationalisation, with their concomitant 'push-down' and homogenisation impacts on culture, are vital to understanding why historians construct national and cross-cultural pasts the way they do.

Secondly, and possibly more importantly, cross-cultural comparisons are frequently an intrinsic part of the past, given that historically contemporaries undeniably made comparisons between different countries and cultures. Such comparisons frequently sought to connect, delineate and order cultural identities. In nineteenth-century colonial New Zealand, for example, we find evidence of attempts to retain as well as sever cultural links with Great Britain.[6]

In addition, across nineteenth-century Europe and the colonies, there was an observable awareness of cross-cultural developments, with a nation's degree of advancement and civilisation being constantly reassessed in contrast to other nations – a practice particularly noticeable in the case of national crime rates, punishment regimes and legislative development (see Pratt, 2002: chapters 3 and 4). In the case of Victorian drunkenness legislation, for example, international comparisons were rife.[7] As McLeod has noted, English legal reformers regularly invoked comparisons with European licensing laws in order to illustrate the diffident nature of British law and force legislative progress (Macleod, 1967: 235). Interestingly, these comparisons were used to illustrate national divergence in order to push for higher levels of legal congruity between different countries, with the suggestion that one's own legislation was lagging behind more 'progressive' countries, serving as a catalyst for action.

As we see, therefore, the 'unity' vs. 'divergence' dichotomy is not merely an artefact of late modern academic debate, but is in fact an inescapable element of our cultural pasts. Certainly the different driving forces behind these contemporary comparisons – frequently overlooked by historians – ought to furnish a rich feeding ground for future research in comparative crime history. For these reasons, modern debates about cross-cultural research are of central importance to studies in comparative crime history, and while admittedly revealing many methodological and philosophical dilemmas for the cross-cultural historian, also pave the way to new opportunities for studies in crime history, where the potentialities of travelling simultaneously across time and cultural space remain an exciting area for future exploration.

> 'But the great difficulty is this,' interrupted the Psychologist. 'You can move about all directions in space, but you cannot move about in Time.' [The Time Traveller replied] 'That is the germ of my great discovery. But you are wrong to say we cannot move about in Time.'
> (H. G. Wells, *The Time Machine*, 1895: 10)

Notes

1. This research has been sponsored as part of the Bright Future Scholarship Scheme. The author would like to thank the Foundation of Research, Science and Technology in New Zealand for their ongoing support.
2. See, for example, the following journals: *International Journal of Sociology and Social Policy, The International Annals of Criminology, International Journal of Comparative and Applied Criminal Justice, International Criminal Justice Review, International Sociology* (Karstedt, 2001); conferences: 'International Feminist Conference on Women, Law and Social Control', Mont Gabriel, Quebec, 18–21 July 1991 (Hahn-Rafter and Heidensohn, 1995), 'How Does Crime Policy Travel?', Keele University, 21–22 June 2001, 'Comparative Crime Histories', British Academy Conference, Keele University, 16 July 2002, 'Crossing Borders', British Society of Criminology Conference, 17–20 July 2002; societies: International Sociological Association (ISA) (Albrow and King, 1990), International Research Associates (INRA), International Social Science Council (ISSC) and International Federation of Data Organisations (IFDO) (Scheuch, 1990).
3. However, as Stan Cohen argues, the transport of crime control policies is often not as benign or benevolent as Karstedt suggests, often constituting a form of 'malignant colonialism' whereby unsuccessful and obsolete western crime policies are transported regardless of their failure in the western context to Third World societies (Cohen, 1982: 98).
4. See 'conferences' above, note 2.
5. 'Connections from Local to Global', New Zealand Historical Association Conference, Canterbury University, New Zealand, 1– 4 December 2001.
6. For example, see 'New Zealand and English ladies: a critical comparison', *The Christchurch Press*, 24 December 1904, p. 5, and Bollinger (1959: 23–7).
7. See also British and Colonial Foreign Statutes relating to the Penal and Reformatory Treatment of Habitual Inebriates (Being a Supplement to the *Report of the Inspector of the Inebriates Acts for the Year 1901* (1902)), 1903 [Cd 1747] xii, 419; Dunstan (1988: 105); McKenzie (1896: parts I–III).

References

Albrow, M. 'Introduction', in Albrow, M. and King, E. (eds), *Globalization, Knowledge and Society*. New Delhi: Sage, 1990, pp. 3–16.

Albrow, M. and King, E. (eds) *Globalization, Knowledge and Society*. New Delhi: Sage, 1990.

Archer, M. 'Resisting the revival of relativism', in Albrow, M. and King, E. (eds), *Globalization, Knowledge and Society*. New Delhi: Sage, 1990, pp. 19–33.

Beirne, P. 'Generalization and its discontents: the comparative study of crime', in Johnson, E. H. and Barak-Glantz, I. (eds) *Comparative Criminology*. New Delhi: Sage, 1983a, pp. 9–37.

Beirne, P. 'Cultural relativism and comparative criminology', *Contemporary Crises*, 7, 1983b, pp. 71–391.

Berger, P. and Kellner, H. *Sociology Reinterpreted*. Garden City, NY: Anchor, 1981.

Bollinger, C. *Grog's Own Country*. Wellington: Price Milburn, 1956.

Cohen, S. 'Western crime control models in the Third World: benign or malignant', *Research in Law, Deviance and Social Control*, 4, 1982, pp. 85–119.

Dunstan, D. 'Boozers and woozers', in Burgmann, V. and Lee, J. (eds), *Constructing a Culture*. Fitzroy, Victoria: McPhee Gribble/Penguin Books, 1988, pp. 96–123.

Findlay, M. *The Globalisation of Crime: Understanding Transitional Relationships in Context*. Cambridge: Cambridge University Press, 1999.

Galtung, J. 'Theory formation in social research: a plea for pluralism', in Oyen, E. (ed.), *Comparative Methodology: Theory and Practice in International Social Research*. New Delhi: Sage, 1990, pp. 96–112.

Giddens, A. *Runaway World*. London: Profile Books, 2002.

Godfrey, B., *Do You Have Plane Spotters in New Zealand? Issues in Comparative Crime History at the Turn of Modernity*, paper presented at the British Academy Comparative Crime Histories Conference, Keele University, 16 July 2002 (see expanded version in Chapter 1, of this volume).

Gottfredson, M. and Hirschi, T. *A General Theory of Crime*. Stanford, CA: Stanford University Press, 1990.

Hahn-Rafter, N. and Heidensohn, F. 'Introduction: the development of feminist perspectives on crime', in Hahn-Rafter, N. and Heidensohn, F. (eds), *International Feminist Perspectives in Criminology: Engendering a Discipline*. Buckingham: Open University Press, 1995, pp. 1–14.

Heiland, H., Shelley, L. and Katoh, H. *Crime and Control in Comparative Perspectives*. Berlin: Walter De Gruyter, 1990.

Johnson, E. H. and Barak-Glantz, I. 'Introduction', in Johnson, E. H. and Barak-Glantz, I. (eds), *Comparative Criminology*. New Delhi: Sage, 1983, pp. 7–17.

Jupp, V. 'Comparative method', in McLaughlin, E. and Muncie, J. (eds), *The Sage Dictionary of Criminology*. London: Sage, 2001, pp. 45–6.

Karstedt, S. 'Comparing cultures, comparing crime: challenges, prospects and problems for a global criminology', *Crime, Law and Social Change*, 36, 2001, pp. 85-308.

Karstedt, S. 'Durkheim, Tarde and beyond: the global travel of crime policies', *Criminal Justice*, 2, 2, 2002, pp. 111–23.

Leavitt, G. 'Relativism and cross-cultural criminology: a critical analysis', *Journal of Research in Crime and Delinquency*, 28, 1, 1990, pp. 5–29.

Lodge, D. *Small World*. London: Penguin Books, 1985.

Lowenthal, D. *The Past is Foreign Country*. Cambridge: Cambridge University Press, 1985.

McKenzie, F. *Sober By Act of Parliament*. London: Swan Sonnenschein & Co., 1896.

McLeod, R. 'The edge of hope: social policy and chronic alcoholism 1870–1900', *Journal of the History of Medicine*, 22, 3, 1967, pp. 215–45.

McLuhon, M. *Understanding Media*. New York: McGraw-Hill, 1964.

Mandelbaum, M. *The Problem of Historical Knowledge: An Answer to Relativism*. London: Harper Touchbooks, 1967.

Melossi, D. 'The cultural embeddedness of social control: reflections on the comparisons of Italian and North American cultures concerning punishment', *Theoretical Criminology*, 5, 4, 2001, pp. 403–24.

Nelken, D. 'Whom can you trust? The future of comparative criminology', in Nelken, D. (ed.), *The Futures of Criminology*. London: Sage, 1994, pp. 220–43.

Nelken, D. 'Understanding criminal justice comparatively', in Maguire, M., Morgan, R. and Reiner, R. (eds), *The Oxford Handbook of Criminology*. Oxford: Oxford University Press, 1997 edn, pp. 559–73.

'New Zealand and English ladies: a critical comparison', *The Christchurch Press*, 24 December 1904, p. 5.

Newman, G. 'Problems of method in comparative criminology', *International Journal of Comparative and Applied Criminal Justice*, 1, 1977, pp. 17–31.

Oyen, E. 'The imperfection of comparisons', in Oyen, E. (ed.), *Comparative Methodology: Theory and Practice in International Social Research*. New Delhi: Sage, 1990, pp. 1–18.

Pratt, J. *Punishment and Civilisation*. New Delhi: Sage, 2002.

Scheuch, E. 'The development of comparative research: towards causal explanations', in Oyen, E. (ed.), *Comparative Methodology: Theory and Practice in International Social Research*. New Delhi: Sage, 1990, pp. 19–37.

Schlosser, E. *Fast Food Nation: What the All-American Meal is Doing to the World*. London: Penguin Books, 2002.

Sheptycki, J. 'Insecurity, risk suppression and segregation', *Theoretical Criminology*, 1, 3, 1997, pp. 303–15.

'Summit calls for cut in farm subsidies', *The Times*, 29 August 2002, p.13.

Sztompka, P. 'Conceptual frameworks in comparative inquiry: divergent or convergent?', in Albrow, M. and King, E. (eds), *Globalization, Knowledge and Society*. New Delhi: Sage, 1990, pp. 47–58.

Teune, H. 'Comparing countries', in Oyen, E. (ed.), *Comparative Methodology: Theory and Practice in International Social Research*. New Delhi: Sage, 1990, pp. 38–62.

'The Earth Summit is not a pointless talking-shop', *The Times*, 28 August 2002, p. 16.

Tilly, C. *Big Structures, Large Processes, Huge Comparisons*. New York: Russell Sage, 1984.

Wallerstein, I. *The Modern World System I*. New York: Academic Press, 1974.

Wallerstein, I. *The Modern World System II*. New York: Academic Press, 1980.

Winch, P. 'Understanding a primitive society', *American Philosophical Quarterly*, 1, 1966, pp. 307–24.

Index

abilities, successful policing 135–6
academic property rights 7
academic shrinkage 196
academic theory, fault lines 6
accommodation industry 148
affect structure, urge for violence 45
age-related definitions, juvenile
    delinquents 112–13
aggressive masculinity 76
Albrow, Martin 199
Anderson, David 18
anomie theory, predicted increase in
    homicide 82
anonymisation, travel revolution 92, 95
Ansell, Samuel 170
anthropology, and violence 46–7
anxiety, about violent street crime 63
apologetic autobiographies 137
Archer, M. 207, 208
Army Discipline and Regulation Act
    (1879) 163–4
Arnot, Margaret 20, 39
Arrow, Charles 128, 130–1, 133, 135,
    137

Articles of War 160–1, 170
assaults, Wurttemberg (1880–1900)
    103f
auditor-general, Prussian army 165
Australian story 13
autobiographies
    nineteenth century categories 137
    policing 127–32
Axel Lund, Paul 146

Bandits 21
Bayley, David 18
Beck, U. 5
Bedford, Duke of 168
Beggs, Thomas 111
Beirne, P. 203, 207
Belgium, juvenile institutions 112, 117
biological explanations, violence 37–8
black economy, seaside resorts 148
Blackpool, policing 145–56
Blackstone, Judge 173
Blok, Anton 21
bogus policing memoirs 127
Bokkeryders 21

Bottomley, Horatio 169
boundaries, in violence history 39–44
Brierley, Ben 152
Britain
    juvenile delinquents
        criminal liability 112, 115
        institutions 117, 118
    military law (1866–1918) 159–74
    moral panic (1972) 60–1
    see also England
Britishness 13

Canler, Louis 133, 137
capital punishment 17
career success stories, police 130
carnivalesque parade 180
Carpenter, Mary 119
Cassellari, R. 133, 135
Caton, S 47
CCTV 198
celadores de la playa 153
chain gangs 188, 191
Chamberlain Committee 171, 172
charities 155, 198
charivari tradition 180, 188
Chelmsford Chronicle 57, 59, 61, 62
child abuse 37
Child Protection Act (1912) 113
Child Welfare Act (1896) 113
childhood, romantic view 114
Children Acts (1908, 1933 and 1948)
    114
Churchill, Winston 168
civilisation 4
Civilisation and Its Discontents 38
civilising process 23
    changes in punishment 16
    decline in interpersonal violence 89
    decrease in homicide 82–3
    eradication of local culture 24–5
    and masculinity 84
    shifting patterns of violent
        behaviour 20
    travel revolution 96–7
    violence history 44–5
Claude, M. 133, 134, 136, 138

clean slate reforms 191
clothing, prison 182, 183
cock fighting 181
Colchester, moral panic (1765) 57–9
colonial experience, comparing 8–9
colonial legacy 15–16
Colonies Agricole (Mettray) 117, 120
Commanders-in-Chief, military
    discipline 162, 163, 165, 167–8, 172
commissions, military 166
Committee on Prison Rules and Prison
    Dress 182
community self-policing 48
community service orders 183
community violence 43
comparative criminology
    British and American military law
        159–74
    cross-cultural research 195–210
    homicide rates 72–85
    juvenile delinquents 110–20
    moral panics 53–70
    past and future of 2–7
    policing memoirs 125–42
    policing the seaside holiday 145–56
    railway traffic and violence 89–106
    research studies 16–26
    shame, modern penal systems
        178–92
    strategies for 7–16
    violence 36–48
conferences, modern 196, 200–1
conflict resolution 78–9
conflict theories, predicted increase in
    homicide 82
Consolidating Act (1866) 117
contemporary debate, avoidance of 17
convict lease system 187, 188
The Convergence Theory 197
cop culture 125
corporal punishments, in military 164,
    166
The Corporation (Blackpool) 151, 152
The Countrey Justice 112
court of military appeals 174
courts martial 160–1, 164, 174

crime
    globalisation of 198
    surveys 21
crime control measures 57
crime fiction 139–40
crime policies, modern 198–9
crime rates *see* homicide rates
crime reporting, street crime 54
crime statistics 20, 101
crime themes 65–6
criminal justice
    centrality of nation state 19–20
    national characteristics 14
    Weisser's survey 21
criminal liability 115
criminals, familiarity with, policing
    memoirs 134–5
Crimineel Wetboek 113
critical autobiographies 137
criticisms, of police by authors 137–8
cross-border crimes 198
cross-cultural research 195–210
    comparative research
        anecdote concerning 201–2
        future of 208–10
        methodological implications
            203–5
        nature of 202–3
        ontological considerations 205–8
    globalisation
        internationalisation of
            knowledge 196–9
        localisation of knowledge
            199–201
Crowder, Enoch 170
cultural convergence 197, 200
cultural differences 1–2
cultural heritage 199–200
cultural relativism 207–8
cultural shifts 4
cultural values, shaming 183, 187, 190
culture
    criminal victimisation 14–15
    equivalent meanings 206
    importance of in explaining
        violence 45–6
    repressive functions of 45
    as social force 3
    and violence 76–7
    see also cop culture
cultures of violence 43
Cunningham, Hugh 116

The Daily News 62
Daly, Martin 37–8
Darling Report 171, 172
Darwinism, and violence 37–8
Das, V. 47
Davis, Natalie Zemon 113
Dean, Trevor 21
death penalty, military justice 174
Deflem, Mathieu 19
detection 136
Detective Anecdotes 139
detective fiction 139–40
Déviance et société 20
discernment, juvenile delinquency 112
discipline and justice, military law
    163–9
Discipline and Punish 17
disruptive forces, travel revolution
    91–2
diversity *see* universal/divergence
    debate
doli incapax 112
domestic homicide 80–1
Donzelot 119
ducking stool 180
duelling 47–8, 180
Dupin 139
Dupont Bouchat, Marie-Sylvie 19
duration, moral panics 61–2
Durkheim 82
Dyett, Edwin 169–70

Earl Marshals 160
egalitarianism, railway revolution 91
Elias, Norbert 44
elites, transnational mentalities of 48
Ellice, General Sir Charles 166
emancipation, railway revolution 91
The Emergence of Carceral Institutions 17

Emsley, Clive 18–19
England
    policing memoirs 125–42
    vigilante activities 192
    see also Colchester; London
Englishness 6, 12–13
Enlightenment 4, 5
entertainment value, policing memoirs 140
entrepreneurial skills, East End detectives 132
equivalent meanings 206
Eurocentric modernity 4–5
European integration, English distinctiveness 6
European violence history 41–2
Evans, Richard J. 17
evolutionary theory, violence 37
executions *see* military executions; public executions; state executions
exemplary autobiographies 137

familial violence 48
familiarity, as basis of comparison 8–12
families
    juvenile delinquents 118–20
    travel revolution 95
family group conferences 192
family members, killing of 74
Faralicq, René 129, 133–4, 138
fear factor
    seaside resorts 147
    violent street crime 63
female juvenile delinquents 115–16
fiction, crime and detection 139–40
fictional aspect, policing memoirs 129
Fielding, John 115–16
figuration 44–5
flogging, abolition of 164, 166
forensic knowledge, decline in homicide 77–8
formative incidents, policing memoirs 133–4
Foucauldian gaze 89
Foucault, Michel 17

France
    juvenile delinquents 112, 115
    policing memoirs 125–42
Frank, Leo 190
Freud, S. 38
Fry, James 167
Fuller, Robert 130
functional understanding, of culture 3

Galtung, J. 205
gambling, seaside resorts 149–50
Gannon, Luke 153
Garland, David 17
garotting panic 55–7
Gattrell, V.A.C. 9, 17, 20
gendarmeries 19
gender
    criminal liability 115–16
    legal practices 20
gender perspective, homicide 84
George, Duke of Cambridge 163
George Routledge and Sons 128
Georgia 185
girls, criminal liability 115
global criminology 205
globalisation
    internationalisation of knowledge 196–9
    localisation of knowledge 199–201
Golden Mile 153
Gran Casino 149–50
gun control, research into 17–18
Gurr, Robert 8, 10, 41

Habitual Criminals Act (1869) 57
Hackney Wick Academy 117
Hamon, Louis 130
Harris, Lord 169
historical time periods, moral panics 69–70
Hobbs, Dick 132, 134
Hobsbawm, Eric 21
homicide
    evolutionary theory 37
    research on 22
    social theory 81–4

homicide rates 72–85
  empirical findings 74, 75f
  explaining continuities 75–7
  explaining discontinuities 77–9
  explaining the violence that
    remains 79–81
  research into 17–18
  Wurttemberg (1880–1900) 102f
honour
  changing concepts of 78, 79, 84
  cultures of 48
  and masculinity 76
Hooligan 54
hooliganism 111
Hôpital Général 116
hostility, generated in moral panics 65
House for Progress and Education 117
House of Refuge for Orphan Girls in
  London 115–16

identity politics 12–15
Ignatieff, Michael 17
Improvement Act (1879) 151
incommensurability, problem of 207
independence, in policing memoirs
  138
Industrial and Reformatory School
  Acts (1850s and 1860s) 113
Industrial Schools Amending Act
  (1861) 117
industrialisation, predicted increase in
  homicide 82
infanticide
  16th to 20th century
    distribution of 76f
    frequency of 75f
  development of forensic knowledge
    78
  evolutionary theory 37
  time-specific homicide 77
institutional identity, police forces
  141–2
institutional loyalty, police authors
  137, 138
institutions, juvenile justice 116–18
insults, change in perception of 78

integration, travel revolution 92
internal tendencies, violence 38
international cooperation, police 19
International Criminal Court 198
international perspective, violence
  history 39–44
interpersonal violence 23, 89–90, 104–6
interpretation, policing memoirs 129
interrelatedness, of society 89
Irwin, James 184–5

Jackson, Moana 5
Jervis, Richard 133
Jevons, Thomas 119
Johnson and Barak-Glantz 203
Johnson, Eric 20
Judge Advocate General 160, 162, 163,
  164, 165, 166, 172
judicial norms, transmission of Anglo-
  attitudes 15–16
judicial statistics 20
Jupp, V. 202
justice and discipline, military law
  163–9
juvenile delinquents 110–20
  families 118–20
  institutions 116–18
  legal processes and language
    112–16
Juvenile Offenders Act (1847) 113

Karstedt, Susanne 23, 205, 208
Kaspersson, Maria 22–3
Kernan Report 171–2
Killingray, David 18
King, Peter 23
Kinloch, Lieutenant-Colonel 167–9
knowledge
  internationalisation of 196–9
  localisation of 199–201
Ku Klux Klan 188

language, juvenile delinquency
  112–16
law-breaking, moral panics 68
Lawrence, Paul 25–6

legal processes, and juvenile
    delinquents 112–16
legal systems 25–6
legitimate man hunts 133–4
legitimate violence 24
Lejeune, Philippe 129, 137
Lenman, Bruce 20
Leonards, Chris 118
Liang, Hsi-Hui 19
lifespans, moral panics 64
literary trends, policing memoirs
    140
local diversity, globalisation 199–201
Lodge, David 196
London, moral panic (1862) 55–7
Lowenthal, D. 208–9
Luc, Jean-Noël 18
Lütdke, Alf 18
lynching 184–5, 189–90

McDonalds 197
McLeod, R. 209
McLevy, J. 134
macro-level analyses 11, 203
mafia 21
Malcolm, Joyce Lee 17
male homicides 75–6
managerial mentality, policing
    memoirs 132
Mandelbaum, M. 209
Mannheim, Hermann 20, 183–4
Manual of Military Law 160, 163
Maori, challenge to Pakeha historians
    7
Maori methodology, need for 5
Margarey, Susan 113
María Christina, Queen 150
Mars, Gerald 146
Marxism 82
masculinity
    and civilising process 84
    and violence 75–7
Massachusetts Articles of War 161
Mazower, Mark 18
media
    creation of moral panics 55–65

see also crime reporting; police-press
    relationship
medical explanations, crime and
    violence 40
medical knowledge, decline in
    homicide 77–8
Mellaerts, Wim 21
Melossi, D. 207
Menius, Justus 111
Mensur 48
Metropolitan Police 130
Mettray (Colonies Agricole) 117, 120
micro-studies 11
middle class, distaste of shaming
    punishments 180–1
military
    crime histories 24
    see also soldiers
military commissions 166
military executions 161, 162
military law (1866–1918) 159–74
    background 160–2
    discipline and justice 163–9
    postwar recriminations 171–2
    total war and two systems found
        wanting 169–71
Mill, John Stuart 181
minority plea, France 112
mobilisation
    decline in interpersonal violence
        89–90
    development of weak ties 96, 97
mobility, cultures of violence 43
modernisation, decline in
    interpersonal violence 89–90
modernity
    decline of shaming punishments
        180–4
    Eurocentric 4–5
Moltke, General von 166
Monkkonnen, Eric 20
moral entrepreneurs, moral panics
    66–7
moral panics 53–70
    continuities in patterns of 62–5
    creation of 65–8

parallels in 23–4
pattern of 55–61
similarities in 61–2
youth and violence 111
Morrison, Bronwyn 22
mugging 61
municipal civilian police 19
Mutiny Act (1689) 160–1, 163

Napoleonic Code 19, 112, 113
narratives
    of improvement 130
    of violence 41, 46–7, 48
national characteristics 12–15
national data, analysing 8–12
national identity
    reaction to globalisation 199–200
    violence 40–1
nature/nurture, analysis of violence
    37–9
Neighbourhood Watch 198
Nelken, D. 203, 204, 206
neo-welfarism, juvenile justice 114–15
Netherlands, juvenile delinquents 113,
    117
New York, moral panic (1976) 59–60
New Zealand
    colonial experience of crime 8–9
    national characteristics 13–14
Nordstrom, C. 46
Northumberland, Duke of 168
Norway, juvenile delinquents 115
novels, popularity of policing memoirs
    141
Nye, Robert 20

The Observer 56
Oeconomia Christiana 111
On Duty with Inspector Field 136, 139
open personality 44
Oram, Gerard 24
the other
    possibility of comparison 2–4
    the right to study 7
The Oxford History of the Prison 17
Oyen, E. 204

Pakeha foundational myth 14
Pakeha historians, Maori challenge to
    7
parents, juvenile delinquency 119
Parker, Geoffrey 20
past, preservation of 199–200
Paterson, Alexander 182–3
Pearson, Geoffrey 54, 111
Pecqueur, Constantin 91
Peel, Sir Robert 130
Penal Codes 112, 113
penal institutions/policies,
    comparisons 17
Penitentiary House for Young
    Delinquents 117
permeability, cultures of violence 43
Pershing, General 170
Peterson, Linda 129
Philanthropic School 117
physical theories, crime and violence
    40
Pick, Daniel 20
Pilkington, Hugh 56
pillory 180
plane-spotters 1
plantation owners, disciplinary control
    185, 186
Pleasure Beach 152
poetry, expression of violence 47
police
    comparative studies 18–19
    post-Second World War English 14
police/press relationship, moral panics
    67
policing
    decline in violence 9, 10
    seaside holiday resorts 145–56
    transnational 198
Policing the Crisis 55, 60, 68
policing memoirs 125–42
    autobiographies as a genre 127–32
    fact or fiction 139–42
    publications 127f
    and self image 133–9
political interference, military
    discipline 174

postmodern fracture, global 200
postmodernists
   Eurocentric modernity 5
   historical enquiry 6
practices of violence 47–8
Pratt, John 24
pre-industrial mobility 105
Primo de Rivera dictatorship 150
Prisons Act (1865) 57
private prisons 198
privatisation, of homicide 74
property crime 20, 22, 105
protection rackets, seaside resorts 147
providential plots, loss of and interest
   in policing memoirs 141
Prussian army 165
psychohistory 38
psychology, and violence 38
public brawls 79
public executions 180, 181
punishment
   changes 16–17
   cleavage between scientific
      knowledge and bureaucratic
      experts 184
   see also corporal punishments;
      shaming punishments
push-down effect, globalisation 199,
   200

quantitative comparisons, of violence
   42

rail network (1845–1900)
   access to 94f
   development of 93f
   volume of usage 94f
railway traffic 23, 89–106
   changing mentalities 90–5
   and violence, Wurttemberg 98–104
   weak ties
      development of 95–8
      shift of interpersonal violence
         104–6
rank and file mentality, policing
   memoirs 131–2

Rasphuis 116
Rauhe Haus 117
Recollections of a Detective 140
recorded violence, examining 9–10
Reformatory Acts (1902), Sweden 113
rehabilitation, reform through 183–4
Rehabilitation of Offenders Act (1974)
   183
reintegrative shaming 179
Remarks on Criminal Law 119
Report of the Committee for Investigating
   the Alarming Increase of Juvenile
   Delinquency in the Metropolis 119
research, into history of crime 16–26
researchers, comparative 204
residual violence 79–81
restorative justice 24, 178–9
Riehl, Wilhelm Heinrich 92–3
right, to study other's histories 7
rioters 155
Risk Society 5
ritualised forms of violence 47–8
robberies
   moral panics
      Britain 60–1
      Colchester 57–9
      New York 59–60
   with violence 54
Roberts, Lord 167–9
Rousseaux, Xavier 19
routine activity theory, decline of
   homicide 83–4
Rowbotham, Judith 24–5
Royal Commission, military discipline
   165
royalty, San Sebastián 150
Ruff, Julius 21, 41
rural life, travel revolution 95
Russian Army 165, 166

Saint-Siminonists 91
San Sebastián, policing 145–56
seaside holiday resorts 25, 145–56
seasonal pattern, moral panics 63–4
Second Texas Mutiny 170–1
self image, policing memoirs 133–9

self-help, Victorian police 137
sense of mission, policing memoirs
    132, 134
sentencing, by courts martial 164
Shahar, Shulamith 115
shaming punishments 24, 178–80
    decline of 180–4
    renaissance of shame 190–2
    Southern United States 184–7
        post-bellium penality 187–90
Shanks, Major-General David 172
Shore, Heather 25–6
Simmel, Georg 91–2
Singha, Radhika 25
Slim, Private 164
Small World 196
social areas, seaside resorts 152–4
social behaviour
    diversity of 207
    travel revolution 92, 96
social capital, railway traffic 96
social class
    policing memoirs 130–1
    travel revolution 93–5, 96
    see also middle class; underclass
        culture; working class
social control
    decline in homicides 84
    travel revolution 96–7
social crises, moral panics 68
social distance 96
social ethnography, travel revolution
    92
social life, railway traffic 91
social problems
    global perception of 197–8
    juvenile delinquency 111
social relationships, travel revolution
    95–8
social science, universal 205
Social Science History Association
    Conference 18
social theories
    crime and violence 40
    and homicide 81–4
society, interrelatedness of 89

sociologists, global perspective 199
soldiers, homicide rates 77, 82, 85
Somers affair (1842) 161–2
Southern United States
    post-bellum penality 187–90
    a shaming and shameful region
        184–7
Spain, criminal liability 112, 115
spectacle of suffering 180
The Spectacle of Suffering 16
The Spectator 56
Spencer, Philip 162
State Board of Corrections 190
state civilian police 19
state executions, Southern United
    States 190
statistical studies, violence 42
stereotypical offenders 61
stigmatic shaming 178, 179
strong ties (social), railway traffic 96
A Study in Scarlet 140
sub-national case studies 11–12
subcultures
    police 125
    of violence 77
suicidal murders 77, 81
superstition, railway traffic 92–3
supra-national comparisons 15
surveillance, violent street crime 64
Sweden
    homicide frequency 79
    juvenile justice 113
Sztompka, P. 205–6, 207

A Tale of Two Cities 15
taxation, seaside resorts 148
television, over-representation of
    violent crime 54
territoriality, travel revolution 95
Teune, H. 207
threats, change in perception of 78
thrill of the chase, policing memoirs
    133–4
time-space dimension, railway traffic
    91
time-specific forms, homicide 77

timing, moral panics 61–2
Toribios 115, 116, 119–20
transnational crimes 198
transport technology, impact of 95
travellers, travel revolution 95, 96
Tuscany, juvenile institutions 115

underclass culture, and violence 76
underworld credentials, policing
    memoirs 134
United Kingdom *see* Britain
United States
    military law (1866–1918) 159–74
    see also Southern United States
universal/divergence debate 205–10
universals 3–4
urbanisation, predicted increase in
    homicide 82
Usborne, Cornelie 20

Vael, Claude 19
vigilance committees/clubs 187, 188
vigilantism 192
Vincent, David 128, 141
violence
    comparative perspectives 36–48
        developing methodologies and
            agendas 44–8
        national and international 39–44
        nature/nurture debate 37–9
    decline in readiness to use 78–9
    and masculinity 75–7
    railway and decline of 23, 89–106
    surveys of 21
violence-vol hypothesis 22, 24

violent street crime, moral panics
    53–70
visitor numbers, San Sebastián and
    Blackpool 148–9

Walton, John 25
wars, decline in homicide 85
Watch Committee (Blackpool) 151, 152
weak ties (social)
    railway traffic and development of
        95–8
    shift of interpersonal violence
        104–6
Weisser, Michael 21
whipping bosses 185, 186
white collar crime, San Sebastián 148,
    150
Wilde, Oscar 182
Wilson, Margot 37–8
Wolseley, Viscount 165
Wood, John Carter 23
working class
    autobiographies 128, 141
    violence 76–7
World Summit in Sustainable
    Development 198
Wurttemberg
    data 98–9
    development of crime 101–2
    rail traffic
        development of 100–1
        modelling impact of, on violent
            crime 102–4

Zehr, Howard 20